The Paradise of
TEXAS

Clarksville and Red River County 1846-1860

Volume I

Richard B. Marrin
and
Lorna Geer Sheppard

HERITAGE BOOKS
2007

HERITAGE BOOKS
AN IMPRINT OF HERITAGE BOOKS, INC.

Books, CDs, and more—Worldwide

For our listing of thousands of titles see our website
at
www.HeritageBooks.com

Published 2007 by
HERITAGE BOOKS, INC.
Publishing Division
65 East Main Street
Westminster, Maryland 21157-5026

Copyright © 2007 Richard B. Marrin
and Lorna Geer Sheppard

Other books by the authors:

Abstracts from The Northern Standard *and* The Red River District *[Texas]:
August 20, 1842-August 19, 1848*

Other books by Richard B. Marrin:

*A Glance Back in Time: Life in Colonial New Jersey (1704-1770)
As Depicted in News Accounts of the Day*

Going to Court in Texas: Riding the Circuit, 1842-1861

Passage Point: An Amateur's Dig Into New Jersey's Colonial Past

*Runaways of Colonial New Jersey: Indentured Servants, Slaves,
Deserters, and Prisoners, 1720-1781*

All rights reserved. No part of this book may be reproduced or
transmitted in any form or by any means, electronic or mechanical,
including photocopying, recording or by any information storage
and retrieval system without written permission from the author,
except for the inclusion of brief quotations in a review.

International Standard Book Number: 978-0-7884-4241-4

THE PARADISE OF TEXAS (VOL. I): CLARKSVILLE AND RED RIVER COUNTY

Introduction. 1

Clarksville: A Small Texas Town, 1846 -1860 5

Red River County and Clarksville: Their Histories 6

The People and From Where They Came. 7

The Town and its Public Square. 10

The Country Side: Resources, Industry and Agriculture. . . .27

The Wilds of Red River County. 57

Getting Around Texas: The River, Roads, Bridges
and Someday the Railroad. 59

Weather in Red River County 81

Clarksville: A Seat of Learning 95

Religion and Morals 103

Health and Medicine 113

Law and Lawlessness 125

Entertainment in Clarksville 149

Holidays in Clarksville and Red River County 165

The Sporting Life 189

No Man is an Island: The World
outside Red River County. 203

The Rest of Texas 205

        (i) East Texas 205
        (ii) Central Texas 209
        (iii) West Texas 226

The International Scene 234

Within the United States 236

On the Horizon 249

End Notes 257

Indices 301

INTRODUCTION

The Northern Standard, a weekly newspaper published in Clarksville, a small town in the northeastern corner of Texas, was barely three years old when the independent Republic of Texas voted to annex itself to the United States as its 28th state. The journal had been founded in August, 1842, by Charles DeMorse, a twenty six year old Massachusetts born, Connecticut educated, New York lawyer and veteran of the Texas Revolution. He was to remain its editor, publisher and owner for the next 46 years. During his tenure at *The Standard*, the paper would grow to become the second largest in circulation in Texas and DeMorse himself would be hailed as the *Father of Texas Journalism*.[1] Throughout its almost half century of publishing, *The Standard* captured, in contemporaneous accounts, pictures of an emerging Texas, from the days of the Revolution until the threshold of the 20th century. Like a mirror into the future, it has reflected those images for us to gaze upon in the 21st century.

Clarksville had been founded only a decade before the newspaper had and was proving itself to be a prospering settlement. A number of its prominent citizens, convinced that a newspaper would be beneficial to the town's continued growth, had recruited DeMorse to start one. He proved to be an excellent choice. Few men would love Texas more, nor be more devoted to her best interests, than was DeMorse. He had come to Texas in 1836, a young lawyer from New York's fabled Wall Street, as part of a brigade of volunteers from that City, intent on helping Texas win her independence from Mexico. He served first as a lieutenant of Marines in the Texas Navy and later as a major in the Army. After Independence, DeMorse resumed the practice of law, not in New York, but in Matagorda, Texas, a settlement of 1,650 transplanted New Englanders at the mouth of the Colorado River as it emptied into the Gulf of Mexico. He also began dabbling in newspapers, becoming a journalist for *The Daily Bulletin* in Austin, reporting on the activities of the Texas legislature.

DeMorse and Red River County must have gotten along

well because he spent the rest of his life there in its county seat, Clarksville, reporting first hand on the town's activities, the marriages and deaths of its citizens, the celebration of its holy days and holidays, the progress of the crops, the moods of the weather, what the merchants in the Square had to sell, and on a hundred other threads that, woven together, present us with a tapestry of the day to day life of the Texas settler/pioneer in 1846, more than a century and a half ago.

If that were all *The Standard* provided, an album of snapshots of one of the hundreds of small towns then popping up across Texas, it would still be a very valuable entry point into the Past. Happily, *The Standard* provides us with even more. DeMorse kept up the practice of law during the time he published *The Standard*. In Texas then, judges and lawyers, usually twice a year, would ride the "circuit", going from county to county, spending a week or more in each county seat, trying cases. DeMorse welcomed the chance to visit the Red River Valley, the Upper Trinity and the Upper Cross Timber regions of North Texas, as far south as Dallas and Fort Worth. It provided him the opportunity of soliciting new subscribers and advertisers for *The Standard* as well as to dun the tardy. He also reported back to his readers as to conditions in these new settlements on the frontier. These dispatches back to Clarksville, accumulating over years and years of his court visits, accurately chronicle the growth of these towns from the days they were laid out. He called his letters home to his readers "Editorial Correspondence". They preserve in print the matters of interest and curiosity occurring in these towns, warts and beauty marks alike. DeMorse's narratives of his trips, crisscrossing Northern Texas, are eye witness, first hand accounts of the settlement of this section of Texas.

Without any doubt, *The Standard* provided its readers, then and now, with a full offering of what was happening in Clarksville, Northern Texas as well as the rest of Texas, America and even the world of the mid 1800s. As DeMorse explains in one of his frequent subscription drives:

> *We call attention to the reduced price of our*
> *paper. Unsurpassed by the quality of reading matter by*

any other paper in the state, clearly printed on better material than is used by any other paper in the state, we have put it within reach of all the citizens of our District who have any desire to keep themselves informed of current events or to read the mass of instructive miscellaneous matter which all well conducted newspapers now introduce into their columns. The progress of the world, comprising the progress of civilization, science and art, is developed in the newspaper and no where else. No man who would keep himself in a fit state to perform his duties as a citizen or to perform his part in the social organizations of the community in which he lives, can possibly dispense with a public journal.[2]

CLARKSVILLE: A SMALL
TEXAS TOWN, 1846 -1860:

An ideal society should turn out educated, healthy, industrious, law abiding citizens, who, while independent and self reliant, are also yet good neighbors, gratefully acknowledging, and yielding to, a Higher Authority. If this is correct, a society comprised of such citizens should, absent misfortune, thrive and be productive and, the more societies like it that are gathered together, the greater the advantage to all within the greater community and to the Future's well being.

Were Clarksville and the other new towns in Texas, a century and a half ago, such societies? Scientists can see back into time, toward the Big Bang, and view the elements of matter that emerged to form everything we know, (and all that we do not know, as well) today. Were we able to travel back into time, could we see, like the scientists in the formation of Clarksville and its neighbors, evidences of these essential societal traits in operation? Who were the people of Clarksville and the other villages beginning to pop up around Texas and what were they like? From where had they come? Were they self reliant? Good neighbors? Lawless or lawful? Healthy or ailing? A few but of scores of questions about the people who settled Clarksville and towns like it across Texas.

What did small western towns themselves look like 150 years ago? How were they laid out? Where were the stores, blacksmith shops, saloons, the homes of its citizens? Clarksville should be typical. Was there crime, gun fights in the street, as in the movies? Was there fun? Were the woods full of wild animals and Indians? What did farmers raise and what did they do with it when they raised it? What holidays did the people celebrate? Did the children go to school? Our questions are endless when comparing yesteryear to us today in a new millennium.

The items of *The Standard*, detailing daily life in the new settlements, become for us magic carpets back into time, providing answers to some of those questions and giving clues to the solutions of others.

The first page of *The Standard* was given over to national and even international news. The second page of *The Standard* was unfailingly devoted to what DeMorse thought to be the items of interest for his three principal markets: (a) the town of Clarksville, (b) the surrounding Red River Valley and the Northern Texas regions, from the Arkansas border on the east to the always moving westward Indian frontier on the west (c) and as far south as below as Tarrant and Dallas Counties. That was where the local news was found and, in the local news, we can "find" the Clarksville of 1846 -1860, a prototype of most Texas towns of the period.

Red River County and Clarksville: Their Histories prior to 1846

Red River county is the mother county, in whole or part, to thirty nine present day Texas counties. Today, after giving birth to her litter of counties, Red River County has been reduced to roughly a thousand square miles of gently rolling prairie and timberlands.

Its earliest settlers, of course, were Indians, as long as 2,500 years ago. The Caddos lived there when the Spanish and French probed the area, but departed at end of 1700s because of an epidemic and the belligerence of the neighboring Osages tribe. By the 1820s, Indian newcomers from the East, Shawness, Delaware and Kickapoo, pushed by an expanding white population, settled along creeks that still bear their name. They remained there barely a decade before the wave of white settlers pushed them west and north into the Indian Territory across the Red River.

American hunters and Indian traders had come to Red River county as early as 1815, claiming that it was part of the Louisiana Purchase of 1803. In 1818, the Jonesborough and Burham's settlements were established. It took Claiborne Wright, six months on a self made keel boat, *the Pioneer*, to come all the way from Tennessee, with his family and his two married slaves, Jin and Hardy Wright. They put down stakes, along the Red River, near Pecan Point in 1816, joining George and Alex Wetmore and William Mabbit who had settled there earlier that year. By the mid 1820s, the settlers had begun to move from the river locations to the prairies. In 1833, James Clark and his wife Isabella Hanks Clark founded Clarksville.

When Texas completed its annexation to the United States in February, 1846, Clarksville was still a hamlet, not much more than a dozen years old. It stood at the edge between the pine forests of East Texas and the lightly-wooded and highly-fertile black land prairie that stretched westward, seemingly forever. It was an outgrowth of the first permanent American settlement in Texas at Pecan Point in 1815, not too far distant from Clarksville, on the Red River. Before that, it had been the home of Indians and the roaming grounds of the elk, buffalo, mustang and numerous other wild animals.

The town had been named after the village's founder, James Clark, a Tennessean-born adventurer of Scotch ancestry, and his wife Isabella. Its springs, just south of today's town square, earlier had been the camp grounds of friendly Delaware Indians, visited by Indian traders, Clark among them. Later, Clark was to purchase, from his friend Henry Stout, who had been granted the land by Mexico, some acreage near those same springs, as part of a plan to sell lots on it and build a town. He convinced an immigrating family, that of Isaac Smathers, to stop and settle there. As an inducement, he gave Smathers a choice lot and enlisted the efforts of neighbors to erect, in a single day, a log house for him. The next day, they built a house for Clark as well and the town of Clarksville was off and running.

The People and from where they came

Clarksville claimed to have a population of 750, but it may have exaggerated it a bit so as to boast itself a town. The 1848 census showed just 633 persons in town, 422 white and 204 slaves and five not described, which probably indicated free Blacks. As small as this might seem to us in a metropolis, like Dallas or Houston, it was a large population in Texas at the time. As the county seat, Clarksville had a sixth of the total population of the entire county of Red River, which had a white population of 2,316, a slave population of 1,456 and 19 free Negroes. Texas had a population of 100,508 whites, 35,038 slaves and 229 free blacks.[3] Within three years, by 1851, it had all doubled. The population of the county had increased to 5,374 and the State to 200,000. However, to put things into perspective, as impressive as was the growth of the Nation's 28th state, it had still but a tiny fraction, less than one per cent, of the United States population of 23,298,000.

Who were these people who lived in Texas in the 1840s and 1850s? A New Orleans newspaper, the *Picayune*, gave a romantic, flattering image of Texas, its citizens and beauty, that DeMorse proudly reprinted. It is an apt introduction for today's reader to the Texas of a century and a half ago:

> *From the result of personal observation, we have long been of the opinion that Texas was not only a great state, but that she was destined to be still greater. Her population is young, active and remarkably intelligent, comprising principally in the middle and western divisions, the picked men of the agricultural class of the whole United States.*
>
> *You sit down at a table with a farmer, who wears a long beard, don't comb his hair and sports a red flannel shirt, mud boots and greasy buckskin pants. You are surprised, ere much of the hot coffee every Texan has with his meal of corn bread and venison chops have been eaten, to find that your host is an educated man, has traveled, has perhaps been in Congress or the Legislature of his previous state, that he takes several newspapers. The Texans are famous for that, and their papers, taken as a body, are the best edited and printed of any country papers in the United States. He knows what is going on, of the latest date, in the scientific, political, literary, manufacturing, commercial, and agricultural worlds. He has stowed away in some corner of his log cabin or adobe mansion, a collection of standard works and that he can give you more useful*

> *general knowledge and impart more stirring active original ideas than any city individual you have ever seen.*
>
> *On discussing with this frank, courteous, hospitable, red shirted, long bearded man, you come to the conclusion that Texas must be the finest country in the world. Your own eyes tell you it is one of the most beautiful. The free play of your lungs tell you that its atmosphere is one of the most purest and bracing. The big glossy coated cattle, running wild in the prairie in winter and summer, the great flocks of deer and sheep wandering in its small valleys, wide sweeps and gently rising hills, indicate its surprising pastoral advantages. The cotton, sugar, indigo and corn, flourishing together on one plantation at the same time, as we have seen, give you an idea of its agricultural treasures. [So too] the abundance of wild fruit and timbers of all kinds and the facility with which wheat, oats and grain of that kind is raised; vegetables of every imaginable species and stock to any amount of the finest kind, you will speedily perceive.*
>
> *Texas is developing all of her resources; she will have enough to do for 50 years to come to carry out this policy. She is big enough for several states. We hope she may be able to "wave" forever.*[4]

Of course, all early Texans did not fit this description. There were many other types that made up the population of Texas in the 1840s and 1850s. There were a few Indians, among them. Some were peaceful, like the Choctaw, Caddos and Delaware in the north and east, and some wild, warlike ones, Comanches and Apaches among others, in central, south and west Texas. Settlers from Mexico, introduced into Texas as part of Spain's, and then Mexico's, defense to an encroaching United States, lived in San Antonio, a mostly Mexican town. Other inhabitants, the Anglos, were the descendants of the pioneers who had settled in Texas, a generation earlier, while it was a state of Mexico, before the Revolution. After 1846, new settlers came in waves from all the other twenty seven states of the Union. More were from the South, than the North, and the southern planters brought with them their slaves, without whom growing cotton would be physically and economically impossible. Emigrants from foreign lands came too, many from Germany and France, but from all of western Europe.

Most folk in the Red River Valley region of Texas were farmers, tillers of the soil, raising cotton, wheat and corn and grazing livestock. "Groceries", cotton gins and lumber and grain mills, became centers of tiny settlements, scattered throughout the countryside. Clustered in towns like Clarksville were the merchants, professional men, "mechanics" and artisans of different sorts, tinners, carpenters, smiths, among them.

The Public Square

Let's take a seat, you, I and the rest of us from the twenty first century, on a bench in front of the Clarksville Hotel. We will get ourselves a copy of this Saturday's *Standard* and, with its help, witness life during the first fourteen years of Texas statehood, from the Clarksville Public Square outward, to the Red River Valley, to all of North Texas, indeed, to all the rest of Texas, the United States and even the world. The view is spectacular!

A public or town square does not form naturally as do the centers of some towns that spring up at a river crossing or near a mill, for example. A square is a planned thing, usually associated with county seats. The court house anchors the square, which draws the citizens of the county to town on a regular basis. Businesses buy up the lots that lie on the square. This leads to more traffic and more commercial interests, which increase the value of the surrounding acreage. That was how Clarksville had started. To induce commercial concerns to set up shop there, a must, of course, for any ambitious, upcoming town, the Clarks had promised that the funds received from the sale of the valuable lots on the public square would be reserved for the construction, in the middle of the square, of a court house for huge Red River County.[5] With the court house, Clarksville was assured of being the county seat. This, in turn, promised activity for the businesses that had had the foresight to purchase the choice sites that surrounded the Court House.[6]

A few years later, in order to attract more citizens and businesses, Mrs. Clark, widowed, and her new husband, Dr. George Gordon, gave away *gratis* or sold at low prices, many of the best lots in town on the purchasers' promises to build stores or homes. Several parcels were sold for as little as $200.

Clarksville still has its public square *i.e.,* where four blocks (Broadway, Pecan, Main and Locust) face inward, to form a square, inside which once was a Court House. It is not there now, having moved to its present site in 1885. The public square in Clarksville is now a small park, with a statute erected to honor the Confederate Soldier and another to the first Protestant preacher in Texas and plenty of spaces for cars to park.

Malls are public squares outside of town and giant discount stores have drained the traditional downtown public squares of their business and bustle, Clarksville being no exception. But it was not always that way. The merchants and professional men sought the choice lots on the square and set up their businesses there. Most everything of importance that happened seemed to happen on the square.

Founder James Clark had laid out the public square near the same springs of the Delaware Creek, where, a couple of decades before, the Indian traders had transacted their business. From reading the local news in *The Standard*, we can visualize the public square as it existed in those first days. It was well used and, in the middle of it, sat the doubled log cabin court house that had been built in 1834 or so. Court was in session, twice a year, for at least a two week period each time, sometimes longer. In a winter term in 1847, the court sat for six weeks and disposed of 450 criminal and civil cases. Activity like that brought to town a flock of lawyers from other counties, as well as the participants in the lawsuits: the plaintiffs and defendants, the witnesses, the jurors and the curious. Politicians, railroad promoters and pedlars of patent medicines and other products took advantage of the large crowds to ply their goods. Often, there was entertainment during these court weeks: balls, horse races and traveling shows. Clarksville was a bustling town during Court week.

Later, toward the end of winter or in early spring, when the Red River rose sufficiently to let the steamers from Shreveport and New Orleans up as far as the Clarksville landing, the town became hectic again. Wagons full of cotton passed through town, on their way to deposit their season's harvest at dockside for the expected steamboats. These steam boats had not arrived empty. Their cargos up river were merchandise for the storekeepers on the square to sell. The town was again busy in early summer, when the students at its three boarding schools and McKenzie College had their examinations and graduations. Parents, relatives, friends from the Red River District and beyond came to see the scholars show off in public forums what they had learned. And, of course, there was always activity when those four horse stages would pull in several times a week from Little Rock, Waco, Austin or Shreveport, loaded with visitors and the mail. Holiday celebrations, like July Fourth, brought people from the country into town. So did the immigrant wagons that had crossed the Red River at Jonesboro from Arkansas and points east. They needed to resupply themselves in Clarksville for the rest of their trip west to the Texas frontier.

None of the first edition structures on the square remain, due to a major fire in 1851, a second one in 1856, and the normal ravages of time, hurried along by man's desire to always build bigger and better. The brick buildings stand today on parts of the square did not follow the second fire by much. Visit the square today and imagine dirt streets, crowded with wagons, not cars, with elevated board walks, instead of sidewalks, and the image of old Clarksville reappears. It is not unrecognizable.

Clarksville, on a major route into Texas for the immigrants who crossed at Jonesboro as well as being the county seat, had a thriving hotel business, at least four of them. One was known as Mrs. Donoho's Hotel, another Thompson's. Two others were on Main Street on the south side of the Square. Sample advertisements in *The Standard* recited the pedigree of the latter establishments and provide some idea of what they might have looked like:

STAR HOTEL,
CLARKSVILLE,
Red RIver County, Texas.

The undersigned, having purchased this large and commodious establishment, formerly kept by Dr. Ward, respectfully solicits a share of public patronage.

The house is large and eligibly situated upon the public square of the Town, and affords private apartments for families, or others desiring them.

An extensive stable, and carriage shed, are attached to the establishment, and plenty of provender always on hand.

Every attention will be paid to the accommodation of travelers and visitors, who may give the house a call.

J. J. Montgomery. [7]

CLARKSVILLE HOTEL.

THE undersigned has taken this house, first built and occupied as a house of entertainment, by late James Clark; subsequently by Mr. Musgrove, and latterly, by Mr. Geo. F. Lawton, as a boarding house. The house is situated on Main Street, east of the Star Hotel.

The house is undergoing repairs and improvements which will make it as comfortable as any other in the place, and will be kept by the undersigned, as well as her skill in the business, plenty of assistance, and a desire to please, will permit.

The table will be furnished with the best the country affords.

A share of public patronage is respectfully solicited.

Cynthia Caton.[8]

On the northeast corner of the square, perhaps near

where the post office stands today, was the new store erected by Rhine & Co., an entrepreneurial empire of some significance in the Town and elsewhere in North Texas, an early Walmarts of sorts during the decade upon which we are focusing.

> *Goods and Drugs...*
> *We call attention the Rhine & Co advertisement in this number. They have on hand and still coming a very extensive stock of goods, which they will open in their new large store on the north east corner of the Square.*
> *Next store is the new drug establishment of McDonna, Rhine & Bros., filled up with a style exceedingly tasteful and inviting patronage with the advantage of a large and entirely new stock, disposed to the best advantage for the examination of customers.*[9]

Many of these businesses advertised in *The Standard*, identified themselves to readers as being "on the square." Sometimes, they revealed the actual side of the square, north, south, east or west, where they were. Even a partial list, taken from the advertising sections of *The Standard*, reveals how varied the Clarksville's businesses community was. For example, if a visitor to town wanted to purchase clothes, he or she had a choice. Alexander's, a ladies dress shop, bragged as having the "tastiest articles in the way of Ladies Dresses that has ever been in Clarksville, laces, fringes, ribbons, and scarfs etc." Mrs. N. C. Hudspith advertised herself as a "fashionable dress maker." J.P. and C. C. Dale, called themselves "merchant tailors" and advertised "ready made clothing of all kinds and qualities." Oliver & Chatfield, proudly displaying a cowboy boot as its logo, offered "ladies', men's and children's shoes, as well as hats of the latest style." W. P. Dickson & Co, located on the East Side of the public square carried "general merchandise" and James Gordon advertised "spring and summer goods." There was a "mattress manufactory" on Main Street, that sold both "cotton shuck" and "spring mattresses." Rhine & Co. were selling three pine pianos and 14 family buggies's and, if the piano went out of key, there was a piano tuner in town, George W. Smith.

There appeared to be enough business to keep two jewelers competitive:

> *silver ware*
> *Peabody Silver works are in full blast. We called in on Wednesday last and saw some Masonic ornaments, which were made and were to undergo the finishing process of engraving and burnishing.* [10]
>
> *We were shown by Mr. B.J. Sneed a few days since, a watch that had been taken by the chain attached, and dashed upon the pavement several times until it became a shapeless mass and the jewels were crumbled. He had completely restored its shape, supplied the missing jewels and all the damaged works and made it as good as new. This is the character of work, we apprehend, which cannot be done by every country watch repairer and proves simply that, if anyone has a watch badly out of order, it is not necessary to send it to New Orleans for reparation.* [11]

If food were the object of the visit to the square, Gilbert Regin had a "food shop: fruits, confections and eatables of various sorts." Mrs. Lee's confectionary with candies and cakes was next to Thomson's Hotel. Mr. John Farret, also a confectioner, had "some choice apples and edibles of various kinds at [his] neat establishment on Main Street." If delicacies and drink were the purpose of one's visit to the square, stop at Simms & Simms which had for sale a "large supply of oysters, salmon, sardines, chewing tobacco, German and Havana cigars, scotch and Maccaboy snuff; pie fruits, preserves, brandy, fruits, wines, syrups, bitters etc; cognac, brandies, scotch, ale, London porter, champagne and champagne cider, bourbon, rye, and corn whiskey. [12]

Physicians clustered about the square as well. Drs. Barry & Moore, for example, had their "medicine & surgery offices" at Mrs. Donoho's Hotel. A surgeon dentist was next door. Wholesale and resale druggists could be found at the south eastern corner of the Square. So were lawyers. All, but a very few, had their offices near the Courthouse: "on the south west side of the public square" or "next door to the District Clerk's" or "next to store of John s Gordon" or even "upstairs in the Courthouse."

The equivalent of today's gas stations and garages were stables and livery stables and Clarksville did not lack them. Messrs. Thompson had a "fine large commodious and well stocked livery stable on Mulberry Street between the Masonic Hall and Church Street", a little south of the square. Darnall and Bryant sold saddles and Hughes and Donoho had a livery stable. There were several blacksmiths to choose among: J&R Raines, John West, Wm. M. Harrison, and Wm. M. Shanahan. F.M. Sims was a "Wagon Maker and carriage repairer" which, when it was taken over by Archimedes McLean advertised that it "was prepared to paint and trim buggies and carriages and also make and repair wagons at the shortest dispatch."[13] Brim's Cabinet Shop and Chair Manufactory also made coffins and took care of funeral arrangements.

Settlements "came and went" throughout Texas all the time during the 1850s, many of them vanishing, not unlike the scores of species that disappear each day in our world ecology. To remain the business center of Northern Texas, Clarksville had to be vigilant. For one thing, it had to look the part of a neat, prosperous community, especially to the immigrants streaming across the Red River from Arkansas and points east, who were looking for a place to settle. Through their unofficial spokesman and civic booster, Charles DeMorse, the citizens of Clarksville encouraged each other to keep their town attractive to these newcomers, including keeping noisy drunks off the street at night.[14] DeMorse, ahead of himself by a century or more, suggested that a portion of the square be made into a park:

> *What do some of the property owners about the Square think of the propriety of benefitting themselves by enclosing it with a substantial railing with heavy*

> *posts and planting out trees within the enclosure. We think it would pay them well for the expenditure.*[15]

Other hints as to how to spruce up the town's appearance were frequent items in *The Standard*. For example, an annual message would urge the planting of attractive trees around the town, calling it "no labor which is more richly repaid:"

> *Ornamental Trees*
>
> *We again urge our citizens to transplant shade trees, the lateness of the spring and the continued rain have protracted the time for it so that they will still do well, if set out with some care and a little attention given to watering them during the summer.*
>
> *The improvement which shade trees make in the appearance of a Town, where general attention is given to its culture, is immense. Anyone will appreciate this who has ever been to New Haven, Connecticut. Everyone appreciates the improvement in the beauty and comfort of each residence which has them around it. We might as well as have our Town noted for its beauty in this respect, as otherwise, and it will enhance the value of the property to have it so. Those who cannot procure the China or the Locust now, can get plenty of the Black Walnut, the Oak, the mulberry and other native varieties, which are immediately about Texas and easily gotten, and then, if they wish the China or the Locust, it is an easy matter to raise any number from seed and we will give seed to anyone who will plant them.*[16]

Clarksville has several cemeteries. One of them, on Washington Street, a block south of the public square, known as the Methodist Cemetery, contains the final resting places of many of Clarksville's earliest, citizens, James Clark and Charles DeMorse, included.[17] DeMorse was aghast at the condition to which what was to be his final resting place had sunk.

THE GRAVE YARD.--

The occasional burials for the last few months, more frequent than ever before in this section have drawn our attention to the grave yard at the Methodist church, generally used by our citizens for the internment of the dead.

We have frequently looked at this neglected place of burial and felt something akin to anger at a forlorn appearance, indicative of a want of proper consideration among the living for those who had possessed their affection or respect while among them. There is no one place of public use which tells a more favorable tale to the stranger of the people he has set foot among than a tastefully laid off, well enclosed, and well treated place of burial.

Our grave yard is greatly neglected, barbarously so. It has less of the attention proper for such a place, than savages would give it, for no flowers are planted, no mound is raised, nor stones are piled upon the graves, to denote that those who be there are cared for, or remembered. Neither the yard, nor the single grave, with two exceptions, are enclosed. The grass grows rank and uncultivated, where the cattle do not tramp it down, but even upon the graves themselves, the cattle tramp, if it suits them.

All this should be reformed. The Church Yard should be substantially enclosed. The portion appropriated to burial should be laid off in compartments with dividing walks.

The Weeping Willow, the China and some Evergreens should be planted out and upon the graves themselves, affection, if there is any felt, for those who once possessed it, should plant pot roses to make cheerful and inviting, those little hillocks which are the last homes of all the human race.[18]

DeMorse also urged the merchants around the public square to present an attractive image to the newcomer, including the placement of attractive signs to direct the would be purchasers to their products or services:

Sign Painting

There are few things after good houses have been erected, which more improve the appearance of a Town, than neatly executed signs designating the various pursuits of the individuals who do business in it. They are at the same time, ornamental, business like, and useful, directing persons from the Country, who have business in the Town, where to find individuals, or make purchases.[19]

Ironically, our best picture of the what the Clarksville square looked like can be found in accounts of an 1851 and 1856 fires[20] which swept through and destroyed much of it:

Fire in Clarksville.

We have this week to report the first serious conflagration which has ever taken place in our town. On Friday morning last, at about two o'clock, the citizens were awakened by the alarm of fire, and attracted by the light proceeded to the public square and found the large building known as the Star Hotel on fire and making a most brilliant illumination. The air was still, hardly a perceptible current, and to that only are we indebted that there is a house left about the square. All of them are wood and highly combustible. The hotel was only occupied at one end room, by Trimble & Hudkins, a law office and was soon consumed, most of their books and papers being destroyed. From the fact so unusual is the alarm of fire in our quiet village and so little the preparation made for indicating it, they [did not arrive] until the hotel was completely enveloped in fire, but few were present and they were looking out for houses filled with merchandise and furniture.

From the hotel the fire communicated itself to the opposite store, occupied by Wm. P. Dickson, with a Masonic Lodge above it, and, spreading easterly and northerly, it then destroyed the law offices of Mills & Murray and A. Morril, the confectionary of George Fredson, the tailor shop of Wm. Crittendon and the house occupied by Dr. Geo. Gordon as an office and Thos. R. Wilson's as a saddle shop. The fine house of Mr. Boyce, on one end, and the fine hotel of Mrs. Caton, on the other, were saved by wet blankets and carpets. The grocery store of Mr. J. C. Hart was saved in the same way. As we said before, if there had been a breath of air, the Square would have been swept. The town has no such possession as a fire engine. All the contents of offices and shops, except the office of Trimble & Hudgins were removed. During the progress of the fire, an unsuccessful attempt to blow up a house with powder was made and failed from a want of knowledge for the true manner of doing it. The buildings were most of them small and the actual loss does not exceed 7,000 dollars [later $9,000 to $10,000]. The fire was quite an event in our village life and doubtless will induce the purchase of several of Phillip's fire annihilators, as soon as they can be procured. It originated in the kitchen in the back of the Star Hotel, where some persons were said to be amusing themselves with a small game of cards. Whether the Grand Jury will consider the result to be of significant importance to warrant an inquiry by them into the nature of the game aforesaid remains to be seen. [21]

The square, of course, was rebuilt and life went on. No

one gave any thought that proper fire fighting apparatus and a volunteer fire company, might prevent a recurrence. But in 1856, the town was partially destroyed again as a fire burned two cabinet makers' shops. Had not the wind changed direction at the last minute, the Donoho Hotel, the Court House and a number of other buildings would have been lost. Now DeMorse led the chant for a fire company for the future.

Destructive Fire

Our citizens were thrown into a state of great alarm on Wednesday evening by the breaking out of a fire in the cabinet shop of Mr. J. B. Shanahan, which soon extended to the cabinet shop of Mr. Wm. C. Gaines, both of which were entirely consumed. In Mr. Shanahan's shop, we understand that over $500 of fine furniture, together with a large quantity of valuable materials, all his tools, etc were entirely destroyed. From the nature of the materials, the fire had broken out for only a few minutes, until all chance of saving anything was lost. Mr. Gaines saved all the furniture from his showroom and a few of his tools, but lost a large quantity of valuable lumber and materials for making fine work. The loss falls heavily on both. It is estimated at not less than $3,000. Mr. Shanahan has lost most of his savings from several years of persevering industry. To both of the sufferers, we sincerely extend our utmost sympathy and we earnestly recommend to those who are indebted to either party to come forward and settle their indebtedness. Promptness on the part of their patrons would be a true manifestation of their kindness and it would afford lost material and essential aid.

On this occasion, our town was most providentially saved. Had the wind continued as it had at the commencement of the fire Mrs. Donoho's large fine hotel would have inevitably been consumed by the fire. The burning of this building would have occurred,

> *despite every effort which could have been used, been communicated to the Court house and thence to the other buildings around the Square. Had our town been supplied with a fire engine, the fire could have easily been confined to Shanahan's shop and all danger to surrounding buildings would have been obviated. We sincerely hope that our merchants will make an effort to be prepared against any future contingency.*
>
> *During the progress of the fire we were struck with the idea that some regularly organized fire company should forthwith be got up. There should be some one to take command at such a time. Was it not the duty of our Mayor and constable to appoint as many assistant constables as the exigency of the case demanded? Let the whole affair be a warning to us to be more careful about how fires are secured in our houses and let the gratitude of our heart be offered to God, who holds the winds in his Hands, for preserving our town.* [22]

The merchants and professional men who carried on business in the public square generally lived with their families nearby. Commuting any great distance by horse or carriage was difficult. The lots here offered here for sale were on the south side of town and sat on an elevated prairie overlooking the town:

> *My residence, and the tract of land on which I now live, adjoining the Town of Clarksville on the south, and within 600 yards of the Courthouse square, buildings and improvements generally not surpassed by any in Texas, and containing 575 acres of good land, both prairie and timber, it lying so convenient to the Town that it is the most desirable situation in Eastern Texas. The houses are a large framed dwelling smoke house, stables, etc. There are two good cisterns, and all*

other improvements necessary for comfort and convenience.

J. H. Darnall [23]

DO YOU WANT TO BUY GOOD LANDS

☞ *IN THE VICINITY OF CLARKSVILLE, TEXAS, I offer for sale, from Five to Twelve Five Acre Lots, within four hundred yards South from the court house in the town of Clarksville. The Lots are handsomely situated in a beautiful, rich, high Prairie, from 25 to 50 feet above the level of the Town site and afford a full view of the town and surrounding country for several miles.*

All of which I will sell on accommodating terms. The land will be bound for the payment.

Joseph C. Hart [24]

DeMorse provides us with his assessment of the Town of Clarksville and the County of Red River in 1858, their difficulties and promise alike.

Our town improves a little - not rapidly. Perhaps, however, this slow growth is the surest. At all events, we know of no town in Northern Texas that has a stronger surrounding county to support it, although some of the counties are more numerous. Ours, however, is longest settled and we think exports more value of product than does any other in Northern Texas. This is a point the census will settle, when fully published. Bowie probably competes with it in cotton, but not in general products and no other county, than Bowie, approaches it in cotton product.

Clarksville is preeminently healthy, is handsomely situated in a beautiful rolling prairie country, with rich land. The heaviest settlement of the county is immediately around it, which is perhaps the reason why the town does not improve faster, it being convenient for many of the children educated in the schools of the town, to ride or walk from home, so that there exists no necessity for parents, who have farms on good land, to move into town.

As it is, however, we improve a little bit every year and the improvement is on an entirely sound basis, not at all speculative. We have two large and well kept hotels in the place and several mercantile establishments of a permanent character. One of our heaviest firms, Rhine & Bros, had their storehouse burned a year ago since and have been selling since in a building entirely inadequate to the extent of their business. We see the heavy timbers for the inner frame work of a very large and externally fireproof brick storehouse now being hauled upon the ground; also the timbers for a large residence for the senior member of the firm. The bricks for the walls of the storehouse are now making at the place of J. A .N. Murray, Esq. who has the contract for the walls. The structure will be the largest in our town, although the precise dimensions we do not now recollect.

Three or four handsome new residences are about being finished and a large new school house erected by the Rev. H. C. Barrus. Our town is so divided between the two sides of the Delaware, that a stranger passing through it on a journey, would really not appreciate its full size. It is only since we have commenced writing this article that we have ourselves been made aware of the new buildings now finishing. Three of them are south of the Delaware and our attention has been called to them by seeing their new roofs from the window of our sanctum, which is in the second story of our office

From the necessities of the case, Clarksville, long dormant, must improve. It has social advantages, superior schools, a county around rich in lands and a population of more than average property for Texas, a county which makes good crops more invariably than any other in our State (with the exception perhaps of Brazoria, Matagorda, Wharton and Washington), a county blessed with general good health, with a population whose faces and bodies will show for themselves with good color and fullness of sound flesh. The railroad, which is now a fixed fact, will, in its construction towards this place, from either end, give a flush to population and enterprise, which must result in the more complete development of the very rich capacities of old Red River, the progenitor of the Northern counties and, along with it, in the expansion and improvement of Clarksville .[25]

A year later, there was more progress:

Our town continues to improve. The new Brick jail is nearly completed and from our office building we see the large frame of the new Presbyterian Church, in its commanding position overlooking the eastern part of the town. The large new brick store of the Rhines has taken a fresh start and begins to show its broad sides palpably to those within sight of the Square. Other smaller improvements are going on.[26]

The Country Side:
Resources, Industry and Agriculture

Clarksville and the approximate hundred square miles of the surrounding Red River County had its attractions. For example, it was only ten miles from the Red River, which provided it access to the world, *via* New Orleans. Without the river, the planters could not get their cotton to market or get provisions for a new season. Also, there were thousands of acres of rich virgin farm land, rich and inexpensive, available to emigrants to North Texas, who were looking for a good spot to farm:

Emigration. Those who seek rich soil which they might own - they and their children - are daily to be seen now, winding their ways through the counties [of North Texas]. They enter a country, which pleases the eye and gladdens the heart by its beauty. No man can look upon it and ask if it is rich. That is a proposition self solved at a glance. If, however, they are critical and would know of its products, they see, by the size of the corn stalks, by the yield of the cotton, that they have seen no such country before. And as they move on, they see thousand of acres of virgin soil into which no plough has ever been thrust, still green with the garment of verdure which Nature has given it and wooing with a promise of rich fruitfulness that cannot be doubted. We have the garden of the world, rich enough for millions, now wasting their energies in unproductive regions. Come to it! There can be no more propitious time. The price of land is yet so low that a citizen of an old state would smile derisively at the mention of it. Grain is plentiful and cheap and, in another year, the land will certainly be higher. Food may or may not be as low. Texas is the last field of the Southwest. In all of Texas (we know it well) there is

> *no fairer or richer lands, than in the Red River counties. We disparage no other, for the state has an immensity of fertile lands, but we say, ignorantly or from prejudice, that we believe the Red River Counties to be the choice of all Texas, for all purposes. Yesterday 40 wagons passed through our town.*[27]

Another resource enjoyed in Red River County was the plentiful supply of timber that stood nearby. Red River County was the divide between the pines and the prairie. A neighboring forest was crucial. Without a ready supply of good timber, houses and commercial buildings could not be erected, and farms could not be fenced. Indeed, timbering could be a livelihood of its own. Surplus trees could be cut down, saw milled and sold to the settlers to the west on the treeless prairie, an economic blessing according to DeMorse:

> *Clarksville has a mine of wealth adjacent, which will always draw tribute from other counties adjoining. From as far west as Grayson County, 90 miles from town, wagons are hauling the lumber made by our steam mills. The supply of pine near us is inexhaustible, and there being none of consequence west of us, we must necessarily furnish our neighbors much of the article, for many years to come. The quantity of lumber turned out by these mills, and those which will be erected as fast as the demand may render proper, will do much towards building up our Town and rendering it permanently prosperous.* [28]

DeMorse might have thought the region's supply of timber to be inexhaustible, but it was not. So many thousands of families were settling the prairies of the Red River Valley that the demand for lumber for fencing and home construction was much greater than the supply. Besides, wooden framed buildings, especially those put to commercial use, did not last long. Brick became an alternative. Fortunately, Clarksville and Red River County were blessed in that respect as well. All the ingredients for an endless supply of brick could be gathered locally, including the all important clay. Soon, some were experimenting with it:

> *Brick - Judge Todd showed us on Saturday morning last a specimen of brick from the top course of the kiln he has just burned. This brick is of the very best sort and he says out of a kiln of a 100,000, he does not believe that there are more than 1,000 soft brick. We have always believed that good brick could be made around the Town with proper care and good burning. The last three trials have sufficiently demonstrated the correctness of that opinion. We hope to see more brick made in this vicinity hereafter and a change in the order of buildings erected in and about town.* [29]

DeMorse soon became an advocate of the use of brick around the Clarksville public square, especially the court house that lay in the middle of the square. He built a new office for *The Standard* out of it. We owe him our thanks. Brick buildings, like the dozen or so that constitute the northern edge of the square today, have survived to the present because of the permanency that bricks brought to the town of Clarksville.

> *The point is now settled that good brick can be made here and they should here after supersede wood for the building of all building of pretension to magnitude or costliness. We know that several, ourself among them, have only been waiting until good brick could be obtained at a moderate cost, to erect substantial buildings. If a brick yard of some magnitude were kept up regularly, we believe it would be found more profitable and at the same time, will conduce the improvement of our Town. It would be difficult to get*

> *lumber now for any considerable number of buildings. The three steam mills in operation can hardly supply the up country demand and it would be troublesome to get the [amount] of wood for the improvements now contemplated about Town.* [30]

A safe, unfailing, at least to the diligent, drinking water supply was another gift of Nature, bestowed upon the citizens of Clarksville and Red River County. They did not take their water from rivers or creeks. Nor did they dig wells to the aquifers below or have springs gush it up under their noses. Instead, the townspeople allowed rainfall to run off into cisterns they had dug in the soft rock beneath the Clarksville earth. It appeared very efficient and healthy.

> *Our greatest element of health is pure water, the water that descends after atmospheric purification and is received and retained in cisterns in the solid rock, many feet beneath the surface. It is such water as we have found no where else, so cool that ice is no luxury here. Not so cold as ice would make it, but near it, that ice is unnecessary and no body feels the want of it; so cold that milk from a vessel let down to the bottom of a cistern will make the teeth ache.* [31]

The supply was inexhaustible, nothing less than the prior winter's rainfall, which in Clarksville is usually copious. Effort was required to dig the cisterns, but that was all that was needed to insure plenty of fresh cold water immediately available in a summer drought, without hauling.

> *Water Supply*
> *The summer has been an unusually dry one, the creeks and water holes immediately about town having gone dry. Those individuals, who did not attend to*

> *filling their cisterns during the winter, and those who having none, always rely upon their neighbors, have been put to inconvenience about water and have to get it hauled. But those who have cisterns, including three quarters of the families in Town, have enough for themselves and, as for others, they can procure, as it is procured in hundreds of other towns, by hauling.*
>
> *Parents who have withheld their children from school from a fear of a scarcity of water can send them along. They can have plenty of the best in the world water, pure from the rock receptacles which receive it from the heavens.*
>
> *Every family should have one large cistern or two small ones. With this preparation, not a costly one, there would never the inconveniences about water. The editor of this paper who has relied upon one moderate sized cistern for several years, to supply his office and residence, requiring a large supply has never been a problem, but once, for a few days, and would never have been then if he had not supplied other families. We would not exchange the reliance of this town for water (we mean the rocky substratum in which the cisterns are excavated) for the best springs in the State. We can have as much water as we want because cisterns can be made as large as we want and the winter rain will fill them and from these we have cold water, the purest in the world.* [32]

A frequent bragging point of DeMorse's about Clarksville was its healthy climate. By this, was meant the town's freedom from cholera and yellow fever epidemics that periodically inflicted the rest of Texas. The use of cistern water played a greater role in that, than the townspeople would have suspected, although some were beginning to guess.

> *Clarksville has no local cause for sickness and*

has the best water in the State, being pure rain water, contained in cisterns, excavated from the solid rock. It has been noted that where cistern water is used, Cholera does little or no damage. [33]

In 1848, nearly 3,000 people, five sixth's of the population of Red River County, lived outside of Clarksville on farms or in one of the tiny settlements scattered over the thousand plus square miles of the county, a few of which - Savannah, Robbinsville, Halesboro, Madras, Millville, Maple Springs, Albion, Rowland - have survived. Often, these hamlets were little more than a general store or grocery, a cotton gin, perhaps a lumber or flour mill and a few scattered houses. According to the 1850 census, Red River County had seven "manufacturing facilities" - *i.e.*, producing goods worth $500 or more a year. Together, they employed fewer than a hundred people. This comprised the industrial base of the county. Examples of these businesses have been preserved in the advertisement pages of *The Standard*:

GRIST MILL.

The undersigned respectfully inform the public that they have now in operation 2½ miles from Clarksville, near the residence of Gilbert Clark, Esq., a superior grist mill, running two pairs of stones, with a fine bolting cloth, brought from Cincinnati expressly for the mill.

They will make as good Flour and Meal as can be made in the county, and will usually have a supply on hand for sale. All persons taking Grain to the Mill may depend upon having it ground well, and with all reasonable dispatch.

Look & Gregg [34]

LUMBER

The undersigned proprietors of the Steam-Circular Saw Mill near the Town of Clarksville respectfully tender their acknowledgments to their friends for the liberal patronage bestowed upon them during the past season and solicit a continuance of the same from their former patrons, also from the community in general. They will keep constantly on hand a large stock of Lumber embracing almost every description, and all orders for any particular kind will be filled on the shortest notice.

They have now on hand several thousand feet of dried lumber and will endeavor to keep a supply for the benefit of those who have to haul their plank to a distance.

PRICES, ON TIME

Square Pine Lumber	$15.00 per M.
Sheeting Plank	7.50 ....
Gum Plank	30.00 ....
Black Walnut Plank	40.00 ....

CASH PRICES.

Square Pine Lumber	$12.50 per M.
Sheeting Plank	6.00 ....
Gum	25.00 ....
Black Walnut	35.00 ....

H. D. WOODSWORTH, Esq., of Paris, will act as our agent for Lamar County.

Montgomery Barnett & Co.[35]

CLARKSVILLE GIN MANUFACTORY

We understand that this establishment whose advent as a new branch of mechanical employment in our neighborhood, we were much pleased with, has

> *succeeded fairly equal to the expectations of Mr. Patterson, and he has enlarged his capacity for business, by a co-partnership with Mr. J. J. Snider, of our town, a notice of which will be found in this day's paper.*
>
> *Mr. Patterson tells us that he is constantly receiving orders from a distance, including orders from the Choctaw Nation, and has as much business before him as he could desire.*
>
> *There is one decided advantage in employing these gentlemen, instead of purchasing abroad. They set up their work and start it. If there is anything wrong, they are there to remedy it, and if there is any serious defect apparent after a lapse of time; as they warrant their work, and are to be found easily, the warranty is of some use. It will be seen that they promise as good gins as can be got anywhere in the Union.* [36]

The bustle businesses on the public square and the developing industries on the outskirts of town were secondary activities compared to agriculture. Farming was Red River's attraction. The 1850 census counted 166 farms in the county. DeMorse was proud of the county's fertility - the "Paradise of Texas", he called it - and did not hesitate to boast of it to the arriving emigrant:

> *We occupy as beautiful a country as the sun ever shown upon. Our soil is a rich and productive as a man could desire. Our climate is as salubrious as any in the world and our crops are as promising as we have ever seen them. We have harvested a most abundant crop of wheat. The corn crop has never been finer and the cotton promises a yield of a bale or more an acre.*
>
> *Emigrant, do you desire a beautiful home in a rich, healthy and picturesque country, a country*

abounding in good society and the best of schools? Then come to Red River county, Texas. You can get land cheap and provisions for nearly nothing. [37]

Land was, in fact, inexpensive, even compared to other places in Texas. For example, in central Texas, around Austin, farm land in the immediate vicinity of the town - that is, from one to ten miles outside - cost $10 to $25 an acre. In Red River county it could be had for $2 an acre. Compared to other parts of the United States, buying land in Red River county was a smart choice. People from the East could sell their worn out lands at high prices - there being a demand for land in the populated East - and use the proceeds to by many times for acres of fertile virgin soil.

The first farms of Texas bore the impressive name "plantations", a description common in the American South at the time and once even used in the North and in England. Commercial interests, the doctors and the lawyers, schools, patriotic, religious, and social life might all cluster about Clarksville, especially its public square, but it was the agriculture of the plantations of Red River county that was key to the region's economic health.

The Red River Valley region had a long growing season- 234 days - and sufficient rain - 49 inches a year. There was plenty of good land available and affordable for all:

DO YOU WANT TO BUY GOOD LANDS?

I will sell 900 acres of rich prairie and timbered land, elegantly situated one mile south from Clarksville, handsomely improved, with one hundred acres in a high state of cultivation -dwelling house, corn, cribs, stables, &c. &c.

I also offer 1200 acres, lying within 2½ miles southeast from Clarksville. This tract is beautifully situated, two-thirds of which is high, rich prairie, the balance is rich bottom land, heavily timbered and well set with cane.

Also 800 acres, 4 miles west from Clarksville, near J. W. P. McKenzie's. This tract is principally second bottom cane land, 40 acres of which have been in good cultivation, and I do contend that it is the best stock farm in Red River County.

I will also sell 1500 acres of Black Oak and Hickory land, situated 4 miles north of Clarksville. This tract is well timbered and watered, and adjoins the Clarksville Prairies, which warrants the timber to be valuable. This tract also affords two delightful situations for farming. All of which I will sell on accommodating terms. The land will be bound for the payment.

Joseph C. Hart [38]

Sometimes the entire plantation was for sale, land, houses, tools, slaves etc., as was the case with the pioneer Pecan Point Plantation, which had to be sold when the owner died. Its "for sale" advertisement in *The Standard* gives us a good idea of how extensive they could be:

In our own county [Red River] we have the advertisement of Matthew Watson, executor of Hamilton, offering to sell the magnificent plantation, known for 20 years or more as the Pecan Point place with all the Negroes, Tools, work animals and agricultural implements, corn, etc. It is a rare opportunity: 1500 acres, 640 in high state of cultivation with Overseer's house, Negro cabins, frame gin house, with gin and mill attached, new cotton press, also 7,300 acres of unimproved land on Red River, good for cotton; 1,476 acres in Cass county; Robert Hamilton's head right certificate; 74 Negroes, men women and children.[39]

For you curious readers, the plantation sold within a month to Matthew Watson, Jr. It brought $17.50 an acre. He bought all of the slaves with the exception of some thirty of them who were sold to planters in Bowie and Arkansas. They were all sold as families. The sale of the slaves brought in $106,000.[40]

Cotton was the principal crop in the American southland and in Texas, anchoring the State's system of commerce and trade. In 1849, the U.S. crop was worth $65 million, requiring a slave population, valued at $150 million, to raise it. The economies of England and New England were as dependent upon it as was the South and Texas. Without sufficient cotton, their mills closed, their citizens idle and hungry, and they had no goods to sell to the people of the American and English countryside or empire, which, after all, was the basis of their economies.

> *Every class of our citizens are duly interested the good crops and remunerating prices for the farmer. All are, to a certain extent, dependent on the products of the earth. Unless the farmer has the means as a reward of his industry of supplying himself with such of the luxuries and comforts of life, as his necessities demand, the merchant, the mechanic, the professional man, all suffer with him and, therefore, it is with no small degree of pleasure and thankfulness to the Giver of all Good that we have to record such an agreeable change in the weather.*[41]

During 1840s, Texas farmers turned to cotton and, by the end of the 1850s, they exported thousands and thousands of bales of the staple. The progress of the cotton crop was of interest to everyone and *The Standard* would give reports on it frequently, even weekly at crucial periods.

Crops - Red River county

At Pecan Point in Red River country, there will be a bale made to the acre, on 200 acres. On the place of Thom. C. Forbes, black prairie land, there will be a bale made to the acre on 35 acres and 12 hundred pounds to the acre of the remaining 40 acres of cotton. He picked a 1000 pounds to the acre the first pick. On the next place of Hopkins and Hamilton, there will be a bale to an acre on 265 acres. On the prairie lands of R. M. Hopkins, there will be a bale to the acre on part and 1200 pounds on the average, and 40 bushels of corn to an acre. One more rain would have made corn yield 50 bushels to the acre. Wm. Ralston in the neighborhood has picked 1400 pounds off acres of prairie, and has 1000 more to pick. Col. English in the Savannah settlement, in this county, on sandy land, made 1000 to 1200 pounds to the acre. Judge Wootten, just below, on sandy land, makes 800 to 1000 and plenty of grain. The bales we speak of are calculated at 500 pounds. One more rain in July would have made the prairie lands average 2000 pounds of seed cotton to the acre.[42]

DeMorse was interested in agriculture[43] and maintained an extensive garden of his own. However, whether this made him an authority on raising cotton is questionable. Nevertheless, he preached about it frequently. For example, in July 1847, he touted a "Mastadon cotton" that had been tried in Red River County for the first time that year and found to be "of the finest character" and "whose growth so far exceeds of the specie heretofore used here." DeMorse was convinced that the Mastodan would dominate in North Texas. It suited the local soil and climate; its yield was much better than any other; its bolls were much larger, and hence "the quantity presented to the grasp of the picker at each place is much greater than of the old sort and the results must necessarily be the ability to gather a larger quantity at the same space and time and with small labor." He urged the region's merchants to bring up a large quantity of this seed, the next winter, as the demand would be overwhelming. However, a month later, DeMorse sheepishly had to admit that one drawback of Mastadon cotton was that not a single bale of it had been purchased by the London cotton mills. There was no market for it. No one wanted it. Another great idea spoiled by the facts.

Of course, a near blunder of this magnitude might intimidate a lesser man from uttering future recommendations, but it did not stop the Editor of *The Standard*. Just a few years later, he championed a new type of cotton.

Prout Cotton

We have been shown a specimen of Prout Cotton grown on the plantation of A. J. Titus, Esq. . The limb was about a foot in length and had on it 35 healthy bolls, blooms and squares. We have not the least doubt from the appearance of the specimen which we saw that the Prout cotton will "turn out" more than twice the common cotton now generally in cultivation. The planters should all endeavor to get a start from the seed of this cotton next year.

We have seen a specimen of Prout cotton grown on the plantation of William H. Harrison, 5 miles west of Town. We are unable to decide between his specimen and the one sent in by Mr. Titus. We don't think there can be any difference. They couldn't be better. There is not room on the branches for any more bolls. We hope Messrs Titus and Harrison will raise enough of this cotton to supply the rest of the planters with enough seeds at the next planting. We would be pleased to hear how this cotton "turns out." Let us hear from you gentlemen. [44]

Cotton might have been the king crop, but it was not DeMorse's preference for the farmers of the Red River Valley region of Texas. He urged them to grow wheat.

WHEAT

While upon this subject, we will request again that more wheat should be raised by our farmers. It is a surer crop here than it is in most of the Western states and we have a home market for all over the neighborhood consumption. In the Choctaw nation and in the counties of Bowie, Cass, Harrison, Rusk, Upshur, Smith, Cherokee, and Shelby, we can always find purchasers.[45]

There were a couple of reasons why growing wheat made good sense. There was a strong local market, a number of military posts to be supplied, a great number of provisionless immigrants arriving in the state and, when the wheat was milled into flour, it could be exported to New Orleans by river. What really made wheat attractive, however, was a bit of farm equipment that would revolutionize agriculture, the reaper invented by Cyrus McCormick. With it, a single man, with three horses, could cut 15 acres a day. Before that, a farmer could not get enough help to harvest wheat, either because the needed men were either working at their own farms or because using slaves would interfere with the cultivation of the more important staple, cotton. A second invention was the thresher. Raising and cutting more acres of wheat resulted in more bushels of wheat that had to be threshed before milling. Technology provided that to the small farmer in a "wagon like vehicle of unusual appearance, - Emery's Wheat thresher - highly commended for portableness and of their comparative performance, being worked by two horses and threshing 250 bushels a day."[46]

Wheat

Have our farmers grown enough wheat? We think not, after having made some inquiry. There is an eager demand for flour now in the counties below and we are satisfied that there is not enough wheat of last

> *year's crop to supply it. For eight years we have urged our farmers to grow more of this grain and yet they will not make a main crop of it. Why we cannot tell. It is by far the surest crop raised here, except oats. There is less trouble in cultivating it than cultivating either corn or cotton. It is a most profitable crop, particularly suited to the character of our prairies and yet hardly a farmer cultivated it, except as a convenience. We wish very much that some wheat farmer from one of the northwestern states with capital and energy would come here and show what can be made by attention to wheat mainly and other grains secondarily. The profits of such farming, thriftly and industriously carried on, would be immense and the example would tend to benefit this region of the country. Just so much land as a man can prepare and seed, with all the labor at his command, he can readily reap in a few days with a machine reaper. Then, with a patent thresher, it is soon prepared for the mill. Then we have home consumption, garrison consumption for Towson, Washita and the posts west of Washita to Brazos and all of Texas, south of us, for a market. Add to this for years to come, the increased home market from an immense immigration. And, when all this fails to consume the market, cutting, threshing and grinding our wheat at the earliest moment, we can send our crop to New Orleans in early June, in advance of the northwestern crop and command high prices as the only fresh flour in the market.*[47]

Of course, if enough wheat is grown, reaped and threshed, then more mills would be needed to convert it into flour. DeMorse recognized and urged progress in that endeavor as well.

> *There is only one defect about the valuable conversion of our surplus wheat crop into money. We have not yet the right sort of flouring mill. We need a*

> Merchant Mill, a steam mill with all the necessary
> fixtures and devoted entirely to grinding wheat, corn and
> rye. The establishment of such a mill would give an
> impetus to wheat raising, which would be beneficial to
> the District and, we should suppose, beneficial to the
> mill owner.
>
> Will no one try this speculation?[48]

DeMorse did all he could to encourage the sowing of more wheat. He distributed seeds of experimental breeds. He solicited and published crop yields from farmers, publicizing the productivity of Northern Texas. He even awarded annually a silver goblet to the farmer in the region with the best crop and published promising candidates:

> Our farmers should measure their wheat crops
> and report them to us for publication, giving the yield
> per acre and the method of preparation of the ground
> for the crop, which we doubt not was all in cases
> indifferent enough. We want to show what kind of wheat
> or rather what quantity our land will produce, even
> when unprepared in the proper manner.[49]

> Judge Dillahunty has sent to us some heads of
> wheat which average some 93 to 103 grains in a head.
> Can anybody beat this?
>
> Measure your crops and send in your reports.
> Let's know what Northern Texas can do![50]

Cotton was the money crop in Red River county with wheat and corn strong seconds. The cotton was mostly for export, the wheat, by and large, for sale to emigrants and the corn fed to the slaves. Fruit and what DeMorse would term "garden vegetables", on the other hand, appear to have been raised for local consumption, both on the farms as well as in the gardens of townspeople, DeMorse himself being a perfect example.[51] Of the many types of fruit that was raised in the county, apples seemed to be the favorite. They were sold in town for 75 cents a bushel and, if DeMorse's enthusiasm is to be believed, were essential to the good life:

> *Red River Apples*
>
> *Our friend William Enmonson presented us today some Golden Pippins, raised by him on his place on Pine Creek. Last year was the second bearing. They ripen late and keep through the winter nicely. The gratification in receiving such compliments is enhanced by the evidence that some attention is being given by our farmers to raising this noble fruit. There are few enjoyments which attend more to attach men to the soil, and especially young men to the place of their birth than a rich plentifulness of fruits and flowers, gratifying the higher sense, mingling the mental with the animal taste, while satisfying the animal appetite, ministering to the sense of beauty.[52]*

DeMorse applauded the availability of fruits other than just the apple, again suggesting that fruit production was a hallmark of any civilized society.

> *Nothing more marks the advancement of a country than the plentifulness of fruit in its market places.*
>
> *We recollect that four years ago, when we first came to Clarksville, nothing of the sort was ever offered for sale in the Town, save perhaps, some poor distressing looking representations of the watermelon species. Now rarely a day passes that wagons are not standing about the Square with peaches on it or melons. These, it is true, do not constitute a variety of fruit to boast upon, but we are merely referring to the*

plentifulness and quality of what we have and must be considered with reference to the newness of the county. The watermelons are frequently of the finest order. They are brought from the sandy soil ten or twelve miles from Town. We do not believe the black land immediately around us to be favorable for their growth. The peaches are of fair quality, not the best, but frequently very good.

The apple, plum and pear orchards are getting near their maturity. We were presented some this summer with some fine specimens of the large yellow and red plums. Apples have been growing in some two or three places on the river for perhaps 15 years, but in the prairies, few of the orchards were bearing at all until last year, and then but scantily.

In the fall of the another year, the visitor to Clarksville, may see upon the street wagons of apples for sale, giving another notable example of the union of the products of the north and the south, in this favored region, a union so strongly exemplified by the remarkable yield of wheat.[53]

Garden type vegetables were also grown for the table, not export, throughout Red River county. Some of them were quite large and DeMorse did not hesitate to brag about them, challenging others to match or best them. Indeed, some of the specimens might be of record proportions. If you doubt it, pretend you are in the "vegetable section" of a frontier supermarket and jot down the size of some of the following, to compare to the produce in your neighboring super market today.

RADISHES

Benj. Crownover, Esq., has brought us some specimens of Blossom Prairie radishes raised upon his place. The largest is 16 inches and three quarters around, and weighs two pounds and three quarters; another one weighs two and one-half pounds. [54]

☞ *We acknowledge the receipt of a large Radish, weighing four pounds and measuring eighteen inches, sent us by Samson Smith Esq.*[55]

We have upon our table an ear of corn from the plantation of John Robbins, plucked last Monday. It is 11 and ½ inches long and has on 976 grains and weighs one pound nine ounces. We are told there are many more of the same august proportions in the same field. We think this will pass for corn anywhere.

We have also upon our tables some cotton bolls deposited with us by Mr. Wm. S. Johnston of this vicinity who says he has plenty more of the same sort. They were plucked last Wednesday and the largest measures 6 inches and 3/8th around. Somebody is requested to do better, if he can. Mr. Johnston challenges any one in the vicinity to show more cotton from any one acre in their farm than he will show from one acre of his at picking time.

We acknowledge the receipt of a fine mess of sweet potatoes from the farm of E. P. Wallis. They were of excellent size and flavor and we should suppose quite forward.

Acknowledge also the receipt of a muskmelon from Mr. A. J. Rice, weighing twenty five pounds and measuring 35 and ½ inches around one way and 37 the other. Has plenty more of the same sort.

If all the above are not evidence that we raise something in this region in the way of corn, cotton, potatoes and muskmelons, we are no judge of such matters.[56]

BEET THIS WHO CAN!

There were presented to us on Thursday last by Wm. Sims Esq., two beets, the growth of his garden.

One measuring 22 inches around and weighting 11 pounds, the other, smaller in circumference, weighting nine pounds.[57]

Peaches

Our friend Joseph Taylor presented us with several peaches a few days ago, which were the largest we have ever seen, five of them weighting over three pounds. Thus, it will be seen that our soil is not only adapted to the growth of cotton, corn and wheat but also superior fruit and vegetables in rich profusion.[58]

BIG POTATOES

There rests upon our table, a Yam potato raised by Dr. A. J. Redding of this county measuring 18 inches in length, and 21 inches in circumference and weighing 13 pounds. Have you anything more to say?[59]

Egg plant

We have on our table an eggplant sent in by James C. Caldwell, Esq. which measured around the middle 22 ½ inches - from the stem around the bottom 24 inches, but this seems to us to be a large one, but is said to be an average specimen from the garden or, at any rate, there were many more that were as large.[60]

Capt. J. E. Hopkins of this County has sent to us some specimens of potatoes, beets, turnips and radishes - the last two the growth of this fall on new land, which are astonishing large for the length of time grown - turnips sown in September. We have not tape line convenient or else we would give you the circumference. He challenges competition. The vegetables are in our office and can be seen.[61]

DeMorse, reluctant to have the region rely so heavily on cotton, urged the farmers to experiment with other crops, which we today would find unusual for Texas. For example, the acorns of the forests of East Texas:

> *The Pecan Mast, which is now beginning to fall, will prove a source of considerable profit to western Texas the present season being very abundant, and considering the dryness of the season, of excellent growth. We understand that many individuals west and south of us are turning their attention to the gathering of this fruit, with a view to ship it to foreign markets, and, indeed, it would not surprise us, if it should prove of greater value to the west than the cotton crop to the planters of that staple in other portions of the State.*[62]

Tobacco was another experiment. It never really caught on in Red River region, failing probably because of the climate.[63] Nevertheless, some farmers tried it:

Maj. De Morse

> *I herewith send you a copy of my Texas tobacco, agreeable to request, and from the results of my experimentation have no hesitation in believing that our hickory barrens will produce as finer tobacco as any country whatever, and, for quantity per acre, will surpass that of anywhere it is now raised as a stable commodity. This year, I have raised two crops from the same stock. The last, if anything, heavier than the first cutting. The weight of the last I would thing would approach 100 pounds to the acre. Our thicket land on the Sulphur will produce tobacco, equal in quality to the best river lands in Virginia, if the same care be taken in its curing. This experiment has been made by me to convince our people that there is absolutely no necessity for the importation of this article. Its cost to this county,*

> in 1856, according to the best data, amounted to over $8,000, exclusive of segars [cigars] and a surplus can be exported.
>
> Wm. Williams[64]

For a while, in the 1850's, sugar cane, usually associated with places like Cuba and Louisiana and another crop that could decrease the county's reliance on cotton, became all the rage.

Chinese Sugar cane, referred to as sorghum sucre, was very popular across the nation. Sugar could be made from the dried stalks, and, reportedly, it could be grown far north as Massachusetts. It required principally dry soil and hot sun. Maturing in fewer than a 100 days, from time of sowing of seed, it could be used either for sugar or feeding livestock. Supposedly, it yielded 4,500 gallons of "vinegar" or "syrup" to the acre, a rich molasses which, DeMorse pronounced, as having the taste of the sugar houses molasses. A portfolio of *Standard* items, in chronological order, present the ascendancy of Chinese Sugar Cane in Northern Texas:

> *Texas Sugar*
>
> *We have been furnished by the Rev. Jas. Sampson, with a specimen of the sugar made by Henry Jones, on Caney, Matagorda County. It is really beautiful. We have never seen better in our life. It is light colored, very lively and large grained. The grains have that bright sparking look that we see in the best flint loaf sugar. We invite examination by those who take pride in home production. Will not some of our farmers in the timberlands or in the prairies with a skirt of timber on the North, try the cultivation of the cane? It would be a great saving of money to raise our own sugar as we do our own wheat. We have no doubt that it could be successfully raised in the timber lands of Titus county and probably in Red River and Bowie.[65]*

> *Sugar cane has been successfully and profitably cultivated in Harrison county by Col. Rene Fitzpatrick, formerly residing in this county, near Jonesboro. He made 6 barrels of sugar and 300 or 400 gallons of fine syrup from 2 acres of cane.*
>
> *Cannot some of our sandy land farmers try this? It might perhaps succeed in the timber lands and is certainly worth a trial.*[66]

> *The Chinese sugar cane – promising.*
>
> *We have a small patch in our garden, which has grown well and matured seeds. The quantity is too small for experimentation on the juice. We have cut some of the tops to let it seed again, as it is said it will, and we have planted two or three weeks since, from the seed of the first crop, to see how a second crop from seed would mature. This last planting is about 3 inches high.*[67]

The farms had live stock, of course, of varying kinds.

> *Hogs*
>
> *Red River county against Hopkins - Mr. Wm. S. Johnson of Jonesboro writes to us that he has raised a hog, which he killed on the 11th instant, at three and a half years old, weighing 402 pounds. The hog was only put up in December last to fatten. He wishes this to be a challenge for Hopkins county to meet.*[68]

Texas is not known for sheep, but it was not from lack of effort by DeMorse to have the Northern Texas region adopt sheep raising and thereby substitute wool for cotton as its principal crop. He explained why:

Wool Growing

Several times within the last five years we have endeavored to impress upon our readers, the inevitable profit to the individuals who would engage in it, as well as the great advantages to this section of the State, of an investment of capital in sheep and the growing of wool for market.

Sheep do fine here and of little expense, except for herding, and upon any of our considerable prairies, but particularly on the south side of the Sulphur, would make a man an immense return on his investment and necessary attention. Then again, the wool bears so much better, from its greater value per pound, the expense of transportation. We have many times endeavored to impress upon our citizens the folly, as well as the uselessness of relying upon cotton as a product for market, when we can diversify in so many ways more profitably, the flavor of the district.

We see no man of capital turning his attention to wool growing, which would be the most profitable of all occupations in the District.

Cotton is an indifferent dependence, burthened as we are with expense and delayed in the transportation. The wool market will not be affected as the cotton market by every arrival from Europe, today bearing a high price and tomorrow ruinously depreciated, but will vary little and can be counted upon with a reasonable degree of certainty as to value.[69]

DeMorse cited examples of the profit involved. John D. Pitts, on his farm in Grimes county, had in a single year increased his flock from 122 sheep to 229; Pitts sold thirteen of these sheep to Thomas H. Duncan, residing on the Guadalupe, six miles below Seguin. In twenty two months, they had increased fifty two head, which averaged five and one quarter pounds of wool per shearing. At sixty to ninety cents a pound prices in 1854, that was between $150 and $200 bonus cash yield on a flock that kept profitably multiplying in number and size. But, all of DeMorse's careful reasoning was to no avail. The planters of North Texas never became interested in becoming shepherds, however compelling DeMorse's logic was.

Today, Texas is synonymous with cattle, especially the Longhorn. That image, however, was still in the distance, to emerge in the post Civil War period. Yet, in the early Anglo days in Mexican Texas, Red River's principal market commodity was cattle. By the 1820s, small herds were being driven south to San Antonio. Then, during the next decades, cotton became the most important agricultural product of Red River county. Cattle still were raised, but they were the eastern breeds of beef, descended from English stock brought over by the early colonists. The Longhorns, which we associate with Texas, were wild still, a breed apart from their European cousins. They had been brought to America by Columbus from Spain, where they had been introduced by the conquering North African Moors in the 1400s. Escaped and abandoned animals, over several centuries, formed huge herds in South Texas, awaiting to be discovered by the Texan.

Although not Longhorns, Texans continued their attention to cattle in the 1840s and even engaging in some of those "cowboy" type activities that would be their hallmark a dozen years later. New Orleans needed beef and Texas supplied it. The cattle were not driven eastward, but floated there on specially built boats. Cattle raising was a promising business for Texas as the *Galveston Civilian*, reprinted in *The Standard*, explains:

> *The beef trade of Texas seems to be steadily increasing. The number of cattle shipped by sea to New Orleans within the past 12 months, varies little from 10,000. In addition, from the means heretofore used to bring cattle from the mainland to Galveston, there are now two steamers being built with special reference to this trade - one at Louisville, Kentucky, and another, the*

> hull of which was built at Lynchburg, now being
> completed at this port. Between 2,000 and 3,000 beeves
> are now necessary to supply this city and the number
> will increase yearly. Stock raising is perhaps the best
> business followed in Texas. Some of our distant readers
> will scarcely believe us, when we say there are men in
> Texas who receive more than $10,000 annually for
> beeves, the rearing of which cost nothing but the labor
> of branding and herding. They live upon the
> spontaneous growth of the soil, not even requiring salt
> of their owners [70]

The Standard, of course, encouraged the industry, as it did all things that benefitted Northern Texas. The favorable economics, enjoyed by one early rancher, served as an example.

> *Profits of Stock raising.*
>
> In 1842, a gentleman in Brazoria county who
> does not like to see his name in print, but for whose
> entire validity we will vouch, gave half a league of land
> not worth more than $4,000 for 1000 head of neat cattle.
> Since that time, he has supported his family and
> improved a farm worth $4,000 to $50,000 from the sale
> of the produce of the herd, which has now - besides the
> number sold - increased to 7,000 head. Of this number,
> he has sold 4,000 at $4 each for a total of $16,000 in all.
> He estimates that the number previously sold brought
> $10,000. Readers abroad must understand that the
> cattle have no food in this country, save what is
> furnished by natural pastures.[71]

The immense vegetation of Texas and its open ranges were what made cattle raising so economically attractive. Nature fed the herd, man protected its growth and harvested it at their leisure. That was not the way it was back in the crowded Eastern states or elsewhere in the United States, as the following article from *DeBows Review*, reprinted in *The Standard*, points out:

Texas as a Grazing State

The beneficence of her climate, operating upon soil of unsurpassed fertility, must render Texas the garden spot of our favored country. In Tennessee, Missouri and the vast Northwest, nearly two thirds of the year is devoted in a unremitting effort to provide the necessary food for the livestock during the winter. This effort involves an immense capital, severe and constant labor and frequent exposure in the cold temperatures to attend the stock. These energies are bestowed too upon lands which cost from $20 to $70 an acre, while Texas presents the most beautiful picture of eternal pastures, which beneficent providence has prepared to her hands and which needs not the labor and capital necessary to put the woodland of the Middle States into grass. The cattle on a thousand hills roam over these natural meadows and require no care save salting and herding in a period of Northers. It is not possible to exaggerate the importance of Texas in her grazing capacities, for while her lands are rich and cheap, her prairies are ever green, and mules and cattle may be reared at a price that would seem to be incredible to the grazer of the Middle States. The cotton and sugar planters on the coast, as well as the planters on the states on the lower Mississippi furnish a safe and profitable market for the mules and cattle raised on the table lands that may be readily purchased at $1 to $5 an acre, which in their deep soil and mellow climate are crying aloud to the rich as well as the poor of other countries. Come and Occupy![72]

When gold was discovered in California, another new market for cattle opened up. The demand for beef there was great and the gold with which to pay for it readily available.

The number of cattle driven across Texas to California was a trickle compared to the cattle drives that would follow after the Civil War, but those that got there could be sold at large profits:

> *Wentworth who left here [San Antonio] here some time ago with stock for California , we learn, has arrived at his destination without accident or loss. Cattle are in great demand and he will recognize a handsome profit in his stock. He was offered, before getting into San Francisco, $120 per head, which he refused.*[73]

But, driving cattle westward across Texas to California could also be extraordinarily dangerous. The people of Clarksville learned that only too well, when a number of their citizens, joined such a venture organized by Howard Rhine of Clarksville, part of Rhine & Brothers, the energetic North Texas merchant and entrepreneur family. Brad Fowler, a lawyer from Paris, who had been a companion of DeMorse's on the Northern Texas court circuit, was among the adventure seeking, working their way to California "attendants" hired by Rhine to manage the herd. He reported to *The Standard* readers a great many curiosities encountered on the first leg of their trip west, Clarksville to El Paso, including the horrible ambush by Apaches that claimed the lives of some of their number.

Agriculture was not as foolproof as DeMorse suggests. A promising crop of any kind could be cut down at any time by any one of a number of pests. Locusts, army ants, cut worms. cotton worms, birds and grasshoppers were among the villains. Red River county appeared to be spared any of these ravages during the first decade of Texas' statehood. However, regions to the south were not so fortunate, as *The Standard's* exchange papers reported.

> *We learn through The Huntsville Banner that the Cotton Worm is doing great damage to the cotton crop*

> in that region. We are informed that within the last few days they have made their appearance in this county. This certainly looks rather unpromising.[74]

> We regret to learn that the crops have been seriously injured by the cut worms and birds. Many planters have been compelled to plant their corn three or four times and their cotton has been cut down, as if the army worm were ravaging the country. Many of the gardens have been desolated by these destructive insects.[75]

> Grasshoppers
> Nearly all out western exchanges bring lamentable accounts of the ravages of the grasshoppers on the crops and grass. In many places every blade of grass, every plant of corn, entire wheat and oat fields have been destroyed by these merciless freebooters. In some places, after they had nothing left to feed upon, they have sought out new regions in which to exercise their filibustering propensities. The farmers have taken advantage of their temporary withdrawal and replanted their crops. In places visited by them, their devastation is little worse that the locust plagues in Egypt. What renders this visitation more deplorable is that there is one for which there is no easy remedy.

> In this region, we are still exempt from the plague, but we cannot say how long we may remain. That we are so we do not believe to be attributed to any great extra amount of merit on our part, but in the long suffering patience of a merciful God.[76]

Weather also a big factor as to whether the farmer would thrive or suffer. Too much rain was bad; too little rain was worse. In 1854, for example, the whole of Northern Texas - probably the entire southwest - suffered for want of rain. The corn crop was lost. The cotton crop was "passable, but not under any circumstances a good one." It affected more than just the crops. "The creeks are fast getting dry and the grass beginning to parch and rain will soon be needed for the health of the grazing stock."[77] But both deluge and drought built character, and clever farmers would find a way around them:

Rain

For nearly a month, shower after shower has poured down upon this locality, keeping the streets continually wet and, worse than that, deluging the devoted crops of corn and cotton. Our cotton crop will only be half as big. Ploughing of late has been impossible, except for a day at a time, and the only course now for our farmer is to prepare as much ground as possible during the summer and in the fall sow wheat exclusively and endeavor by transporting flour to Shreveport and the counties below us to realize money at the same time they usually get returns on their cotton.

This can be done by industry and energy and it should be a rule of life never to bend to temporary adversity but the higher the impending wave, the greater the effort to rise upon it and ride safely over it.[78]

The Wilds of Red River County

One did not have to go too far out of Clarksville to go hunting or fishing. There were still a bit of that left in northern Red River county, near the adjoining, sparsely settled, Indian Nation. Of course, it was not like just twenty years before, when Red River county was the roaming ground of elk, buffalo, mustangs and numerous other wild animals. It sufficed, however, for sport and food, as the following handful of accounts attest.

Piscatory

Some of our citizens have already commenced the summer sport of fishing. In a little lake on CutHand bottom, about 7 miles from town they caught on Thursday last some of the finest perch and trout ever seen in the southwest and plenty of them. We had been lamenting prior to last summer that our region was destitute of this type of recreation, without a travel of 13 or 14 miles to Red River to catch catfish, which we look as like sitting at the end of a wharf and catching toad fish, but the experience of the last summer and the commencement of this season prove fish as well as game can be found in abundance near enough to town for convenience. [79]

The Chase

Game is more abundant in the woods near Town than has been known for years heretofore and we are induced by the "sights" of birds, venison etc. which we see occasionally, to believe that hunting is now not only pleasant, but profitable. [80]

Small game is abundant about here now, and hunters shoot in the vicinity of the Town, great quantities of Ducks, partridges, Squirrels etc. We also hear an occasional bear hunt in the bayou. [81]

pigeons

There has been for the week or so past an extensive pigeon roost in the pine woods between the Steam Mills. Many of our citizens have availed themselves of the chance to kill them at night. It has been several years since the pigeons have been here previously. In the winters of 1842-43 and 1843-44, they roosted in the same vicinity. [82]

There were dangerous animals around as well, especially wild cats or panthers. When the Red River was low, they would come across it from the Indian Nation, looking for a favorite food, pigs.

Red River panther

On Tuesday night last, Mr. Walter S. Spencer and Pat B. Clark, being out hunting near Roland, on Red River, the dogs started what the hunters thought to be a fox, followed it about three miles when it took a tree. Supposing it at last to be a large cat, they chunked it out of three trees successively and, at last, the dogs, four in number, seized it and killed it, when it proved to be a panther nine feet from the tip of the nose to the end of the tail and very large in the girth. When the dogs seized it, it was slightly wounded by a fall in the left fore foot, discharged from a pistol. The hunters had but one load left, and were obliged to leave the work mostly to the dogs, who had a severe contest, although only one was badly bit. The hunters assisted in the affray by hitting the panther occasionally with sticks. [83]

Killing a panther

Early last Sunday morning two panthers were discovered in the cotton field on Dr. Gordon's Red River plantation below Rowland in this county. They were immediately pursued by Mr. James Clark with his dogs. One of them took a tree some 200 yards outside the fence, when Mr. Clark shot in him in the side by a discharge of one barrel of his shot gun and the panther dropped and was finished by the dogs. The other panther got out of sight and was seen no more. The animal killed was near 10 feet from the nose to the end of the tail long, was enormously large and fat and very gray on the head and the neck, probably a veteran long accustomed to feed on the pigs of the neighborhood. His tusks, two inches in length, has been shown to us. The hogs, belonging to the plantation, had been turned into the field for protection and had been repeatedly missed of late, sometimes pigs, sometimes full grown hogs. When the panthers were started, they had just killed and were eating a hog and pieces of the pig as large a man's hand were found in the stomach of the animal killed.

This is the second panther killed on this place within a year. The place has been settled some 20 years and is immediately adjacent to the landing for this town, known as Roland, in a region one would suppose that these wild foragers of the woods would avoid. It may be that they come from the comparatively unsettled region of the Choctaw side opposite, the river having been low for a long time, as to interpose no obstacle, and of late frozen over. [84]

Getting Around Texas: The River, Roads,
Bridges and Someday the Railroad

It is difficult for us today to imagine a Texas without highways and airports, connecting and making manageable the enormity of the State's geography. A century ago, it was the railroad that was the modern wonder. It and the telegraph wires that ran alongside the track would revolutionize communications and travel within Texas and to the outside world. A town's success or failure depended on how close it lay to the passing tracks. However, totally forgotten is the time, a generation before even the rail road, when internal transportation depended on the rivers of Texas. Indeed, the rivers themselves are nearly invisible today and, when recognized, more resemble the abandoned "canals" scarring the Martian face, than the infrastructure of the 1850s. How many in Dallas - once called the City of the Three Forks of the Trinity- know the location of those river beds today? Dams, lakes, flood control, irrigation and development, all have done their part to the withering of Texas rivers: the Brazos, Colorado, Sabine, Trinity, Guadalupe, San Antonio, Nueces, Rio Grande and, of particular importance to the people of Clarksville and the Red River Valley, the Red River, with its Sulphur Creek.

The Red River is 1,360 miles long, the second longest in Texas. It stretches from the Mississippi and the Gulf of Mexico on one end, north to Arkansas, west across the entire state of Texas and then into the mountains of New Mexico. A key to Clarksville's success was the landing or docks the town had on the Red River, which permitted Texas to hook into the river commerce. The landing was just ten miles north of Clarksville. It had some stores, warehouses and its own name, Roland. A passing mention of it by DeMorse provides some identity to it and its residents:

> *Roland.*
>
> *This little river town is improving. The road from here to Roland is at present comparatively good or could be made so at a very trifling cost. While on this subject, we would honorably suggest to our Chief Justice the propriety of establishing an election precinct at Roland. It is wanted very much by the people in that neighborhood, who, when they vote at all, are compelled to travel some 10 or 12 miles to do so, crossing Pecan bayou in their route, which is, at times, almost impassible.*[85]

You will not find Roland on the map today, or even in the memory of the oldest citizen. But, it was there, at Roland, where the Red River planters and Clarksville merchants received the seed, equipment, manufactured goods and other necessities and luxuries they had been ordered the autumn before. As the Christmas holiday season approached, Editor DeMorse had his own visions of sugar plums running through his mind and Roland on the Red River was the key to his Christmas Wish's becoming reality:

> *Our townsmen, Rhine & Bros, are the owners of the Fanny Fern. We hope the first trip she makes to Roland that her enterprising owners will have a corner, well stored with oysters, a few fish, salmon stowed away in ice and such a supply of Irish potatoes as that this county can get, at least an abundance to plant at an early season.*[86]

It was at Roland also where, in winter and spring time, as the "navigation" of the river permitted, the planters would send by steamboat or flatboat their cotton down the Red River to Shreveport, where the Red River joined the Mississippi. From Shreveport, the market in New Orleans was only two days away by steamer. After the cotton was sold in New Orleans, it would be stowed on sailing ships and sent to the cotton and textile mills of either New England or London, where thousands upon thousands of workers waited to turn the nature's fiber into fabrics of fashion.

Although the Red River was by far the best means available to the farmer to send his crop to market and to receive his supplies in return, it was still a very difficult, often unreliable, route. The river was not deep and it was obstructed in places, with accumulated fallen trees and growths of vegetation, called *rafts*. Usually, the river began to rise in January or February, peaked in mid-spring and then declined until, by early summer, boats became rare. Sometimes, late fall would bring some more rains and the river would again be briefly "boatable." It would follow logically that, if ample rains brought navigation, droughts would hinder it. Texas river traffic was highly dependent upon the weather. We are fortunate because, in this fifteen year span from 1846 through 1860, we encounter the best and worse of weather's effects upon the river and the economy of the region.

For example, in the spring of 1846, the river was reported as "running red" which, we are told, "indicated a good stage for boats." Presumably, the river was gaining the color, for which it was named, from the red clay in the banks, not usually washed into the water, unless it was swollen. The river was regularly navigable at the necessary seasons for the rest of 1846, all of 1847 and 1848.

> *The Red River has been bank full the past week, and is still high with the prospect of continuance for some time.*
>
> *On Monday, the Fulton arrived at our landing and, on Tuesday, the Buffalo, bringing large lots of merchandise for Clarksville.* [87]

However, beginning in late 1848, a new weather pattern set in, the likes of which had never been experienced even by the same "the oldest citizen" who was always quoted on those occasions, when no other record books existed. As described elsewhere, the weather turned very wet - unusually large snow storms in the winter and steady, monotonous rains for months on end. The rivers, of course, responded accordingly.

At first, the affect of the precipitation on river traffic was welcomed. It allowed the planters to get their cotton off to market quickly so as to get the best price and, at the same time, permitted an easy and long steam boating season. This, in turn, created competition among the steamboats, resulting in lower freight charges for the planters and merchants. DeMorse applauded that "Old Red" had served Clarksville well that winter, with "almost uninterrupted navigation and the freights are at reasonable rates."[88]

Unfortunately, there can be too much of a good thing. It kept raining and raining in 1849 and the river rose and rose, until it flooded plantations along the river, disrupted the mail and began to be an overall nuisance. DeMorse quipped that the "sweet stream" - the Red River - was *only* 16 miles wide at Fulton and that they were considering chartering "a small schooner" to be sent over to the region "where Fulton used to be" to pick up the mail. It was to get worse:

Red River. . .

Old Red commenced rising on Sunday and, by Thursday, was bank full with a liberal promise of an overflow.

At 11 o'clock yesterday, the water was running over the plantation of Hamilton & Rainey at Pecan Point and was still rising.

From Travis Wright's landing, we learn that he was moving everything back from the warehouse, fearing an overflow. [89]

The extraordinary period of heavy precipitation ended in

the autumn of 1850. The next three years normal rains restored regular commerce on the river. However, lest the Planters grew too complacent, Mother Nature displayed her fickleness. In late spring of 1854, a drought began and, in consequence, the level of the Red River dropped. It was to be the start of a two-year cessation of river traffic, which brought hardships along with it. The cotton, picked in the fall of 1853, remained stacked up at the river landings, waiting for steam boats that never came. No boats meant no supplies from New Orleans and, among those affected was DeMorse and *The Standard* which ran out of paper and could not publish for a number of weeks, until wagons hauled in a new supply on the longer, more expensive overland route. To the west, past Sherman, the Red River was "as dry as a bone - not water enough for a horse to drink." It was drier than the ubiquitous "oldest pioneers of the sources of the river had ever seen or hear of." It began causing some shortages in town:

> *Red River*
>
> *The rain, which fell during the middle part of last week, was insufficient to render Red River in boatable condition. The rise at Roland, our landing, did not much exceed 5 feet. Should we have another good rain in a few days, the river would probably be in boating order for this section of the country. This event would be hailed with pleasure by most of our citizens, as stocks of merchandise of all kinds, especially of groceries, are getting low. Coffee has been selling here for some time at 25 cents a pound and scarce even at that price.* [90]

It did not get better. The drought continued and low water threatened worse problems than higher coffee prices:

> *The river, our only dependence as a means for getting cotton to market, is now at the low water mark. Our merchants and planters have been suffering*

severely of the past 12 months by the unprecedented continuance of low water. Had boats been in readiness to take advantage of the rise in the river, which we have had this spring, our cotton may have all been at market, but this not having been the case, our cotton still lies at the various landings or houses. [91]

Happily, in August of 1856, some two years and three months after the drought had begun, the skies opened up often and long enough for the drought to end and Red River to return to normal. The news of copious rains in the western part of the Red River valley, filling the tributaries of the river, reached Clarksville before the rise in the river did:

weather

We had a rise in the river of between four and five feet, before the rain which fell on Tuesday and we think it highly probable that now there will be a sufficient rise to permit large size boats to visit our landing at Roland. Since writing the above, we have seen a gentleman who returned from Roland yesterday evening. He states that the river has risen more than 15 feet with considerable drift wood running. A Gentleman from Bonham, who arrived in town this morning, reports that a vast quantity of rain had fallen in that section on Tuesday evening and night, so that the prospect is now very favorable for a good rise in Red River, sufficient to let boats come up and take off the accumulated cotton of two years crop from the different warehouses along the river and at such rates as planters can afford to pay. [92]

DeMorse, no more a river man than he had been a planter, was determined, nonetheless, to dispense advice about transportation, just as he had done with agriculture. The steamboats out of New Orleans and Shreveport were charging what DeMorse believed to be exorbitant rates. Freight charges, together with the size of the crop and the market price, determined how well or how poorly the planter did that season. Remember that Democrat DeMorse proudly claimed that his paper was "opposed to all chartered monopolies." What the river needed, according to DeMorse, was some competition, ideally home funded. Outraged at how much he had to pay in freight for a small parcel, DeMorse preserved to us, a century and a half later, the economics of the river traffic:

Extortions

Few persons elsewhere have any concept of the outrageous charges for freight made by steamboats on the Red River. We have been charged a dollar and half freight for one box of claret, one dollar and a half on a cheese about 20 pounds, weight, half a dollar on a loaf of sugar and, yesterday, we were presented on getting home with a little package containing stereotype plates, weighing two and 3/4 pounds on which one dollar freight was charged from Shreveport to our landing. All freight is charged $2 a barrel from New Orleans to the landing and everything less than a half barrel is charged as if it were a half barrel, no matter how small the packet or parcel. Boats in this trade pay for themselves in a year, or a little more, and then after all profits are net. This is not on account of delays incident to the navigation. They come within a few hours of the appointed times. A little more competition would benefit out citizens and would ensure profit on newcomers who would prices a to a fair rate, say one dollar and a quarter per barrel and fifty cents for a hundred weight.[93]

DeMorse's wish came true. Two new boats were bucking the "Combination" on the river, as DeMorse referred to the price fixers. DeMorse predicted that "the action of the people has already had its effect. The Combination can go out, back out or go under, as it pleases. One of the three, it will have to do." [94]

DeMorse urged the planters, as matters of both economic necessity and social virtue, to build their own flatboats to ship their cotton down river, avoiding the "exorbitant" prices of the Combination. He then suggested that the merchants, who paid the same high rates for their supplies, "should club together" with the planters, which would provide cargos for the flatboat's return up river after delivering her cargo. He predicted that the cost per bale would be between $1.50 and $2.50 per bale cheaper that the $4 per price of the controlled steamers. DeMorse saw two other benefits to home built flat boats:

> *It will allow the crop to be shipped with less delay, than by steam boats, and in consequence, in our obtaining better prices at market. Another result will be that steamboat owners and captains, who are disposed to extort upon the necessities of our local situation, will find themselves powerless and will be very apt to become more reasonable in their demands.* [95]

Another way to "out compete" another, is to provide services that he cannot. The concept of using flatboats was a start, but not being steamer propelled were not as reliable going upstream. Special, smaller, specially designed for the upper river boats were needed. Built by local Red River planters and merchants, these steam boats could get up river, where the larger steamers with their greater drafts could not, when the river was low. The best of them drew only 13 inches of water when without cargo. They were able to carry 1,000 bales of cotton down river and needed only 3 ½ feet of water. Coming up the river, they could land at Rowland with 2,000 barrels of freight and need only 2 feet of water. It also had cabin accommodations for 40 passengers. The *Texas*, "owned by citizens of the District" was one of them. The *Choctaw* was another. DeMorse had come up on her from Alexandria, Louisiana "when no other boat in the trade could get up." He pronounced her a "pleasant boat to travel on" and "worthy of patronage."[96] The *Jim Turner* was a third that had been built for the up river trade. She and the others that were "built for this trade and owned, or partly owned, by the citizens of our District are boats that should be patronized in preference of all others, so long as their charges are reasonable."[97]

Roads were responsible for the shorter haul, that is bringing the cargos to and from the river landing. Local citizens and newcomers traveled them on horseback, wagon or stage. Thus, maintaining the region's roads became a matter of both necessity and civic pride. Editor DeMorse became a constant and bitter critic on the subject. He enjoyed being in the public eye and the role of spokesman/ crusader appealed to him. He had been the first Mayor of Clarksville and, when Texas joined the Union, was to have been Red River's representative in the Republic's Legislature. He used the power of the press to speak directly, in print, with his readers to lobby those in charge of remedying the situation:

The Roads

As soon as the corn crop is laid by, laborers upon the road ought to be called out. The roads in our county are in such condition as to reflect serious discredit upon the character of our population. Little muddy sloughs are permitted to obstruct the passage of the main roads through the country, which bridges ought to be placed over without delay, and the still more important bridges over the creeks have been swept away during the heavy rains of the last two months

Upon the road from here to Paris, the obstructions to traveling commence within three hundred yards from town and within a space of three miles there are no less than four places requiring bridges. This work has to be attended to. It is the duty of the Overseer of the Roads to see it done. They have plenty of means to do it and fortunately the Legislature has placed upon the District Attorney the responsibility - and have given him to power - to compel attention and we are entitled that it be applied as it should be, if the roads are not kept in order.[98]

Roads are among the many things we take for granted today. They are built and maintained through tolls or gasoline taxes. It was not always so. Governments, least of all the federal government, were not in the business of building or keeping roads. Companies could obtain charters, however, from the government to build private roads, known as turnpikes, which would charge a toll for their use. The citizens of the locality to be served by the turnpike, bridge or other improvement bought the stock of the company and thus shared in both the costs and the profits of their own road system, hopefully in a more satisfying fashion than we, as taxpayers, do today.

In Red River county, one crucial route was from Clarksville to Roland, its town's landing on the Red River. Over it had to travel the cotton to be sent to market and the next season's supplies. It was in sad shape:

> *Turnpike Road to Roland*
>
> *Every winter we hear a tremendous growling about the horrid road across the bayou between the town and the landing. Freight is detained, cotton wagons bog down. There is a desperate complaint and a stranger would suppose that the first time the roads got dry, big work would be done on the road. Well! A public spirited citizen wrote out a charter for a turnpike road so that the expense of a long bridge across the bottom and some other comparatively light work, might be well and permanently done and paid by the tolls of the wagons and horsemen, passing and re- passing. It is a perfectly safe investment. All those living along the road, our merchants in town, and the warehouse keepers at the landing and more than half the cotton planters in the area deeply interested; and, yet, after diligent inquiry, we do not hear of one practical movement has*

> been made except to get Subscribers for the stock. How can we ever expect our county improve with every man folding his arms in apathy, and waiting for bridges to grow over creeks and railroads to come right to his door and solicit the honor of his personage? Communities, cities, towns or counties are not built up this way. Action is wanted. This county is amply able to build twenty such roads from Clarksville to Roland. Let us have it done! [99]

A road in the other direction, towards Mount Pleasant and the south was also needed:

> A charter was also given to construct a road between Clarksville and Mount Pleasant. The road from here to Mount Pleasant will pay a rich dividend upon the stock, concentrating, as it will, nearly all the travel from the lower country. We presume there will be no lack of subscription to it. The amount of necessary expenditures is not large and the road is very much needed. The lack of a good crossing at Sulphur between this place and Mount Pleasant has, for three years, prevented us from having stages from Clarksville to Marshall, connecting with the line to Shreveport.[100]

The Delaware Creek flows just south of Clarksville. It is barely noticeable today, although bridges are necessary in several locations to cross over it. DeMorse described the Delaware in 1856, when it was at its mightiest:

> The stately Delaware which meanders through our town is a sort of inland sea right now, sweeping around the bridge magnificently. Ordinarily its depth varies for 0 to 2 ½ inches, except in the holes which keeps itself for the domestic convenience of our citizens, from one to three feet in depth. [101]

In the 1850s, one could not come to Town from either the west or the east without having to cross a bridge across the Delaware. The Town was managed by a "Corporation."[102] The bridges were under its control.

> *What is the corporation of Clarksville doing? Is it doing anything? A good many tax payers wait patiently for an answer. It looks to the uninitiated that the "City Fathers" were perfectly satisfied with their greatest improvement of encompassing the Square with drains and never expecting to do any more. Had achieved enough. In the meanwhile, the principal bridge of the town is making preparations to depart with the first or second rise of the Delaware, and is, at present, without side rails to guard wagons or foot passengers from going into the creek below on some dark night.*
>
> *Speaking of bridges reminds us that the bridge across the Delaware, between the residence of Dr. Gordon and the prairie, is out of order and the bridge near the residence of William Crittendon is in wretched fix. Are their no road commissioners in our county or is there no one who will take the trouble to report them.* [103]

It was the bridges leading into town that especially concerned and embarrassed DeMorse.

> *We have intended for weeks to call attention to the wretched state of the long bridge over the Delaware and of the bridge at the eastern entrance of the town. Others may be in as bad condition. We have not crossed them lately. It seems strange that when people along sparsely settled roads throughout the country are willing and able to keep good bridges at the crossing of the creeks that we here at the oldest town of Northern Texas, boasting a sort of Metropolitanism, cannot or do not*

> *keep our own bridges in such condition as to permit reasonable people to pass over them without apprehension for the safety of their persons or their horses. Surely, if we have no corporate authorities, subscription enough can be easily obtained by some public minded citizen to put them all in repair and put substantial hand rails on the long Bridge. The reputation of our town should have some connection with our self respect, and our reputation will suffer with strangers, if we cannot do better. There are plenty of persons about town having leisure, but a moderate amount will be required of each individual citizen. Will some body act and entitle himself to public thanks?*[104]

If pressure from the press was not enough, DeMorse used his knowledge of the law to bend stubborn Commissioners to the will of the People, for whom DeMorse was their self appointed spokesman.

> *Look Out*
>
> *We wish to give road commissioners and others who have a duty to perform in relation to the roads fair warning, that a gentleman of our acquaintance entertains a deliberate intention to report everyone liable to fines to the District Attorney at the next session of the District Court. The law has been examined and the fines are severe and recoverable upon motion. Fair warning now to all of you who are responsible for the wretched state of the several bridges over the main road from town. Everywhere we travel in contiguous counties, we find evidence of labor on the roads. Red River, the oldest settled and most able, does least.*[105]

Clarksville's public square became a stop on stage coaches, carrying both mail and passengers, into and out of the interior. The Mississippi River, gateway to points eastward, was five days away by stage via "Mr. Hanger's line of Mail Stages from Clarksville to Little Rock, connecting Northern, Texas with the world east of the Mississippi." The coaches were said to be "comfortable and regular in their passage" and were especially recommended to "immigrants with families, desiring to come to northern Texas, [who] will find this the most comfortable and expeditious route, coming up the Arkansas and White rivers and thence by stage here."[106]

Another stage route was from Clarksville to Jefferson, the most important port of the time in Texas, where one could connect passage to Shreveport. The stage stopped at Mt. Pleasant and Daingerfield en route. In 1856, the Clarksville - Shreveport route became a direct one and suddenly made Clarksville closer to civilization:

> *Stage through to Shreveport*
>
> *We are glad that, at last, a direct line of communication has been opened between this place and Shreveport. We are satisfied that this line will repay well the enterprising proprietors. Our citizens, going and returning from New Orleans, can now, with little fatigue, accomplish the journey in three days. Letters and papers will travel that route in about half the time.*[107]

Among the many conveniences which we take for granted today is the mail service. DeMorse did not. Probably it lay at the center of his frustration about the state of the roads and bridges, since the mail had to travel over both. In the 1840s and 1850s in Texas, the mail was not very reliable at all. This caused great stress to the person whose newspaper business required fresh news being received from the outside in time for the next edition as well as its customers regularly receiving their paper in the accustomed mail. Mail service touched DeMorse's pocket book, more so than some of the other items about which he preached. Consequently, he was especially vocal on the matter, especially just after Annexation:

> *This section of country is rich, is becoming densely populated, and is entitled to better usage than it gets from the Post Office Department.*
>
> *We know no reason why our mails should go like Robin Hood's path through Sherwood Forest, in every direction except a straight one from the place of departure to the place of destination, and we trust that unless good reason can be shown for it, the matter will be remedied as soon as practicable.*
>
> *By making Clarksville the distributing point for Northern Texas and running the new county routes as already ordered, our whole region of County will be supplied with as much mail facility, as the extent of its communications warrant. The mail to Clarksville would be the main bulk, and the Stage would pass through Jefferson and the County Seat of Titus County, serving their wants and then the ordinary bags for horse conveyance would be amply sufficient to carry off the remainder.*
>
> *By the way, while writing upon this subject, we would be glad to learn, if any one can give us information, why the routes to the new Counties are not established. Seven straight new counties near us, and not a mail route through any of them. The route was authorized by law and expressly ordered by the Post Master General, but not one of them attended to.*
>
> *Under our own little National government [Republic of Texas], we could have cursed and growled and have it, though we never had to. Our government was in extremest poverty, always running one route through each county; but to have to bear with such outrageous imposition under a Government of the magnitude of that of this Union, is deplorable indeed. There is wretched mismanagement, or absence of any management at all, somewhere. In sober truth, we are most shabbily treated.* [108]

DeMorse did not limit his ire to Washington and its bureaucracy. He was frustrated by the lack of speed or accuracy of the post. "How", he asked aloud, "in these days of railroads and electric telegraphs in our own country," could he "receive the mail from the capital of Mexico, 12 days earlier than from Austin, the capital of the State?" The local Clarksville Post Office came under attack also.

Clarksville Post Office

This office, very well managed in many respects, is certainly in one respect an imposition upon the community. There are two mails a week that come in at 12 o'clock noon, and immediately after opening them, the postmaster goes out of Town, to his dinner, keeping those who may have matter in the mails, waiting a long time for their letters or papers. As we write, we have just been refused the use of the key to the outside door, which we wanted in order that we might get to our box, which opens to the outside of the boxes. A little after 12 o'clock, we went to the office and it was closed. At two o'clock having been there and waited for some time, we sent to a house where the postmaster was at a dinner party but could not get the key. Of course, this delays us from selecting news for the community if any of it comes by the mail and we have to issue tonight (Friday). The mails from Boston arrive here usually after dark. If the citizens are at the office just after the mail has arrived and is opened, they get their communications. If not, the post master goes out of town for supper and they must wait two or three hours more. Now we understand that mails and post officers are suppose to be for the benefit of the community and not for the accommodation and profits of either Contractors or Postmasters. So viewing it, we demand that the intention of establishment shall not be rendered nugatory, and we shall not cease our representations upon the subject, until the delinquencies are all corrected. If the contractors and Postmaster will not remedy them, we shall try higher authority, with a few signatures along with ours. [109]

Despite all of his efforts to boost and improve river traffic, build more roads, erect better bridges, DeMorse knew what the real answer was. Bridges and roads needed constant repair by the citizens. The river was seasonal and could be crippled by drought. Without regular clearing out of rafts and other obstacles to navigation, it was also dangerous as a number of sinkings proved. And on top of its unreliability and peril, it was expensive, the freight price being set by a monopoly. Railroads were the solution. [110] " If we had a railroad in the county", DeMorse lamented, "we would be independent of Old Red and its "sharks."

> *Red River is now at its lowest stage at Rowland. It will require considerable rain, west of this, to make the river navigable. Those merchants whose goods have been lost, or materially injured, by the sinking of the Jim Turner and the Preston will doubtless be somewhat inconvenienced before they can receive their spring and summer supplies, which they will be compelled to order as new. Had we anything like "fair play", the navigation of the Red River would long since have been so improved, as that such accidents that we are called upon to report, would be of rare occurrence. The immense amount of agricultural products to be exported from the whole valley of the Red River - including beef cattle, horses, mules, wheat, flour, corn and cotton - and the vast amount of goods that have to be imported to satisfy the necessary demands of our rapidly increasing population, imperiously demand that the facilities for imports and exports be greatly enlarged. We do not believe that these facilities will ever be afforded for the navigation of Red River. We must march on with the improvements of the times. Railroads alone can accomplish for us all that we desire. Had we but facilities for importing and exporting, such as are to be*

found in some of the older states, our population would be quadrupled. Our lands would soon reach something like their intrinsic worth and the resources of our State would rapidly become developed. With all our drawbacks, from the great fertility of our soil, we can boast of as independent a population as can be found anywhere in the Union. [111]

But DeMorse knew that a rail road was not realistic for some years to come, and he did not feel the Red River Valley region could not risk retarding its rapid development by waiting for a railroad line to be built. The river, he reasoned, with all its deficiencies, was still the better alternative.

The Red River or a Railroad - The Raft.

We received on Friday evening of last week a letter considering the relative advantages of the removal of the Raft [obstruction in the Red River] or the construction of a railroad.

That a railroad can be easily constructed between Shreveport and this place, we have no doubt, and that it would make Clarksville an important place, we doubt just as little, but the next consideration is, where are the means to come from to build it? Capitalists will not invest without prospect of a profit, and there would not be business enough to employ two trains of cars constantly, upon such a road, for ten years to come. By the expiration of that time, we believe the road can be profitably constructed, and whenever it can be profitably done, we doubt not that it will be done, and then little dependence will be placed upon the river, whether the Raft is out or in, as a medium of transportation.

A railroad terminating at Clarksville would make it an important point and very greatly advance the importance of Shreveport. The station at Clarksville

> would be near enough for the business purposes of
> Fannin and Lamar and, at the same time, suit the
> convenience of the Choctaw Nation. Beyond Bonham
> westward, the natural medium of transportation is the
> Trinity River, which we doubt not will be made available
> within three years.
>
> But, at present, we think it would be useless to
> look for the construction of a railroad between
> Clarksville and Shreveport. We must rather put our
> energies to the work of the removal of the Raft, which we
> hope our citizens will keep in view, and the means for
> which they can get from Congress, by proper action.[112]

Keeping the rivers opened, until the railroad could be brought in, was the essence of DeMorse's strategy for Northern Texas.

> *Our future*
>
> The Red River raft is to be opened by the contractors
> and kept open five years for the sum of $100,000, appropriated
> by Congress. At the end of those five years, the population of
> Upper Red River, the products and the consequent navigation,
> will have become so immense that it will never be suffered to
> closed again. The Upper Red River region is unsurpassable
> upon the globe and it will rapidly develop now. We shall
> inevitably have the line of the Pacific Railroad through our
> midst. It is its natural course and nothing but the most wretched
> mismanagement could turn it aside. And between an open,
> improved navigation of the river and the railroad facilities,
> which will open upon us ere long, we shall have a locality
> unsurpassed upon the earth for its productiveness, health and
> beauty, stretching from Red River on the east and north to the
> beautiful prairies of the Upper Trinity and its tributaries.[113]

DeMorse looked even farther into the future. He envisioned a Clarksville, not only a hub for *intra* Texas trade, but also a stop on the railroad to be built that would cross the country to California.

> *But this is not all. Our county lies directly in the route of the great Pacific railroad which the necessities of our country will yet compel to be built. El Paso, the only practicable route across our part of the northern continent to the Pacific, does not vary 15 or 20 miles from a due western course from Clarksville.*
>
> *How pleasant for the people of Clarksville in a few years to step into the R.R. Depot and witness the daily cargos, of all the riches and luxuries of the east, to witness the customs, manners and faces of specimens from all the eastern lands - and, if we wish, to take a little pleasant excursion on the cars and be off to California.* [114]

Weather in Red River County from 1842 to 1860

Climate can be either a blessing or a bane and, often, the line between "enough" and "too much" of a good thing is very thin. Today, Clarksville's climate is relatively mild, with sufficient precipitation to permit large scale agriculture. Winters are moderate with only occasional cold waves, while the summers are typically long and warm. The average mean temperature is 64 degrees. The mean temperature in January is 44 and, for July, 83. The average rainfall is 43.5 inches. It is not normally a stormy place, except during the tornado season, and then it sometimes be a very stormy place.

Was the climate the same a century and a half ago? Regular weather records do not appear to have been taken in Texas until the 1870s. *The Standard,* however, goes back to August 1842, and each issue usually provided some inkling of the weather outside, sometimes as separate items, other times associated in reports on the progress of the river or the prospects for the crops. Aberrations in the weather patterns were duly noted.

What do these weekly accounts from *The Standard*, reveal to us, more than a century and half later, as to what the weather was like back then? Were tornados and sweltering summers the rule, rather than the exception? Were winters colder with more snow, warmer with no snow or about the same? What about the effects of global weather patterns, such as El Nino? Can *The Standard* provide us proof of the influence of these forces on local weather more than a century and a half ago? Like artifacts unearthed by archaeologists, can these fossilized weather reports from *The Standard* help us answer questions like that?

The Standard's first report on extraordinary weather was in January 1843. Huge winter "freshets" - the surges from rivers and creeks, fed by torrents of rain and swollen beyond their banks - swept away everything in their path, including the town of Jonesboro on the Red River. The overflow had been "greater and more destructive than is within the recollection of the oldest settlers in this section of country, a period of 23 or 24 years. It is, at this time, probably fourteen feet higher than has ever before been known." [115]

The rush of water, propelled down river at great speeds, by the ever increasing flooded river, must have been a sight for the ages. We have DeMorse's account of one eye witness report:

> *The gentlemen who went from here to the landing at the first receipt of the news [that the Red River was rapidly rising] found the river quite high, but not out of its banks, and were in time to see the second and greatest rise arrive. It came on, not with the gradual swell usually seen, but a heavy column of a body of water, like the outpouring from a swollen and broken sluice, constituting a body of height and front, pressed on by the mass behind, a force and grandeur, not easily described. And, as it came, there came with it tall trees, the growth of a century, not broken, but discharged from the bond of earth about them by its dissolution in this resistless volume of waters. Thousands of acres have probably been carried away and the channel of the river changed in many places. Opposite Jonesboro, we are informed, that a great mass of earth has been carried off.*[116]

The winter of 1843 that began with this destructive freshet was an extraordinarily cold one across Texas. In mid March, several inches of snow fell in Clarksville and the cold was described as "intense." Northern Texas got off easily, compared to the normally warmer South. At Galveston, for example, the ground froze and pools of water were covered with ice half an inch thick. One man perished of cold on the prairie below the town and another nearly lost his life. The shoreline of Galveston Bay was literally strewn with frozen fish, forced upon the beach in the surf by the violence of the wind.

Next summer, 1844, unusually high temperatures predominated:

> *The weather for the last two or three weeks has been more oppressive than we have ever before felt it, during our residence in the Republic. The thermometer has been at 90 in the shade and 141 in the Sun.*[117]

The heat was accompanied by drought and the people, live stock and crops of the region, all suffered mightily:

THE DROUGHT

> *It is now 8 or 9 weeks since this region of the country has been visited by anything like a good, seasonable rain. Springs and creeks are dried up and the few cisterns almost exhausted. Man and beast are in a state of suffering.*
>
> *Most of the citizens of Clarksville are dependent upon hauling water two or three miles, from holes in the creek, which will, we are told, soon be exhausted.*
>
> *Crops are seriously injured; planters say they will not make more than half their crop of cotton.* [118]

Unusual and freakish weather, as that experienced in 1843 and 1844, is always interesting to the reader. Good weather, on the other hand, rarely earns much mention in the newspapers. That must have been the case from 1845 through 1848 because *The Standard* rarely reported on any abnormal weather conditions. Red River was high enough for river traffic at the right seasons and the crops had the correct blends of water and sun to prosper. Everything was perfect.

However, the following three years, 1849 through 1851, were not so benign. In fact, it was to be a 30 month span of changing weather extremes, on which *The Standard* reported. A fickle Mother Nature - or perhaps an unrecognized El Nino - was to blame for the dramatic change.

Rain in Northern Texas is by no means a rarity. Clarksville and the Red River Valley can be rainy places, but that is not necessarily a curse to an agricultural region. Some years, however, it can be *very* rainy. In fact, Clarksville held the Texas record for annual rainfall, 109.38 inches in 1873, more than two and a half time its normal. The average in Texas is about 27 inches.

The year 1849 must have been a wet whopper as well. No detailed records were kept, but a year long litany in *The Standard* is proof enough that it was severe. Actually, the terrible year began in 1848 with an early dusting of snow in the first week of November, followed in December by an early winter storm without parallel, the worst experienced by the townspeople, since they had come to Texas.

Winter in Earnest

Clarksville has never before, since we have been resident in it, had such a Visitation of regular Northern Winter, as came down upon on Tuesday night last and continued until yesterday morning in its severity. It came in the form of sleet which covered everything exposed. The smallest twigs of the trees were covered in ice, in the quantity of ten times their own bulk, while the larger limbs and fences and house tops, showed a regularly increased surface of an inch thickness. A look out upon the prairie gave to the sight a look a utter desolation, an appearance worthy of the Russian wild in the dead of winter, except, perhaps, in that there would be more snow, while this was all ice. The trees about town, broken by the unusual weight, look, as we suspect a chapparal looks, after a raking with heavy artillery.[119].

Oaks of at least a half a century standing about our house, which had no appearance of having suffered before from any cause, were dropping their heavy branches with a sullen crash during Wednesday night, and the following morning, laying fences low before them. A stately pecan which was the front yard ornament of a neighbor and perhaps the largest tree about Town, is a perfect "sight", the least imaginable resemblance to its proportions on Tuesday at mid-day. As for the ornamental growth in the yards which had not yet attained much size- the Arbor Vitae, the magnolia, the Weeping Willow, their heads are bowed to the ground and rest upon it the weight which the stems are insufficient to hold erect. Bushes and vines are trailing low in their frozen suits.

From the country, we learn that the damage to the timber has been serious and that the roads are full of frozen branches.

It is a general remark with those who were raised in the North of the Union that they have never before anywhere seen so much ice upon the timber.

Disagreeable as it all has been, between sleet and rain it has not been very cold. The thermometer in our back room, where there was no fire, was at two degrees above the freezing mark and placed outside, fell to only 2 ½ degrees below. [120]

The New Year, 1849, started off poorly, DeMorse complaining that the "the weather has been more inclement in this region for the last three weeks than we have ever experienced before, in a residence of 13 years." A few weeks later, the Editor *pro tem,* who filled in for DeMorse and had lived in Texas for twelve years, concurred. Sleet and very cold rains, sometimes hard, sometimes just drizzling, were to last all winter

With Spring, came the need to plant the next crop. The dispenser of disagreeable weather, however, announced that it was not ready to withdraw by sending three waves of lengthy, violent hail storms in a single day!

Extraordinary Hail Storms

We have had a strange wet cold spring and our farmers have suffered by it. There has not been heat enough to bring forth garden vegetables in their proper season. They are at least a month behind their proper time.

On Sunday last, about 2:00 p.m., a storm of wind and rain blew up and the hail as large as from small rifle balls to small hens eggs came dancing down and rebounding from the earth like balls of India rubber. This passed by in half an hour and later in the afternoon, came on another blast, the hail coming down this time in a way to exemplify the old term "as thick as hail." The fact is, it came nearly as thick as the rain drops and a most furious storm it was for three quarters of an hour or more

At about midnight, there was another storm lasting for perhaps two hours, accompanied with as heavy a wind as we have ever noticed. [121]

Spring, 1849 brought rain, rain and more rain.

Rains

We have never before in our lives witnessed such continuous rains, as has poured down on this region for the past 6 or 8 months, and it still comes almost daily and the mud and the water stand in our streets, as though it were mid winter. It is, indeed, most disagreeable, and, for months, it has been a matter of wonder that the country around us has not been sickly. But it is remarkably healthy and that is a great reason for thankfulness.

The crops, of course, are suffering. Corn, there

> will be plenty of, although some persons will make scarce any. Cotton, unless we have some dry weather in the next few days, will be hardly a fourth crop and, even if the rain ceases, will not be more than a half crop. Wheat in this county, Lamar and Fannin is a failure. [122]

> The 4th of July celebration was "passed by our citizens in a mixed manner, first listening to the Senatorial address of Col. Clark, then in sheltering themselves from one of the semi-daily showers which has greeted us for the first six months." [123]

DeMorse was at the breaking point. He had only one comparison left to make to communicate to the world outside how awful the weather had been for the past eight months or more and he expressed it in the headline: "The Floods - One of the Olden Times and the One Present." In the article he reported that the night before "the heaviest continuous rain we have known yet, in the series by which we have been favored, came down and fairly deluged everything, carrying off two of the bridges over the Delaware, leaving only the long bridge which is equal to none at all."[124]

All this water had to go somewhere and everywhere there was flooding. The Delaware Creek, normally a benign, docile stream, where, before the coming of the White men, the Indians had camped and where the Clarks began the Town of Clarksville, became a raging "torrent", washing away the bridges that crossed over into the Town. At the village of Rowland on the Red River, a dozen miles north of Town, the waters rose 27 feet in one night from what had already been flood stage, inundating the warehouses that lay at the landing.

The Rivers and Creeks

> Everything like a watercourse in this part of the country has, during the past week, been swelled to overflowing. Even the little Delaware that winds

> through our Town, usually a diminutive stream a foot or two deep, has been running, like a mountain torrent. We recorded last week how it carried off substantial bridges, placed above its natural bed, and again, during this week, it has risen, as before, carrying off ground fences in its vicinity.
>
> Red River rose at a point, north of this, 27 feet in one night and is now, at our landing, one feet over the floor of Bryarly and Co.'s store.
>
> The presumption is that all the plantations below the raft and some above it, are overflowed and the crops ruined. [125]

The Year 1850, at first, appeared to be a copy of 1849. Northern and Central Texas were hit by another large snowstorm, which was followed by a winter of rain, hail storms, a late frost and a wet, wet spring. Then, Mother Nature had a surprise up her sleeve. From cold and wet, she changed to hot and dry.[126] DeMorse reported that the weather has been very hot, "warm enough to make a Negro weep", that there had been no rain for some weeks and that the earth was "perfectly parched with the intense heat." A report from *The Standard* in the first week of September characterized the last month's weather as having been "the warmest ever known." It noted, however, that there had been "a large change" in the weather and that it was now comparatively "cool and pleasant." Little did *The Standard* know that this was the beginning of still another weather aberration - a frost in mid October, followed in a few days by cold weather that was "quite Greenlandish - cold enough in all conscience to suit a Patagonian."

The winter of 1851 seemed normal. Had El Nino or some other long term weather pattern perhaps moved on? No. It was only the final turns in a most erratic and peculiar stretch of unusually extreme weather patterns in Texas from late 1848 through February 1851. The cold fall and early winter changed to having "nearly summer heat in mid winter." DeMorse pointed out that the temperature in mid February in his unheated office was 70 degrees and that the Weeping Willow outside his window already had small leaves and that "the plum trees [were] pushing out their buds." It would not stay that way. A couple of weeks later, the winds of a severe late February storm "blew so cold" that, according to eyewitness Demorse, "the little snow birds sought shelter within doors, and, knocking at the windows, came in." One came in that way to DeMorse's own home, two at his office. This period of aberration came to a fitting end with a late frost in early May.

During the next few years -1851 through 1854 - the weather returned to being generally pleasant. There were periods of extreme weather, to be sure, some "smart visits from Jack Frost", late Springs and hot spells when "man, beast and vegetation were all quailing under a heat which placed the mercury in the thermometer at 90 degrees" for several days in a row. However, compared to the array of constantly changing, out of season extremes of the prior thirty month span from 1848 to 1851, the weather for the rest of 1851 through the summer of 1854 could be termed idyllic. As with the moderate stretch prior the period of aberrations, weather ceased being a regular news item, good weather simply being not newsworthy. The agricultural and river reports, however, confirm that the weather for the next three years was mild, with sufficient rainfall for river traffic and the crops.

But, another multi-month weather pattern was on the horizon: hot, dry weather, leading to drought. In 1854, there had been navigation on the Red River in the springtime, but it was, at best sporadic. By July 1, however, the river was falling and no more boats could come up river. The weather was warmer than usual. It was the beginning of a two plus year drought. Crops were ruined. The rivers dried up and commerce on the river ceased. This brought hardships to the people of the Red River Valley. The cotton, picked in the fall of 1853, remained stacked up at the river landings, waiting for steam boats that never came. No boats meant no cargos from New Orleans and points north, no supplies for the planters, no merchandise for the stores on the public square. Among those effected, was DeMorse and *The Standard* which ran out of paper and could not publish for many weeks until wagons hauled in a new supply. The drought continued through 1855. The little rain that fell, "although it cooled the leaf", did not penetrate into the earth deep enough to do more than keep the crops barely alive. The new year, 1856, however, brought relief with plentiful rains that renewed the earth, filled the cisterns and made the river navigable again.

> *We had a most copious rain on the evening of Wednesday and all Nature is rejoicing in beauty. Crops are all beginning to look remarkably promising. The timely showers which we have had, followed by the genial warmth of the sun, have greatly improved the prospects of the farmer. Wheat promises now to be an abundant harvest. We had a rise in the river of between four and five feet, before the rain which fell on Tuesday, and we think it highly probable that now there will be a sufficient rise to permit large size boats to visit our landing at Roland.*
>
> *Saturday Morning - Since writing the above, we have seen a gentleman who returned from Roland yesterday evening. He states that the river has risen more than 15 feet with considerable drift wood running.*[127]

Besides the welcome rain, the year 1856 also presented within its span of twelve months, extremes of hot and cold, each of which described appropriately by Editor DeMorse:

> *The weather has maintained its severity and these last two weeks may be called "one of the severest spells of cold weather" that we remember to have felt in Texas. It has looked for most of the week that the clouds would like to let out a little of the superincumbent water, but it was so cold that it would not come. During Friday night a little bit of snow fell.*

> *Last night it came - the long delayed - and this morning we have 8 inches of snow by measurement, covering the earth and roof tops and adding bleak beauty to the town. Such a snow has never fallen in Clarksville before during the 13 winters we have passed in it previous to this.* [128]

> *The weather has been on a bust for ten days and the thermometer too high to be spoken of publically. We may refer to its conduct during some northern next winter. But now conversation on this point is not endurable. Men "as thin as two of Cassidy lard the lean earth as they walk along."*[129]

Despite these extremes, normalcy had in fact returned once more to the weather of Northern Texas. The year 1857 was memorable only in that it began and ended with snowstorms. The year 1858 was a gem. There was no freeze that winter. It was also unusually warm all across the United States. DeMorse reported the farmers of New England, who earned their winter living by cutting and selling ice from the lakes and ponds, had had, because of the warm winter, a "crop failure".

The good weather continued in 1859. DeMorse reported in mid January that "the sunshine is bright and the temperature very pleasant. The thermometer in our sanctum without fire being 62 at midday and on the sunny side of this room"[130] and that in February the "weather most decidedly spring like."[131] His peach tree even bloomed. In March, he noted that "the weather is most delightful. We have had very little of what might be termed winter weather, since December, and as the winter months have expired, we suppose we are fairly into Spring. It is warm enough to work or write with open doors; garden vegetation is moving forward. Hyacinths have been long in bloom and rose buds are beginning to disclose the crimson within."[132] Knowing how weather can contain surprises, he worried that "very likely a cold spell of a few days may come during the month; indeed we much fear that peaches and plums, which are nearly out of bloom, will be cut off and perhaps pears."[133] He was right! The end of March turned cold, "on Thursday morning, we had a sharp frost, which wilted the beans in the gardens but we do not think seriously injured young fruit."[134]

April was cold and there was damage done to some of the fruit which had blossomed prematurely. Summer was wet and warm. The river was boatable, if barely, and the crops did well. An early frost in October was followed by an Indian summer, followed by severe cold then warm weather. "We see from the movement of wild fowl from the north, a cold winter is predicted", DeMorse wrote.[135] Again he was correct. On December 10, 1859, he reported "weather for the last five days unusually cold for this part of the country - ground has been covered with snow for more than a week. The weather has been fine for skating, the ice being from three to four inches thick and the boys have had a merry time skating over the Delaware."

A storm on December 18th and 19th, left snow "six inches in depth generally. In hollows there it drifted it was a foot and 18 inches deep. It held its sway stoutly for a week. If one only had been in possession of a dashing sleigh, rich buffalo robes and strings of bells, what a ride could have been."[136] The snowy weather continued into 1860:

> *"Our ride to Lamar commenced on Sunday afternoon the 18th in a rain and concluded on Monday about 2:p.m. in a snow storm. We met, traveling on our route on Monday, only the Stage, and one man in a buggy with a blanket drawn over his head, who inquired whether this was not rather inclement weather. We expressed our conviction that it was rather - about fit for the Arctic Regions. However it was a variety of weather and variety is said to be the spice of life, so we did not complain. If one were never cold he could not appreciate the comfort of a bright fire, which is the most genial invention imaginable at fitting times.*[137]

Eighteen years of incomplete weather accounts from a newspaper a century and a half ago, which contain little scientific data, is hardly the basis upon which to make comparisons between the weather in Texas today and that from 1842 to 1860. Nor should unschooled amateurs, such as we, attempt it in the first place. But, nevertheless, we shall.

First of all, one cannot help but see, over the eighteen year time span, a pattern of periods, 2 to 3 years each in duration, that alternate between good and bad weather. Abnormal weather in 1843 and 1844 was followed by three years of "normal" weather (1845-48), which, in turn, was followed by wet and cool aberrant weather for two and a half years (1849-1851). Normal weather returned in latter half of 1851, continued in 1852 and 1853, to be replaced by another two and a half year span of unusually hot and dry weather (1854-56). A third period of normalcy was experienced in Red River County in 1857, 1858 and the first part of 1859. But, it shifted back to wet and cold in 1860. Do we experience such alternating patterns today? Could an El Nino like global weather pattern be behind it?

Another suggestion that emerges from a review of these 18 years of weather reports is that Northern Texas seems much warmer in the present than it was in the 1850s. The winters seemed colder and ice skating was a popular sport some winters around Clarksville, something that would surprise many today. Temperatures in the summer hot spells of the period were in the 90 degree to 100 degree range for brief periods. Compare this to our summers now that routinely have a dozen days with temperatures in the 100s. Global warming?

Another difference is the relative absence of tornados then as compared to the present. Red River Valley is known today as Tornado Alley, yet in the 18 years of *The Standard,* from 1842 to 1860, only two such storms were reported. One was in Cooke county, west of Gainesville, in 1854 where six lives and much property were lost. Described as "a gale unparalleled save in hurricanes of the tropics", the account of it shows it to be a classic tornado. It knocked down houses, killed cattle, and carried fences out of sight, sparing only those who hid in cellars and the bottoms of dry creek beds. The May 5, 1855 issue of *The Standard* passed on a report from Plano "that Cedar Hills, a small village about 12 miles west of Dallas was entirely demolished on last Thursday night, 29th ultimate by a hurricane. Nine or ten persons were killed and several seriously injured. Fragments of houses, merchandise and human bodies were said to have been found 5 or 6 miles from town."

    Is there any significance in the apparent warming of Northern Texas and the increase in tornados? And what caused the warmer temperatures?

Clarksville: A Seat of Learning

Today, Clarksville and Red River county have excellent schools that educate their young. A century and a half ago, there was no public education, in Clarksville or most other places in the Nation. There were, however, a surprising number of private schools in and around Clarksville. Indeed, from its first days through the Civil War, the town was the major educational center for Northern Texas. The students and staffs of the several schools were a vital part of the community. Upwards of fifty per cent of the Town's white population of five hundred were students from different parts of Texas and Arkansas! DeMorse recognized that it "makes a vast deal of difference in the agreeableness of a town, whether one sees a large number of young people moving about with countenances, yet untouched by care, radiant with the fresh hopes of youth, or whether only matured men, absorbed by business calculations and anxieties, are hurriedly moving onward, careful of only the object then upon the mind and with faces upon which there is no sunlight of smiles and happiness."[138]

Affluent planters would send their offspring, male and female alike, to these schools. *The Standard* was pleased to have some many fine institutions of learning in its neighborhood and DeMorse bragged about them frequently:

Our Schools

We really believe that Clarksville is unequaled by any other place in the State for the excellence of its schools. We do not usually make great news of them, attend examinations or narrate the excellences of this or that pupil, but the truth is that branches of education are taught here, not merely advertised, but taught of a secondary grade only to long established and richly endowed institutions of learning of great repute. For female education, we express our opinion most

> *decidedly that Clarksville is not equaled in its advantages by any other place in the state, or in any neighboring state, and as some evidence of it, that although the population of our Town is no more than 500 whites, our two female institutions usually have each of them from 75 to 100 scholars.*
>
> *Our school for boys or young men in advanced studies, we believe to be unequaled in the state, but we would not express the conviction as positively as in regard to the female schools, though we are confident neither can be excelled.*
>
> *Our Town too is remarkably healthy which, of course, increases its fitness as a place of education.* [139]

The first school in town was the Clarksville Academy, founded in 1842. The Rev. James Sampson was its Principal and a group of local citizens served as its Board of Trustees. It was co-educational, although the sexes were educated in separate rooms. It built a "commodious" school house. However, despite all efforts and perhaps due to increasing competition and some hard times, enrollment had dropped to thirty six in August, 1846, and the school was closed the next year.

Other schools followed, however, among them, the Clarksville Male Academy, or, as it was later renamed, the Clarksville Classical Mathematical and Mercantile Academy.

DeMorse personally endorsed the Academy as well and provided us something of the background and credentials of the instructors.

> *Clarksville Academy*
>
> *We call special attention to the advertisement of this institution which is to be found in our columns. Of the character and fitness of Mr. Russell, who has successfully taught for several sessions in the place, we need not say much. Mr. Anderson who is now here, we*

may properly speak of as eminently qualified to instruct in all the branches, which the two gentlemen propose to teach. His testimonials from Ireland are of the best character. He is a graduate of Belfast University. Where he last taught at Spring Hill in Arkansas, his character as an instructor is very high.

We may considerably say that we do not believe that any other town in Texas east of the Trinity affords such facilities for male and female education as Clarksville does.[140]

DeMorse was in favor of the education of women, far from being a universal practice at the time.[141] His wife, Lodiska C. Woolridge, had been a well-educated woman, having graduated with first honors from The Female College at Clinton, Mississippi.

In Clarksville, there were two schools that concentrated on young women, instructing them "in the higher branches of Female Education including the graces of deportment, as well as of mind."

The advantages for the education of females in our moral, orderly, and rapidly improving Town are such as to claim the attention of all persons within 200 miles of it, who have daughters to educate and would have them receive the care and instruction of ladies eminently fitted to form their minds, morals, and manners, in a place where there are no examples of either fashionable dissipation, on the one hand, or coarse disregard of the courtesies of life, on the other, to taint the thoughts or the habits of the pupil.

Clarksville is the most rapidly improving town in eastern Texas, the largest, the best built and we would not invidiously say the most moral, but certainly having no superior in any of those attributes which constitute a correct and praise-worthy population. The character of the Town itself is proper for consideration in weighing the advantages of its opportunities for education, and especially the education of females. A disorderly place or a dull one in which no attention is paid to the courteous interchanges of social life, are equally unfit for the advantageous training of the manners of a young female.[142]

    One of the girls' schools was the Clarksville Female Academy. It had been begun as the Pine Creek Academy by Robert and Martha W. (Maum) Weatherred in 1840 at Pine Creek, fifteen miles north of Clarksville. It moved in 1844 to Clarksville and renamed itself. Even at its zenith, it had an enrollment of fewer than sixty students. In 1852, it was purchased by a Mrs. Gattis, but the Civil War, with its effects upon enrollment, forced it to shut its doors.

    Another school for young women had moved to Clarksville from Lamar county and changed its name from the Ringwood Female Seminary to the Clarksville Female Institute. The school had been begun in 1844 by Mrs. Eliza A. Todd for the daughters of wealthy planters and had an elementary, high school and the beginning of a college curriculum, with a special emphasis on French. *The Standard* noted, with approval, of the school's move to Clarksville:

Female Institute

We learn from Col. William Todd that arrangements are now being made to remove the institution now known as the Ringwood Female Seminary from Boston to this place. It will open upon the 1st of February next with three assistant teachers of the highest accomplishments. Every branch of instruction to females will be taught which is taught in any other institution of this sort in the United States.

The elegant residence and grounds at present occupied by Mr. M. Harrison Esq. have been purchased

> *and a two story and a half building for the school, sleeping rooms and dining hall will be erected immediately.*
>
> *We are pleased to see the movement. The character of the Ringwood Institute is so high and when we have that and the very excellent institution of Mrs. Weathered & Graham, both in our Town, the place will present such opportunity for education as seldom found west of the Mississippi or excelled anywhere in the United States.*[143]

In 1854, under the new management of John Anderson, the school would merge with the boy's school, the Clarksville Male Academy, and would continue as the Clarksville Male and Female Academy.

The academic year consisted of two sessions of five months each. The first started usually toward the end of January, the second around August, with a month back home for the students in between sessions. At the end of the terms, just before the students return home, there were the dreaded "examinations." Unlike today, where students display what they have learned in tests taken on paper and privately graded by the teacher, the examinations of the 1840's were more public, with family and towns people in attendance. After they were completed, there would be celebrations, concerts that drew "so large a crowd that most could not get in."[144] At night, there would be balls, the forebears, one suspects, of the proms of today.

> *Out town has been lively for some days since. The examinations at the Female Institute drew many strangers to town, who, as well those of our citizens who attended, were for two days more than pleased, delighted with the rare performance of the numerous pupils of the Institution. The recitations were most full and perfect, the music enchanting and the exhibitions of*

painting, wax work, etc in the highest degree creditable to teachers and as scholars. Success to the cause of female education.

After the examinations closed on Thursday evening, a ball came off at the Star, graced by the attendance of any quantity of the fair, and then again the fete was repeated at the Eagle Hotel. In the upper gallery of that establishment, the youths of the vicinity tripped the merry measure of the dance, while on the ground below, in the bright moonlight, which gleamed upon us, as in one of the boasted nights of Italy, Congos of various hue disported themselves in keeping with the measure of the music above, swaying themselves to and fro in the style of dance peculiar to them.[145]

Compare typical highschool final examination period today and those of a century and a half ago:

School Examinations

Our town has been unusually lively this week in consequence of these semi annual examination of scholars of the several institutions of learning in and around the Town. Carriages have rolled in from the neighboring counties, containing parents anxious to have evidences of the progress of their children in those acquirements which render life useful, honorable and agreeable. And we believe they have been fully satisfied. We heard the concluding exercise of the examination of the Clarksville Academy, the public speaking by the boys on Wednesday night. These seemed to afford much gratification to the visitors, who crowded all the standing room in the Church. On Thursday night, there was a most agreeable entertainment in music by the young ladies of Mrs. Anderson class attached to the Clarksville Female Institute, also crowded. On Friday in the morning, we

> succeed in getting to the examination of that institute, which had been transferred from the school house to the Presbyterian church in order to admit the press of visitors. The room was constantly filled to the utmost capacity of its seats by ladies and gentlemen and the exercises were certainly satisfactorily rendered. At the conclusion of the evening, original compositions by the ladies were read and gave the highest satisfaction.
>
> We have never before seen one of the eras of the school to pass so satisfactory or attract so many visitors.[146]

The students at these schools, especially the girls, also participated in many community events of Clarksville. They prepared a flag for the Red River Volunteers to carry, as they marched off to the Mexican War. They held musical concerts, gave dinners and marched as a group in holiday processions in the public square. In fact, on May Day, they were at the center of that ancient holiday celebrating young maidens.

Apart from the Town of Clarksville in distance - it was some three miles to the southwest - and higher in the level of the education than the academies and institutions, was McKenzie College. It was named after its founder and president, John Witherspoon Pettigrew McKenzie, a pioneer in both religion and education in Clarksville. A graduate of the University of Georgia and a Methodist minister, he had been sent in 1836, at the age of 30, as a missionary to the Choctaw Nation, the Indian Territory, now Oklahoma. In ill health, he crossed the Red River two years later and brought Texas its first Methodist Societies. In 1841, he also began this school of higher learning, McKenzie College. Its first school building was a log cabin, 16 by 18 feet, with a log left out on one side to provide ventilation for the students crowed within. A scholar reports that there were two dormitories, one for women and one for men. They were named Graft and Duke after the two carpenters who had constructed them. Later, it expanded to four large buildings on 900 acres. According to DeMorse, "the number of students in this institute [was] greater than any other private school in Texas or perhaps in the Southwest. It is attended by scholars from all parts of Texas."[147] It graduated over 3,300 students by the time its deteriorating financial condition, the poor economic times following the Civil War and the advancing age of its founder and president, all combined to force it to close and transfer its charter and most of its library to Southwestern University in Georgetown, Texas.

Being a religious school, discipline was rigid. Four students were assigned to a room, and they had to take turns at night to study before the single oil lamp in the room. The courses were rigorous, including the languages needed to read the New and Old Testaments in their own tongues, Hebrew, Latin and Greek. There was mandatory chapel before dawn and after dusk. The students took oaths not to gamble, use tobacco or alcoholic beverages, or miss class or chapel. There was little chance that any McKenzie College student would appear at the post examination balls, given by the girls schools in town. Among their promises were not to leave school without permission and not to dance.

Religion and Morals in Clarksville

Clarksville has been associated with the practice of the Protestant religion in Texas from the very first days. In fact, the town has been called "the Cradle of Protestantism in Texas." In 1815, the Rev. William Stevenson, a frontier minister who rode the religious circuit for the Missouri Conference of the Methodist Church, made a pastoral visit to the home of Claiborne Wright of Pecan Point, a member of the newly arrived Anglo Americans who that had drifted below the Red River into Texas. Records indicate that Stevenson's preaching to Wright and friends in 1815 constituted the first Protestant sermons given in Texas. The sermons were to earn him a marker in the Clarksville public square as well as a warning from his friend, Stephen F. Austin, who threatened Stevenson with arrest if he preached his gospel in Central Texas. Texas belonged to Mexico and Catholicism was the state religion. Austin, still almost a decade away from beginning his settlement, feared the illegal Anglo American immigrants, like Wright, who had wandered down from Arkansas, would anger the Mexicans who had stipulated that all settlers in Texas must embrace Catholicism.

Benjamin Clark was a veteran of the American Revolution and brother of General James Rogers Clark, the American leader who captured the Ohio region from the British. He was also a Methodist minister and the father of James Clark, founder of Clarksville. He and another son of his, Gilbert Clark, who too was a part time Methodist preacher, settled in Clarksville and brought Methodism to the village.

Red River County and Clarksville have another claim in the history of Protestantism in Texas. The still flourishing First Presbyterian Church of Clarksville had as its predecessor a congregation organized in June, 1833 by the Rev. Milton Estill. Called the Shiloh Cumberland Presbyterian Church, it had at first been located at the Shiloh Community, about six miles east of Clarksville on what today is Highway 82. Later, it moved to

Clarksville and merged with other congregations to become the First Presbyterian Church of Clarksville. Arguably, Protestantism had its beginnings in Texas with this early day church.

If there were a dominant churchman in Clarksville in those days it was the Rev. John Witherspoon Pettigrew McKenzie. The founder of College which would bear his name, and a Methodist missionary to the Choctaws at Fort Towson in the Indian Territory, he crossed the Red River to establish three Methodist Societies in what was then thought to be Miller county, Arkansas. Two of these were in present day Red River county, Jonesboro and Clarksville. The third was in Bowie county at DeKalb. Tradition has it that McKenzie and a Rev. John Lemeul Lovejoy organized the first Methodist Episcopal Church, South, in Clarksville in 1838. It was located just south of the Square on what today is known as east Church Street.

An item from *The Standard* in 1853 reported that the Presbyterian Church was looking for a larger home and was planning to combine with a couple of social/charitable organizations in the venture. A two story house of 50 by 70 feet, 30 feet high, it was "to be devoted to the triple purpose of a Presbyterian Church, a Masonic hall and a hall for the Society of Odd Fellows."[148]

However, it did not come to past.[149] Instead, the Methodists sold their church on South Street to the Negro Baptist Church, Zion Travelers, and joined with the Masons, to build a two story combination Church and social hall, on North Locust street, a block north east of the Square. The land had been purchased by the Rev. McKenzie, William G. Duke, James W. Sims and Perry H. Flemming, acting as trustees for the Methodist Episcopal Church South, from George and Isabella Gordon. The structure was to be across the street from *The Standard:*

> *The new church and Masonic Hall United, or rather the new building with a distinct hall for each purpose, is now raised and progressing on the lots*

> *immediately facing and west of our office. It is a large building for this part of the county, with fine altitude, which will render its appearance imposing. It will be finished about the 15th of June.*[150]

The Standard's columns also reveal the variety of other Protestant sects and societies that competed with the Presbyterians and Methodists for the soul of the citizens of Clarksville.

> *Our citizens have been much edified, several times of late, by the preaching of Bishop Freeman of the Episcopal Church, who includes Texas and Arkansas within his Diocese. The Bishop is a clear header and eloquent expounder of the Scriptures and of the Doctrines of his Church and produced a marked effect upon large congregations who listened to him.*[151]

> *Clarksville Bible Society*
>
> *The Rev. Mr. Warrener, Agent of the American Bible Society in the eastern part of this state, is in town and, we understand, will hold the Annual Anniversary in the Presbyterian Church tomorrow. The friends of the Bible are respectfully invited to attend.* [152]

> *Preaching*
>
> *Dr. J.F. Hall of Kentucky will preach in the Baptist Church tomorrow at 11 o'clock A.M. and 7P.M.*[153]

> *Drs. Padon and DeSpain of the Christian Church will commence a protracted meeting in Clarksville on Saturday December 31.*[154]

The United States of the 1850s was what one would describe as a Christian country. The 1850 census showed there to be 36,011 churches in America and 210 more in the District of Columbia and the Territories. Church property exceeded $86,000,000 in value and there was one church for every 557 free inhabitants, one for every 646 with the slave population included. In 1854 in Texas, there were some 9,000 Baptists of all varieties, 6,000 Presbyterians, 2,000 Episcopalians, 20,000 Methodists and an unknown number of Lutherans. Except among the Mexican population, Roman Catholics were rare in Texas. Their numbers elsewhere in the Nation were growing with immigration and, as described later, were becoming of concern to American Protestants.

Charles DeMorse was not a church going man, although clearly he was a moral man and a believer in a Deity of some sort. Whenever catastrophe struck - a fire burned a man's uninsured business or a string of crop failures threatened the farmers - DeMorse championed in *The Standard* the concept that, in such situations, the rich should assist the poor, the blessed help out the unfortunate. DeMorse preached an idealistic form of social welfare program, which was far ahead even of the platform of the political party he championed, the Party of the People, the Democrats. Today, of course, the government's assistance of the poor, provided by the income taxes of the more affluent, is a cornerstone of our society.

While regular church going was not his personal preference, DeMorse nevertheless acknowledged and applauded its value:

Sunday School religion

There is not a place in Texas where more attention is given to the moral culture of youth, than in Clarksville. The Sunday School here, which is an honor to parents and teachers, numbers 88 scholars. We have the Gospel expounded regularly every Sabbath by able and pious Ministers, and if the people are not Christians, it is their own fault, for we will venture the opinion that so far as the theory is concerned, religion is as well understood here as it is anywhere. [155]

During the 1850s all the religions of North Texas agreed on one thing: alcohol was evil and needed to be suppressed. Actually, it was a national movement. The Wisconsin Senate, 10-3, had passed legislation making liquor companies responsible for all paupers made directly or indirectly from liquor, a precursor of the product liability suit against, for example, the tobacco companies. The people of Vermont determined that no licenses to sell liquor would be issued in that State for the coming year. A threat was narrowly blocked to deprive sailors of their daily ration of grog. The United States Supreme Court upheld government's right to ban liquor in order to prevent "idleness and debauchery." Many people in the street, and most in the pews on Sunday, agreed with the "punch line" of a witticism of the period:

> *"What's whiskey bringing?" inquired a dealer in the trade.*
> *"Bringing men to the gallows", was the reply.*[156]

Chapters of The Sons of Temperance formed in every county, including Red River, and their members preached, prayed and lobbied for a ban on alcohol and sought "to cause the votaries of old King Alcohol to tremble for the safety and stability of his Kingdom." *The Standard* enthusiastically promoted these meetings and reported on their successes.

> *It will be seen by the advertisement in this paper that the Templars will have a procession of the 28th, on which day, the Rev. Mr. Young will also address the People of the county on Temperance etc. The gentleman's efforts elsewhere are highly commended. We hope he may have a large audience.*[157]

> Mr. Editor...The Sons of Temperance of the Boston [Bowie County] Division, had quite a large procession on the 8th instant and were addressed by Mr. Hewlett in a manner than not only did honor to himself, but to the cause he advocated. He dwelt long and reasoned impressively upon the evil effects of drinking ardent spirits. He also made an eloquent appeal to the ladies, for the benign influence on behalf of the cause.
>
> After the address was delivered, they were invited to the hotel to partake of a sumptuous dinner which had been prepared by the Proprietor. At night, there was a ball given which added much to the enjoyment of those attended.[158]

The anti alcohol movement had its proponents all over, including the frontier:

> *Father Matthews Branch Temperance Society*
>
> On Sunday, the 9th of December, 1849, a meeting was convened in the garrison church of Fort Towson in the Choctaw Nation, by a number of the soldiers of the infantry, at the desire of Rev. Father Marevault, Roman Catholic Missionary, for the purpose of forming a temperance society and proceeded to elect officers for its future governance.
>
> Father Marevault, after mentioning to the soldiers the nature of the society and its benefits, too well known already to be enumerated, 20 in number signed the pledge of temperance.[159]

The efforts were not wasted. In 1854, the Texas Senate terminated all licenses to sell alcohol, permitting each county, upon the vote of its citizenry, the choice whether to allow the sale of alcohol or not, and if so, the terms. Most voted for a version of what came to be known as the "Quart law", prohibiting the sale of ardent liquors in bottles less than a quart size, except for medicinal, mechanical or sacramental purposes.

DeMorse was in favor of the legislation and urged its enactment in all the counties of the Red River Valley. For weeks, he handed out plaudits to counties, like Bastrop, that had banned liquor:

> *On the 10th instant, the citizens of the Town of Bastrop took a vote on the license question. One hundred and twenty eight votes were polled: "For the liquor traffic - 3 votes"; "against the liquor traffic -125 votes" Well done, Bastrop. In the Temperance reform, she deserved the appellation of the Banner Town of the State, being the first to banish liquor traffic.*[160]

Temperance, of course, is not exactly religion, although they were identified together at the time. It is more a moral strength. The citizens of Texas and the United States, however, had purely religious experiences. In April of 1858, there was news from the exchange papers of New York City, reporting on a non sectarian religious revival there among the City's business community. During the work day, merchants, bankers, brokers on Wall Street and men of commerce everywhere put aside their work and gathered for preaching, prayer and song. By May, the revival was reported as spreading westward. By June, it had come to Clarksville and the Presbyterians, in the forefront of the movement, got a lot closer to the new Church they sought:

REVIVAL OF RELIGION

> *While other portions of the country have been greatly blessed with the revivals of religions during the past few months, the state of religion in this place seemed to be as languid as it well nigh could, but it has pleased God to favor this community with which seems to be a genuine work of his spirit. The meeting commenced this week and has mainly been conducted by the members of*

the Cumberland Presbyterian Church. There is a very intense feeling of interest pervading the minds of nearly the entire community; many have expressed a desire to become subjects of divine grace, who heretofore have expressed little interest in spiritual matters and not a few, we trust savingly, converted. The meeting is still continuing and the state of religious feeling, seems to be largely on the increase. The hearts of Christians have been roused from their lethargic slumber, and we anticipate that the numbers who will yet make profession of their faith will be very considerable. For years, the Cumberland Presbyterian Church have had in contemplation to erect a new Church. We learn that upwards of $3,500 have been subscribed towards the erection of a brick church edifice; an eligible situation has been secured and no fears are entertained but that sufficient funds will shortly be raised to pay the whole coast of building.

We understand that the Independent Order of Odd Fellows, intend shortly to erect a Lodge Hall. Should the Church and the Odd Fellows unite, they could erect a building that would surpass in elegance anything of the kind in Eastern Texas. [161]

The revival continued for at least another couple of weeks as *The Standard* reported.

The Revival in Clarksville

We understand that during the late revival in this place, some 26 persons made a profession of faith and some 50 others had gone to the mourners' bench, desiring an interest in the prayers of the church. During the progress of the meeting, which was mostly conducted the Rev. Messrs Dysart and Harris of the Cumberland Presbyterian Church, much solemnity and deep feeling seemed to pervade the minds of all. The Rev. Mr.

Bradley, Principal of one of the female schools in Paris, preached on several occasions with great acceptance by the audience. More than 45 persons went to the mourners bench on the night of Sunday, the 6th instant, after Mr. Bradley's departure for Paris. Several of them have since made a profession of religion and with many of them deep interest is still manifested. We believe that much good has been done and from the feelings which still exist, we are satisfied that much more is left to be accomplished. If Christians would at all times live in the faithful discharge of their duties the presence of God in the conversion of sinners would never be absent from the Church. It is too common after a high state of religious feeling for many professors of religion to relax in their efforts for the conversion of sinners and sinking into a state of apathy to leave it questionable with the world whether or not there is any sincerity in their professions. They should therefore live at all times so that the world would have no reason for doubts on their mind. [162]

Health and Medicine

Old folks say that, without good health, one has "nothing." What was state of health and her hand maiden, medicine, in the middle of the 1800s? Was Red River County an Eden from which illness and disease were barred? Or do we too lightly consider the miracles of 20th century medical science that the world, including Texas, did not enjoy in the 1840s and 1850s.

The Standard invariably contained the "professional cards" of a number of physicians, many of whom were located in Clarksville. Most were in the general practice of medicine. Much notices were short, but a Dr. Ellet provided his education and experience, which helps us gauge the caliber of the medical profession.

A.K. ELLETT, M.D.

C l a r k s v i l l e,

OFFERS his professional services in the several departments of the Healing Art to the citizens of Clarksville and its vicinity.

From the advantages which he has had in qualifying himself for the practice of his profession in the best medical schools in America and several years' attendance upon the Alma House and Hospital practice in Philadelphia, and the Alma House and Penitentiary practice in Richmond, Virginia, together with an experience of 16 years of practice in the South, he flatters himself that he will receive the confidence of an intelligent public, and by an assiduous attention to the duties of his profession, with a desire to please, he hopes to share the public patronage.

He will, unless professionally engaged, generally be round either at his office or at his residence.

> *Office: on the east side of the Public Square.*
> *Residence: the late dwelling of S. Graham .*[163]

A few doctors had specialities like today. For example, Dr. A. B. Hoy was an itinerant "surgeon dentist" and advised everyone that "he expects to remain in Town but a few days, and those wishing operations performed will please call immediately." [164]

The Standard also carried advertisements for local stores that sold drugs and medications of assorted varieties. It provided particulars about patent medicines, which boasted great cures for anything that ailed:

> *THE CHILDREN'S PANACEA.*
>
> *This medicine should be in every family throughout the world. It is sovereign in all diseases to which children and youth are subject. For summer complaints, dysentery, and all other afflictions of the stomach and bowels, it is infallible.*
>
> *Taken in small doses occasionally, it will prevent sickness in any climate. It need but be tried to insure the hearty commendation of mothers. In the southern, western and southwestern states, and in the Tropics, its value cannot be estimated. No other reliable children's medicine is before the public. This supplies a want seriously needed by every mother.*
>
> *Price 25 cents a bottle, with ample directions.*[165]

Clarksville did not have a hospital in those days. Few places did. It was a rarity except in the big cities of the Eastern United States. But, *The Standard* reported a significant surgical operation, probably the first ever performed in Clarksville and Northern Texas. The surgeon made use of the newly discovered "chloroform":

Surgical Operation at Clarksville Hotel

On Saturday last, by invitation, we witnessed at the Clarksville Hotel a very nice surgical operation, performed by Dr. J.P. Minture, who has lately settled in the town. The subject, upon whom the operation was performed, was a Mr. Hoover, about 18 years of age, who, some 8 or 9 months earlier, had his foot snagged, causing injury to some of the bones. It became necessary to amputate the foot above the ankle to perform what has taken the name of Syme's operation, disarticulate the foot at the ankle joint. The Doctor adopted the latter plan and thus the leg is little shortened. [166]

Despite all the advertisements for doctor offices and drug stores, DeMorse nevertheless maintained to the immigrant that Clarksville was so healthy a place that its "physicians [were] idling about the streets for want of employment, despite the recent wet weather." DeMorse blamed wet weather for any sickness the region suffered.

The health of the Vicinage

A few weeks since, when the rain was drizzling upon us intermittently and everything was dropping, sad and somber, and the mud holes looked like lakes of filth, from which any quantity of disease might be expressed among the population, we really were alarmed for the health of the town and had not a doubt, and if by some chance the cholera had come upon us, that our population would be decimated. But the sun has come out last in his majesty and there has no sickness coming out of it, beyond here and there a case. Our Town and the region around them are as healthy as we have ever known them and our doctors lazily lounging around the corners, must either starve or go to California or else get up an epidemic of some sort. [167]

The rest of Texas, however, was not quite as healthy as the Red River Valley. There were outbreaks of influenza which sickened many, although generally they were not fatal:

> *Epidemic in Austin*
>
> *By a letter from Austin under date of January 25, we learn that an influenza has prevailed in that city for some days previous and that it was violent in its character.*
>
> *In San Antonio, it had carried off four persons in one night, including Capt. Highsmith of the Rangers.* [168]

> *Sickness*
>
> *The prevalence of sickness throughout Northern Texas is unexampled and pervades this county to some extent. We are inclined to believe that it has been worse in the timbered counties, than in the prairies, more general and more fatal, partaking of a typhoid character, while in the prairie it is more generally chills and fevers, with an occasional case of congestion. The number of deaths, however, has not been great anywhere. The sickness generally yields readily to medicine, and, where deaths have occurred, we think it was because of lack of medical attention.* [169]

Some outbreaks, however, brought with them great numbers of fatalities. Today, the advances of the first half of the 20th century in identifying and eradicating the causes of many diseases, including the feared epidemics, are taken for granted. It was not always so. A century and a half ago, life expectancy was less than two-thirds what is today, the average age of death for both men and women being under 50. The Cholera Outbreak in Texas of 1849[170] is a good example of the ravages the settlers faced.

The cause of cholera were not known in the 1800s, but its

effects certainly were and were greatly feared. An outbreak had started in the Ganges in India in 1817 and moved westward about 70 miles a month. By the 1830s, it had reached Europe. Mostly, it seemed to strike the poor, the middle and upper classes excepted. Most of the deaths, it was observed, occurred in low, densely populated areas, near rivers. Fleeing from the sickness seemed to be as good as a prevention as any. *The Standard*, citing an overseas account received from its New York exchange paper, reported the disease to be about 75% fatal and that thirty four a day were dying in London from it. It was expected to follow the famine in Ireland. After that, it would be time for America to worry. It could jump oceans. It had in 1832 and 1839 and the spring of 1849 was predicted to see its landfall in New York.

However, the disease moved faster than anticipated, but not in the direction expected. It showed up in New Orleans. From there, it spread westward into Texas and over the course of the next seven months devastated a number of Texas towns, from Galveston in the east to Brownsville and settlements along the Rio Grande in West Texas. San Antonio, however, seems to have had been hit the worst, probably because, obviously unknown at the time, the waters of the San Antonio river that lazily meander through the town and which the citizens used for drinking, had become infected. Over 200 died:

Cholera in San Antonio

A friend writing us from Austin on April 26th says "the cholera is bad in San Antonio. Last Saturday, I am informed, 28 died. The population is leaving the city."

As yet, we have had no cases here, although some say the pneumonitory symptoms are prevalent. [171]

The cause of cholera was not known, although there were views as to both its origin and its cure. Some thought it was produced by drought or, rather, to the dead cattle that died from the drought. Others attributed the disease more to a state of mind, than an invading *bacterium*. The clues, of course, to determining the cause of the disease were there. One resident of San Antonio noted how river water used to be kept for days and would still be fit to drink, but that now, in a few hours, it emitted an offensive smell, similar to bilge water. He said the same was true with rain water. Puddles formed a layer of green scum within a day.

But there was no cholera in Clarksville, although the townspeople nervously watched it spread throughout the rest of Texas. DeMorse publicized the town's freedom from cholera. Rumors of an epidemic in the town had frightened parents with children in one of Clarksville several boarding schools and threatened Clarksville's preeminent position in education in Texas. DeMorse, of course, rose in defense and tended an explanation for Clarksville freedom from disease that was surprisingly accurate:

Health of Clarksville

It would seem that there are some that have a special ill will toward out town, if the fabulous reports circulated against its health are any evidence. Weeks ago, we noticed a false statement of this sort. And since we were informed by a gentleman who had been over in Titus county that some man had passed through that county, stating that he had just come from Clarksville, and that at the shop of our cabinetmaker, he had seen ten coffins making and that persons were dying here at the rate of 4 or 5 a day.

All of this is wholly untrue. Not a person has died in this place for more than 6 months and there is not one person seriously unwell at this time in this place. The fact is that our town is unquestionably one of the healthiest in this state, and has some superior educational institutions in and about it, which draw scholars from a distance. If the place could be characterized as sickly, it would benefit some other

> locality. The fact is that Clarksville is remarkably healthy and will probably compare in that respect with any town in the State. It has no local cause for sickness and has the best water in the State being pure rain water, contained in cisterns, excavated from the solid rock. It has been noted that where cistern water is used, Cholera does little or no damage. [172]

The year 1853 brought to Texas another scourge -yellow fever. An acutely infectious disease, it is caused by a virus transmitted by the bite of an infected mosquito, like malaria is. A mild case can be flu like, but usually it is much more severe, accompanied by fevers, nausea and vomiting. Even today, the mortality rate is approximately ten per cent.

It made its ugly appearance in the City of New Orleans in August,1853. The Charity Hospital there reported forty three deaths from yellow fever in a single day, August 6. By August 26, it was up to 224 a day. Eventually, it would take over 10,000 lives in that city. It also attacked Shreveport, Louisiana and spread up the Mississippi, inflicting settlements along the way. *The Standard* published weekly accounts of the horrible spread. As was the case with cholera, the cause of yellow fever would not be known until long in the future. The readers of *The Standard* feared the illness to be communicative and that it would spread to their state. Their fears were well justified. Yellow fever invaded Texas in October, 1853, visiting Victoria, Matagorda, Tyler, LaVaca, Indianola and other settlements along the Coast. It threatened to move inland.

> *The Austin State Gazette of the 8th inst reports:* "The yellow fever broke out at Cincinnati [Texas] in Walker county on the Trinity about two weeks since and has proven terribly fatal. Out of a population of about 100 persons, there have been ten to 15 deaths and many others were sick at last advice and expected to die. The deaths embraced some of the leading citizens of the place. The place was deserted by all who could get away. [173]

Not knowing the cause of the disease, and believing it communicative, the average citizen literally ran at its approach. *The Standard* even reported that a man in New Jersey caught yellow fever from a pile of old rags from New Orleans. While not fingering the mosquito as the culprit, some citizens recognized that the disease predominated along the coasts and rivers:

> *Fears are expressed by many persons that the yellow fever, now prevailing at Galveston, Houston and Indianola, as an epidemic, will spread into the interior. Such fears are unfounded in our opinion. Two cases have proved fatal in San Antonio. They were teamsters, just up from Indianola, where they contracted the disease, but it has not spread there and we have no fears that it will go beyond the limits of the above towns. Like other evils, it cannot thrive in the pure, wholesome air of country villages and farming districts.* [174]

Clarksville and Red River county, DeMorse was happy to announce, were not visited from the scourge, despite the proximity to the Red River and the Delaware Creek's being just south of the public square. While he "congratulated" the citizens on their intelligence choice of an abode free from yellow fever, DeMorse gave ultimate credit to where it was due, "the Supreme Ruler of the Universe, who has placed us in a land of health and plentifulness:"

Yellow Fever

> *This frequent visitant of New Orleans, this year extends its travels to many other places where its presence is most unwelcome. Our extracts showed last week that along the banks of the Mississippi and the Red rivers, its presence was most fatal - even in little interior towns having no communication with the grand scene of its revels, little villages of a few families in the Pine hills.*

> There must be some generally prevalent cause. It cannot be in all those cases communicative. Quarantine does not seem to be at all effective, for upon the dry and lofty hills of Natchez, where quarantine was rigidly imposed, it has answered no purpose. At Shreveport, it has been most virulent, although seven-eights of the population abandoned the place as soon as its presence was well defined. Yet, out of a population of 200, there was said to be 75 cases. At Galveston and Houston, too, in our own State, the disease is working sharply. At Galveston, up to the 20th ult, there had been 200 deaths and three times that number of cases. At Houston, up to the 15th, there had been 29 deaths.
>
> We, who live high up on Red River, have reason to congratulate ourselves that in all times of general and widespread epidemics, we are free from the scourge, far removed from all apprehension of it and should feel grateful for the exemption from the destroyer, which seizes with such a deadly grip, our brethren below. Both in a sanitary and a business point of view, the exemption is an immense blessing, to be acknowledged with gratitude to the Supreme Ruler of the Universe, who has placed us in a land of health and plentifulness.[175]

While spared the disease, the citizens of Clarksville felt the sufferings of those afflicted. The Townspeople of Clarksville took up an subscription for the benefit of the sick and suffering of New Orleans, which DeMorse pronounced was "a commendable purpose."

A third disease feared across the country was small pox. In 1857, it made its appearance in Red River county. DeMorse assured his readers that it was not in Clarksville, and, certainly not at the Donoho House in Town:

> We understand that Mr. Fleming, living on Pine Creek in this county and lately returned from New

Orleans is down with the small pox and that three or four other persons, living in that vicinity have caught the infection. They have all been brought together and measures taken to prevent, if possible, the spread of the diseases. Nothing of this sort and no other sickness worth mentioning is prevalent in this Town. The place is entirely healthy and the doctors underemployed. The proprietors of the Donoho house has a notice in our columns, some report having gone ahead, that the small pox was in the house or was likely to be. There is no truth in that rumor.[176]

Everything is relative. Clarksville, although spared cholera, yellow fever and small pox, was not entirely immune from fatal diseases. Reviewing more than a hundred random obituaries from *The Standard* yields s some sobering statistics about health back then. For example, on the plus side, it revealed a couple of women who lived to their seventies and three men. Eight other men and women who lived into their fifties and sixties. On the other hand, another 13% of the men died in their forties and 11% in their twenties and thirties. It was not much better for women – 4 % in their forties and 22% between eighteen and thirty nine.

A number of children from two to seventeen were also reported. Infant deaths were about 18 %. How tragic still is the obituary of the three year and old boy: " Little Willie was a good boy and very devoted to his books." Infant mortality - those under two years of age - was reported at about 16% of total deaths:

From what did they die, if not from old age? Obituaries give the causes of death as: typhoid fever, congestive chill, bilious intermittent fever, bronchitis, pneumonia, consumption pleurisy, "died from disease of the heart", sporadic dysenterybrain fever, inflamation of the brain, child birth, congestive fever, an inflammation of the loin, cholera, scarlet fever, hemorrhage of the lung fever, yellow fever; pneumonia, diabetes; spasmodic croup and apoloexy. One poor fellow "died very suddenly not having spoken after he had been found near his house where he had fallen."

Some were protracted illness, one as long as four years. Others just a few days. Others were shot, some died in military service, others in accidents like the 16 year old girl, whose dress caught n fire when she bent down in front of the fireplace to pick something up, or another girl whose calico dress, "distended by hoops" came into contact with the fire.

DeMorse himself was not untouched by unexpected deaths. His wife died at the age of 29 from "congestion of the bowels" caused he said from the rainy weather.[177] His son, Charles De Morse, Jr. aged seven, was killed when kicked by a horse.[178] Three years alter, his daughter was killed by fire.[179] His remaining son would die on the way back to Clarksville from the Civil War.

Personal tragedies aside, DeMorse was correct. All in all the Red River Valley was a healthy region. Indeed, in a pitch to emigrants arriving in Texas and looking for an area in which to settle. DeMorse stressed the over all health of the place as one of the reasons to settle there.

Health.

That health is a blessing of the greatest magnitude is a universally admitted proposition, and looking around us yesterday in the court house, it impressed itself upon us that hardly in any other locality in the State could such another array of countenances could be seen radiate with that type of bloom which indicated, not merely the present health of the possessor, but a healthfulness pertaining to the locality itself. Our physicians are doing less than in any other place we ever lived in before, for in Northern communities known as healthy, that is free of malarious influences, there are still many cases of consumption and inflammatory diseases, which we entirely exempt from here. We assert without fear of disproof, or even contradiction, by those who know, either by trial or personal observations, that there are not three other towns in the State of Texas as healthy as Clarksville and no more so.

Our greatest element of health is pure water, the water that descends after atmospheric purification and is received and retained in cisterns in the solid rock, many feet beneath the surface. It is such water as we have found no where else, so cool that ice is no luxury here. Not so cold as ice would make it, but near it, that ice is unnecessary and no body feels the want of it; so cold that milk from a vessel let down to the bottom of a cistern will make the teeth ache.[180]

Law and Lawlessness

A Republic, be it Rome, the United States or Texas requires its citizens to pay their taxes, serve in the military when required to protect the Republic and to obey her laws.

Courthouses, where violators could be prosecuted and punished, were therefore essential. In those first days, the Courthouse was the first site laid out in a new county seat. Sometimes the lawyers got there before the builders did. Court was held for a while in Wise, Lamar County under a large bois d'arc tree in the summer. A grove of oak trees was the first court in Upshur County as it was in Denton County, when Pickney was the seat. When the county seat was moved to Sherman in 1848, Court was held for a while beneath a pecan tree.

Before Clarksville became the county seat of Red River, Court was held on the second floor of different general stores in the county, first, at Travis Wright's store in Jonesboro, and then at Gunboat Latimer's in LaGrange (now Madras). When Clarksville was voted to be the county seat, Court was moved to a two story log building in the middle of the Square. Clark had promised the structure, if Clarksville were selected, over Madras, to be the seat.

By 1850, however, the Clarksville pioneer court house was dated, dilapidated and undersized. DeMorse, whose home and office were across the square, was both a neighbor, as well, a frequent user of it, being an attorney. But, he was not sentimental about the structure. Calling the old court house, which had been the kernel from which Clarksville had sprung, an "ancient time worn, weather beaten, dilapidated Temple of Justice, [which] has long been an eye sore to the Town and County"[181], DeMorse was happy that it was to be sold to the highest bidder and carted off. He even impatiently suggested that "the boys got up an illumination" and burn it down."

Clarksville built itself a new Court House. DeMorse, self appointed spokesman for the townspeople and the Bar, did not hesitate to express to the County commissioners his ideas on what should be erected[182]. There was a certain logic in what he said:

Our Court House

> The County court will soon decide upon proposals for this building and determine upon its character. In this determination, price should not be the only consideration. Low price may not be cheapness. It is true economy to have good materials, well put together at fair prices, rather than poor materials, put up in an unworkmanlike manner, neither elegant in appearance or durable. We have waited a long time for a court house, are amply able to build one now and should have a good one... We ought to have a good courthouse and should be satisfied with nothing less and a good court house can be put up only with first class workmen. [183]

The new Court House was to be built near the spot of the old one that had been hauled away - that is, right in the middle of the square, center stage, the most important building in town. And it was to be built of brick, the first attempt in Clarksville to use this material and one which the other citizens, including DeMorse, would soon follow in their own new constructions. It was to cost $10,000, soup to nuts, and take about six or seven months to complete. It was to be a good sized structure, "45 by 55 feet with a base of three feet, a lower story of 12 feet to the ceiling, an upper story in which is to be the Courtroom, two clerks offices, 15 feet from floor to ceiling and these with the cornices will give the building an elevation of 33 feet. It is handsomely finished throughout, with seats for the audience. The walls are to be 18 inches thick."[184] DeMorse, sidewalk superintendent, visited the brickyard to check up on those that they were making for the Court House job. He reported back to the tax payers that the brickyard had "succeeded in making a large portion of excellent durable brick, rather rough, but of good color and weight."

Not only was it sturdy, the new Court House was attractively appointed, inside and out:

> *Our new court house is progressing rapidly to completion, the external painting is nicely and looks like nearly done. The painting of the courtroom is also nearly done and the carpenter's work for the Judge's seat, the Bar, the Jury seats and the Audience is finished and present a neat and commodious appearance. The seats for the audience rise from front to back so as to give all a view of the proceedings of the court.*[185]

A sturdy court house was not a substitute for a strong legal system. The administration of justice is essential to any productive society. Disputes among citizens had to be resolved peacefully, fairly, objectively and in a timely manner. Wrongdoers, civil or criminal, had to be brought to order. The public had to have confidence in the justice system, on a local level. That type of confidence in the judiciary was evident throughout the Red River Valley, Clarksville included.

Each county in Texas had its own District Court, with a court house on the public square, with some local lawyers officed nearby. The Judge of the court, the District Attorney who prosecuted criminal actions and many of the lawyers who tried cases in the District Court, however, were all from out of town. They rode what was called a "circuit", going from county to county and trying any cases on the docket that were ready.

During the days of the Republic, the huge Red River District was called the Seventh Judicial District. After statehood, it was renamed the 8th Judicial District, which for some of the 1850s was comprised of the counties of Bowie, Cass, Titus, Hunt, Hopkins, Fannin, Lamar and Red River. DeMorse and his fellow travelers of the Bar appeared fairly regularly in Collin, Dallas, Kaufman, Cooke and other counties as well, some of which were in the 9th Judicial District. As the frontier went westward so did the stalwart band of counsel, often inaugurating court in counties like Parker, Tarrant, Montague, and Wise. It was a lot of running - riding - around.

The Standard of March 29, 1856, gave the schedule for the Spring term:

> *Collin & Titus, both two weeks begin on April 12th*
>
> *Grayson (two weeks)*
>
> *Hopkins (one week) begin April 26th*
>
> *Hunt, one week, begins May 3*
>
> *Cooke is one week and Fannin is two and both begin on May 10.*
>
> *Denton one week begins on May 17th*
>
> *Lamar is two weeks and begins on the May 24th*
>
> *Tarrant is two weeks and begins on June 24*
>
> *Dallas is July 1, until business is disposed of* [186]

The District Court that sat in Clarksville, being the oldest one in North Texas, was understandably busy. It met twice a year, in the early winter and again in early summer and sat for at least two weeks at a time, until the ready docket was finished, or, until the Judge and the non resident lawyers had to move on to the next scheduled term in another county of the Judicial circuit. In 1847, the Court sat in Clarksville for almost seven weeks with admirable results:

> *The District Court*
>
> *We should have stated before this that our district Court adjourned Monday of last week having disposed of about 450 of its cases, leaving about 50 standing over to the next term. This we should call a considerable business for a new country.* [187]

The Judge is at the head of this process. A number of the judges with whom DeMorse for two decades crisscrossed Norther Texas were to become well known. Take Judge John T. Mills, for example. Irish-born, South Carolina raised and educated, John Mills married a Clarksville gal, Mary Jane Vining and was a lawyer in Clarksville before becoming a circuit judge. He later was an unsuccessful candidate for Governor as well as having a county named for him. DeMorse was a fan of Mills:

> *The District Court for this county adjourned on Saturday evening last, after a session of two weeks, in which more than one hundred cases were disposed of. Judge Mills still retains the high estimations our citizens awarded him, at the first circuit he made in this District, and dispatches business with a rapidity seldom surpassed.*[188]

and

> *This gentleman has obtained and deserves the high consideration of the people in the district for his firm, decisive and impartial administration of the law and the energy which he has infused into its execution by the various subordinate officers.*[189]

But it was not just DeMorse who praised Mills. So did the bar. The Jurists Association of the Seventh Judicial District, asked him to deliver an address "upon the character of [the legal] profession and the Duties of Attorneys.[190] So too did the Grand Jury of Lamar County have some kind words for him.

> *The grand Juror cannot consent to return to their homes without giving expression of their sentiments of regard and esteem which they entertain for the Hon John T. Mills, presiding judge. When they take into*

consideration the peculiar disadvantages under which this position of the Republic has heretofore labored for the irregular administration of the law having now assumed of a different, firm and consistent character and that order has been introduced throughout the legal organization of the county, concerning that this improvement has been induced by the capacity and conduct of the presiding judge, the expression of the fact and the acknowledgment of the benefit, they therefore conclude by reassuring him of their high respect and regard for him, both as an officer and as a gentleman. [191]

There was no shortage of attorneys in early Texas. They seemed to have immigrated in numbers disproportionate to their percentage of the general population. None native born or educated. Most were from the southern states. A few like De Morse hailed from the North.

The *Standard* gives us two decades of their "professional" or business cards, from which we can glean a good profile of the members of the Northern Texas Bar. For example, we can confirm that the name lawyers give themselves is the same as today, typically "Attorney and Counselor at Law" or just "Attorney at Law".

The cards also recited each attorney's speciality.

For litigators, that meant principally the courts in which they regularly practiced. During the Republic, when the population was in the eastern counties, it was easy. "Will attend all the District Courts in the Eastern portion of the Republic and the Supreme Court." But with Statehood, came even more settlers. Original counties were divided and re-divided. The original Red River county, for example, was to become 39 different counties. Almost every year, the frontier moved westward and new counties had to be created. Soon, the litigator's beat became more complicated to describe: "will practice in the 6th and 8th Judicial Districts; also in the Supreme and Federal Court at Tyler"; "practices regularly in the District court of Collin, Grayson, Denton, Tarrant, Parker, Johnson, Ellis,

Dallas and Kaufman counties and at the Supreme Court of the state in Austin."

Criminal cases seemed more plentiful than civil matters, although, more likely than not, they just made better press to the folks back home. We each have an image of justice in the early west. It might be a trial held in a saloon, a posse being formed to pursue bandits or a lynch mob taking the law into its own hands. Lawlessness seemed, at least in Hollywood, to go hand in hand with the frontier. In the very first days, that was not always true-- that is, if we can believe what the these folks say:

> *But most attractive of all, and differing from all elsewhere, was the fact that he found the latch key to every cabin door hung upon the outside. There were no locks to the dwelling, or meat house, or corn crib; every comer was welcome to the primitive hospitality --cordial, not passive, hospitality. He noticed that no man feared robbery or wayside danger, but camped out anywhere that fuel could be found, turned his horse on the abundant grass, cooked his meat on a stick, and his hoecake in the ashes and that the little camp coffee pot behind his saddle, furnished him facility for an invigorating beverage.*[192]

For example, a tale of early Clarksville, reported in Pat B. Clark's *The History of Clarksville and Old Red River County, Texas* speaks of a time, just after 1836, when a horse was stolen from a farm just outside of town. This had never happened before. No crime of any nature had ever been reported. There were no laws. There was no sheriff. There was no jail. A "posse" was formed, tracked the thief, captured and brought him back to Clarksville. There, the town's leading residents, in the midst of what is today the Clarksville cemetery on West Washington Street were set to hang the thief from the branch of a blackjack oak tree. One citizen, Dr. George Gordon, however, made a plea for mercy, arguing a horse was not worth a man's life. Another countered with the question that, since they had no jail, they would have to turn the thief loose on the public, if he were not executed. A vote was taken among the large crowd that had formed. Those in favor of the execution stood on one side of the road, those opposed on the other. Two judges, astride a single horse, rode down the road, counting votes. Women were on the jury, probably the first time in Texas. He was acquitted

In the first days, whenever a jail was required, a storeroom or smokehouse that could be padlocked, would be pressed into service. Sometime early on, however, a jail of some sort, sorry as it might have been, must have existed, because we have DeMorse's criticsm of it:

Our Jails

We would the attention of our county commissioners to the unsafe and unsightly building in our town known by the name of the "jail." It is well known to the inhabitants of our county that it is unfit for service, which, at any time, it is liable to be called upon to render. Owing to its unsecure condition, our county, during the past few years, has been put to considerable expense in guarding prisoners, both before and after trial. Prisoners had to be sent to the jails of other counties for safe keeping, thereby imposing on this county additional expense. The time has arrived for making the effort to get a jail, which, instead of being a disgrace to the county can be an ornament to our town. [193]

DeMorse's prayer was answered by forces unknown. The useless structure burned to the ground and DeMorse was not seen to shed any tears and proposals were solicited.[194]

This age of innocence was not to last. An increasing number of crimes of all sorts would be reported during the next decade throughout Texas. No wonder. The population had increased several fold in only a few years and, among the immigrants, were undesirables who were as much fleeing prosecution back home, as they were seeking a new life.

Tiny Clarksville and Red River county were not immune from a rash of crimes that broke out in 1852 and lasted through 1858. Some of the offenses were minor in nature, sometimes even with their amusing aspects. For example, in the following two items, witness criminal defense lawyer DeMorse's bias against the mail thief, whose booty included some subscription and advertising payments due *The Standard*, or how the citizens resorted to self help when a con artist was exposed:

theft

John Wesley Smathers, formerly a mail rider and suspected of depredating upon the mail, between this place and Mount Pleasant during several months of last summer was arrested on Thursday for stealing a purse with $300 in gold, the property of J. F. Harris. Smathers had been purchasing some jewelry and dry goods with some of his ill gotten plunder, but was all the time under surveillance and the purse described by Harris was seen in his possession. Harris procured a warrant for him and Sheriff Bivins arrested him before he left town. He confessed it the theft. The money was all recovered and the young gentleman was committed, with the privilege of $2,000 bail, if he can find it. [195]

The distinguished stranger

A personage made his advent into our town about 3 p.m. on Tuesday, who managed for 24 hours, to make himself eminently conspicuous. Making his descent first upon one of our best dry goods stores, he arrayed himself in a new suit with gold studs and several fine finger rings for which he said he would settle this morning. He went to the grocery and had proclamation made that all who would drink at the expense of the government come in. He announced that he came with credentials from Governor Bell to raise 500 rangers immediately. Adjourning from the grocery to the steps of Dr. Look's new office, he made a speech setting forth the objects of his visit and glorifying his own valor at San Jacinto and in the valley of Mexico very considerably. He made an engagement at the tailor's for 30 sets of new clothes to be ready in six days and spoke for the shooing of 30 horses at the blacksmith shop speedily. So far everything went fine, but the merchant at whose establishment the clothes were purchased, coming in and finding out that they were not paid for, but that, when payment was insisted upon, the gentleman's horse had been turned over and, learning that the gentleman had just started going toward the edge of town on foot, took a double barreled shot gun and, mounting a horse, went after him. As he came up, he addressed his patron by name and asked him, if he were going out riding in the country. The merchant told him he had got out as far as he intended going and requested his return to have an investigation of their business transaction. Taking him back to the store, he deliberately divested him of hat, coat, boots, finger rings and leaving the bird to array himself in his original plumage. He plead strongly for the purpose of retaining the new shirt but to no purpose. He was admirably good humored and, although changing his dress somewhat reluctantly, manifested no anger or chagrin. As he had become suspicious, reference was made to a bill at the Post Office, describing Lynch, the murderer, and a wonderful similarity was discovered. That night the stranger had friends to sit up with him but he made no effort to leave and next morning, he walked around town deliberately and contentedly, trying to sell his horse, until a brace of men rode in armed from Kaufman county and told him that they had come to join his company and desired that he should go back with them and account for a little business transaction there. It seems he had hired aa horse from one of them and, after riding six miles, traded it for the one he rode here. The stranger said he would go with them and be glad to have their company and talked and joked right merrily as off they went together. His written credentials were gross forgeries insufficient

> to deceive anybody and purported to be signed by various notable persons west of this, whose signatures were all in the same hand as the order he gave for his horse. He represented his name as Wright, originally from North Carolina, is about 5 feet 10 inches high, dark complexion, bright black eyes with a suspicious look. Some think him insane and others think him an audacious rascal. He says he has been living near Waco and lost his wife and been sick himself which might account for his insanity, if it exists. He professed to be a Freemason and claimed the Friendship of the Brotherhood.[196]

Other crimes, while not amusing, were nonetheless, non violent offenses, crimes against property, deception[197], counterfeiting[198], smuggling[199] and fraudulent land titles[200], for example. The dearest asset lost to another's misrepresentations might be a maiden's virginity. While not a crime necessarily, it was considered a wrong under the law and DeMorse reports how the case of *Nall vs Russell* for seduction occupied a whole trial day and the jury brought in a verdict of $1,350.

Livestock, allowed to feed in the lush pasture provided by nature, were frequently stolen as well. In the hierarchy of such crimes, hog theft was the least, but it could end you up in the Penitentiary. Cattle stealing was considered petit larceny and not treated much more harshly – a year in the Penitentiary. This, of course, was before cattle became synonymous with Texas and "rustling" a major crime.

Horse stealing was a risk for anyone with a good looking piece of horse flesh that could be sold or traded easily a few towns distant[201], not unlike a popular car model is today. Some thefts were the work of organized gangs[202]. One that operated in the Denton area might have had as many as 17 members, at least according to the five that were apprehended.

A conviction for horse theft usually brought a relatively long stretch in the penitentiary in Huntsville – sometimes as many as four years. Most issues of *The Standard* had at least one notice, often with a reward attached, for stolen horses [203] and sometimes reports of captures.

stealing mules

Green Candle was committed to county jail on Thursday last on the charge of stealing two mules from the range near Wm. Humphreys in this county [Red River] and offering them for sale for $60. The low price elicited suspicion and lead to his arrest. [204]

Burglaries in Clarksville were also reported. In the following instance, the thieves were apprehended by good old fashioned detective work.

On Monday night, the grocery store of W. F. T. Hart was entered into and money robbed of about 450 dollars. The robber, in opening the box with the blade of his knife, let the point of the blade in the box. This was preserved and, on Tuesday night, the pocket knife of a carpenter named Hampton, who was suspected, being observed by a fellow workman with the point freshly broken off. Comparison was mad with the point left in the box and they fitted. Upon this Hampton was arrested, confessed, went to the place of deposit, dug up the money and delivered it, and was confined, on Thursday evening, and is now, we believe, indicted, in conjunction with the Negro man Jeff, the property of Reason Ragin, who is reported as the principal contriver and manager of the robbery. [205]

Clarksville and Red River saw their share of more heinous crimes, from assault all the way to murder. How they were handled usually depended upon who the criminals and who the victims were. It was the proverbial double standard. For example, when a site in Clarksville was selected as the enlisting office for the Rangers, a certain degree of violent behavior was overlooked, and charged off to the high spirits of the enlistees.

> *There has been a movement in Town to raise rangers under the new law, authorizing the reception of 3000 Volunteers by the President. A meeting is to be held today. In anticipation of the serious service upon the Plains, a slight skirmish took place in Town between the leaders, whose eagerness for a fight had become too irritating for further endurance, and so they pitched in to sort of a free fight in which anybody was privileged to take a hand. No serious consequences resulted we believe. And, having blunted the edge of their appetite at home, it is presumed that they are now will take a calm survey of the work before them and march to it, as men go to any other regular employment.* [206]

Wild Indians were no longer of any major concern to the people of Red River county by the time Texas became a state, the frontier being several counties to the west and southwest by then. But, some of the more peaceful Indians from the Indian Nation across the Red River became unruly at times, especially when alcohol was involved. Indians attacking other Indians was acceptable. Indians attacking whites was not.

> *Indians*
>
> *A Choctaw Indian was severely injured by another Indian at Johnson's store, just below old Jonesboro, on Monday last. The weapon used was a revolver, three shots of which were fired two taking effect in the leg of the unfortunate Indian. The attack was unprovoked and cowardly.* [207]

> *Affray*
>
> *On the 9th instant, one of our citizens, Joseph Blackwell, was stabbed in the neck and the side by one*

Ned Johnson, a half breed Cherokee. At the time, his wounds were thought to be mortal, but it is now hoped that he will recover. Johnson had been drinking freely and had beaten and bruised a white man, who was also drunk, for which Mr. B. had ventured to reprove him. Upon this, according to Mr. B.'s statement, Johnson put his hand upon his dirk with the evident intent of drawing it, whereupon Mr. B. hit upon the head with a 4 point weight, but not so hard as to prevent his advance. Before B. could reach the street, he was twice stabbed and but for the timely interference of a passerby would have been killed outright. The affair took place at the grocery of Mr. Wells & Fuller and two lads were its sole witnesses, but so frightened were they that they can give no intelligible report about it.

Immediately afterwards, Johnson mounted his horse, told the bystanders that he intended the death of his victim and rode off. Sheriff Crawford started in pursuit and overtook him in the Bois D'Arc bottom and, as he would not stopped when called, snapped a pistol at him. The weapon misfired and Johnson escaped among the thicket. On the night of the 10th, he was known to have crossed the Red River and he is now lurking some where in the Choctaw Nation. He will not venture among the Cherokees, as he left them about two years ago, to avoid punishment for the murder of an Indian boy. [208]

Drunken Indians were troublesome, but insubordinate slaves were worse. Bands of Negroes, roaming Clarksville streets at night, suggested crime or, horrible to conceive, insurrection, a great fear in all slave societies. A letter to the editor from TAXPAYER voicing such fears and DeMorse's reply illustrate the concern.

Dear Mr. DeMorse
Being a taxpayer, living in the corporate limits of

our town, I want to ask for information on whom devolves the duty of appointing an efficient patrol. During the last winter, there was considerable excitement in the community and the vigilance of the patrol produced a most salutary effect for several months in restraining lawless bands of Negroes from aggregating in and around the town. Now that we are either without a patrol, or if an appointment has been made, it is totally inefficient, our town swarms nightly with the very worst forms of Negroes which the county affords. Thefts are committed nightly and some of them are of the most daring kind, yet there is little or no chance of detecting the culprits. Again I ask 'Whose is the duty to appoint and efficient patrol? Does it belong to the corporation? If so, , have they made such appointments? Does the duty belong to the County Court?'

In reply to the above queries, we would advise [Taxpayer] to make inquiry of our worthy mayor. If the writer has been the victim of any light fingered gentry, we can sincerely sympathize with him, as we also have been favored with several nocturnal visits during the last six to eight weeks. These nightly visitors are in no way particular how they help themselves before leaving the premises. Not having the fear of God before their eyes and disregarding the distinction between meum and tuum[209], *they are equally expert at clearing a clothesline, examining the contents of the smokehouse or stealthily entering your bedroom, rifling your pockets or decamping with your watch, especially if left hanging on the bed head. So deeply indeed are our sympathies with our correspondent that we would earnestly endorse the adoption of such measures, as must necessarily tend to promote and better the state of things in our community.*[210]

Slaves slaying their masters could not be tolerated as the following indicate!

Awful Murder

It is our painful duty to state that our county man, Mr. Gaffeney, who was found dead near his own house, on the road a few weeks since, and who, it was supposed, was killed by a kick from his horse, was basely murdered by two of his own Negroes, who are now in jail at this place. They have not only confessed the fact of the murder, but they have made a full disclosure of all the particulars. They have produced the club by which they had knocked him off the horse and murdered him. [211]

The Standard reported, over the course of three consecutive weekly issues and in some detail, the process of dispensing justice in Texas in the mid 1800s. First, the trial where guilt or innocence was determined. Then, sentencing when the community, through the court, determined the price that had to be paid for breaching societal rules, and, lastly, execution of the wrongdoers, slaves John and Moses, for the murder of William Gaffeney.

Found Guilty

The Negro slaves John and Moses, the property of the late William Gaffeney were this morning placed on trial charged with the murder of their Master, William Gaffeney, on the 24th of march last. They pled not guilty, but their own confession before A.M. Crooks Esq. together with the testimony that was introduced on the part of the State was so conclusive that the jury was but a short time in making up their verdict of guilty. Up to the hour of going to press, the Court had not passed sentence upon them. The prisoners received the verdict with stoic indifference. And to show the perfect nonchalance with which they hurried an estimated citizen out of existence without a moment's warning, they confessed that, in watching the road for their master on the occasion of his *murder, they both fell asleep and were only roused by the sound of his horse hoofs as he road up the road. The two Negroes were appraised at $1,879.16, one half of which was paid by the State to the owners.* [212]

District Court

On Monday last, the Negro slaves John and Moses, found guilty as we stated last week of the murder of their master William Gaffeney, were brought into court in the charge of the sheriff and officials to receive the sentence of the Court. Judge Todd, after stating to the prisoners of the heinousness of their offense and his painful duty in passing the sentence, proceeded to explain to them in language suited to their condition and which they could understand, that the law required that the punishment of death be inflicted upon them and that it behooved them to prepare themselves by every means of grace to meet their victim and their God. After which, the Judge proceeded to pass the formal sentence of death, which was that on Friday, the 17th instant, they should be taken by the sheriff to the place of execution and by him hung by the neck until they were dead. There was a large crowd in the courthouse and the utmost silence prevailed throughout. The prisoners appeared calm and determined, and, with the exception of a slight muscular contraction perceivable about the lips of one of them, there was no outward evidence that anything out of the common order was occurring. [213]

Execution

The two Negroes Moses and John convicted in the murder of Mr. Gaffeney paid the final legal penalty of their crime yesterday at about half past 1 o'clock p.m. There was a considerable crowd to witness the execution and some drunkenness manifest, we are sorry to say.

Silence being ordered by the Sheriff, the man Moses got up and warned his black brethren not to do as he had done, and always, when asked to do anything, however little, to think well over it first. He said he had no desire to kill his poor master till the man beside him persuaded him to join him and told them not to feel sorrow for him because he was going to rest. John said something in an inaudible tone, and, the religious services having been offered by the Rev Mr. Corley of the Cumberland Presbyterian Church and the prayers of all the bystanders of all religious persuasions having been invoked by the Rev. Father Martin of the Catholic Church, the Sheriff commenced disposing the ropes and we left.

The two men seemed both resigned to their fate and not at all alarmed but penitent and willing to expiate their crime, as the law required. On the night before, at about ten o'clock, we passed by the jail and heard them singing a hymn cheerfully, so cheerfully indeed that we at first thought that the sound must come from a residence nearby, but as we got opposite the building and the locality of the sound became defined, we stopped and listened with pleasurable emotions until it ceased.

We are told that the cart drove from under them and that, with little struggle, they passed out of existence.[214]

The public square itself witnessed a few killings. One was the murder of one of its merchants, a jeweler, Charles Peabody, by some other citizens of the town. How it all started has a suggestion of scandal to it:

Awful Tragedy

After ten years or more of freedom from bloodshed, our town was on Sunday evening last, the scene of a most heart sickening butchery.

Mr. Charles H. Peabody, an intelligent, honest, inoffensive citizen, of some weaknesses, but many good qualities, was guilty of an indiscretion a few nights since at the house opposite the Clarksville Hotel, occupied by Miles Husband and his son in law Albert Western. This was much talked about on the public streets by persons who might have found some better subject for continued conversation and Mr. Peabody had been wantonly and publically annoyed by it, until it had raised a feeling of enmity about it between him and Husbands and Western, the murdered man himself certifying that, when he went from town to his boarding house on that day at dinner time, some of the females of that house had shouted after him offensively.

On the evening referred to, Mr. Peabody was returning home from the Square to his boarding house and had passed Husband's house, some distance, when he was informed that Mr. James DeLahunty had been severely choked by Husband on account of some words growing out of his (Peabody's) differences with Husbands. Remarking that he did not wish anyone else to be hurt on his account, and that he would abide the consequences of his own difficulties, or words to that effect, he turned back and going to the middle of the street in front of Husband's house, he said in a distinct tone to Western, as near as can be remembered by the witness nearest them. "Mr. Western, that little difficulty between us, when and how should it be settled?" To this, as the evidence below will indicate, Western responded by jumping out and saying "Now, sir" and discharging a pistol at Peabody. Peabody then drew a pistol and attempted to fire at Western, but the cap exploding fruitlessly, he threw the pistol in that direction and drawing a Bowie knife ran toward Western.

The evidence will then show that he ran about the house without much fixed purpose, until confronted with a new combatant with a brick bat - Miles Husbands- when he attempted to get away, probably feeling he was in a most unequal contest with two and no firearms. But he was not destined to escape so easily. It appears that the poor victim did not know how many enemies he had, who were disposed to hunt him down, even though he had not molested them. The evidence shows that turning to escape he was assaulted by brickbats from unknown enemies, one of which knocked the knife from his hand and one struck him under the eye and left a deep indentation there and by the side of the nose. There was also found on the small of his back, when stripped, a terrible bruise, about 3 inches in length. Stunned and probably stupid with bewilderment, at this hunting down by unseen forces, the wretched man was followed as he attempted to get away and seized by the hair just at the edge of the sidewalk in front of Thompson's hotel and held down by Miles Husbands, while Western, who in the meantime had acquired another pistol, ran up and putting the pistol close to his back above the right shoulder blade, shot him and the ball ranging down toward the heart, he died in a few minutes, making but the single exclamation "Oh God, I am a dead man." The blood poured out in two large pools upon the ground. And after his immediate removal to the office of Dr. Look, adjoining his jewelry establishment, continued to pour out unceasingly until his burial the next day. His shirt was burning when taken off and showed a burnt hole as large as the palm of a man's hand. This scene was witnessed by quite a number of persons, some of whom were at the time of the shooting at the gallery, within a few feet of the murder.

    Directly after the commission of the act, Husbands and Western were arrested and at their examination on Monday and Tuesday before the Mayor and Justice Moore. After hearing the evidence, it was determined that the parties should be bound over to await the actions of the District court, Western in the sum of $1,000 and Husbands in the sum of $500. Those bonds with some difficulty they succeeded in giving and are now *at large.*

On Wednesday morning Frazier was brought before the Mayor upon the charge of being an accessory to the killing of Peabody and was bound over in the sum of $2000. Mr. Frazier, we understand, denied his participation in the affair and therefore we have nothing to say about it. It is a matter to be determined by a jury.[215]

A second killing on the public square in 1857 involved out of towners but it had more sex appeal to it. A parson, by the name of Jones, had eloped from Lamar with another man's wife, after having first defrauded some of his creditors. The law caught up with him in Clarksville where he was arrested, tried and acquitted. Immediately afterwards, he went to the office of his defense counsel, the former Judge Mills, in the Clarksville Hotel. As Parson Jones and his lady friend, left the Hotel, he was shot on the street outside the saddler shop by the brother of the runaway wife. DeMorse, only a short distance away, got to the scene quickly and describe dead body in some detail, the woman's grief at her brother's slaying her lover and the brother's capture just outside of town. The victim did not get much sympathy, however. DeMorse called him the "Reverend Hypocrite" and the body lay on the street for a few hours.[216]

Crime, especially murder, had become so commonplace in Texas that many of the papers carried editorials on the problem, editorials DeMorse endorsed by reprinting them in *The Standard* for his readers. Prevalent in Texas at the time was the usually successful assertion by the accused that he had killed the other fellow in self defense. Interestingly, the public clamor to get tougher on crime is not unlike demands for greater enforcement of the law that we, periodically, hear today.

Increase in Crime

Scarcely and exchange reaches us that does not contain an account of daring robberies or murders. The

> *remedy and the only one for this growing is a more rigid enforcement of the criminal law. Although indictments, we might say, almost by the hundreds, are found by the different courts of the state every year, yet a conviction is scarce ever heard of. Many of the deaths by violence that take place in this state take place from affrays and the survivor is usually acquitted on the ground of self defense. In many instances, the acquittal is just and the accused is entitled to the sympathy of the community, but frequently his claim to such sympathy is more than doubtful. It is time that the men who constitute the juries of our country should begin to act upon the principle that "a just severity is mercy in the end." Men should be taught that it is safer and more honorable to avoid getting into difficulties and that a good character and gentlemanly deportment are a surer defense, than a Bowie knife and a six shooter. But in all cases, where such extenuations cannot be pleaded, the death penalty should be inflicted with infallible certainty. Those who have once tasted "of human blood", like certain wild beasts, ever afterwards have an appetite for the same and are continually seeking an opportunity to indulge their propensity. Until recently, cold blooded murders were rarely committed and the increase of time should produce a corresponding vigilance.* [217]

DeMorse blamed the jurors for failing to do their duty, and, he reasoned, if the legal system fails to punish, then it is probable that private vengeance would take its place.

Another Murder

> *We have the particulars of the killing of Dr. W. N. Anderson, a person of superior intelligence and amiable character, formerly resident of this county, but for many years past of Navarro county. We are disinclined to publish these tragedies and let most pass unnoticed. Fortunately, they do not occur often in this vicinity.*

They would not often occur anywhere in the State, if they were properly punished, but as long as the jurors of the country avoid their duty and give license to crime by acquitting its perpetrators, just so long we may expect frequent recurrences of these acts which are so shocking to humanity and degrading to any people, who pass them by unpunished. We see the termination which must come to pass, if proper legal retribution cannot be obtained. After a while, citizens will be slain, who will be avenged by Lynch law and by deliberate acts of private vengeance. We hold any man morally guiltless, who after his brother or father or some dear relative has been slain, and there has been a criminal avoidance of punishment by the executors of the law, deliberately and cooly avenges his kinsman. Society organized by law owes protection to each member who has yielded something of his personal rights to cement that society and, if it fails to protect him, his original rights revert to himself and he may properly protect himself and those and those who have a natural claim upon him for their protection. It is lamentable morally, but there is no doubt that in some parts of our country the jurors criminally fail in the performance of their duty and allow a false sympathy for the criminal, rather than a proper sympathy for the victim, to sway their verdict, in defiance of the law and of their sworn obligation. [218]

Entertainment in Clarksville

What was there to do for fun in Clarksville and its Red River countryside, a century and a half ago? There were no Dairy Queens, movie houses or malls, except the public square, for folks to congregate and visit. No TVs, DVDs, VCRs or CDs. Most entertainment had to be home grown. Yet, as *The Standard* bears witness, the citizens had a full, wholesome social life.

The ratio of men to eligible women in the first days made marriages - and the accompanying celebrations - somewhat rarer than back East. By the 1850s, however, enough of the fairer sex, home grown or among the thousands emigrating to Texas from other parts of the United States and Europe, were residing on the frontier to make weddings the most common social activity. *The Standard* often published something endearing about the newlyweds, especially if the couple had observed the custom then of sending a piece of the wedding cake (and sometimes wine) to the editor of the paper:

MARRIED

On Sunday, January 3rd, at Richland, Navarro Co., Dr. W.N. ANDERSON, to Miss SUSANNA LOUISA DIXSON.

We are gratified to learn that our old friend, the Doctor, although he has placed himself near the confines of the Indian country, has neither forgotten the affections which soften even civilized existence, nor the consideration due the press, which is equally a mark of social refinement; but, with a thoughtfulness which does him infinite credit and is entitled to everlasting remembrance, he has sent to us, a bridal cake of the most magnificent proportions, and some of that Claret, the love of which we hope will never desert us in this life.

> *He who provides for the creature comforts of the Printer is a more than ordinarily considerate man, and deserves to lead a happy life and extend his name to the ends of the earth.* [219]

Aside from weddings, there were other social activities for the citizen to enjoy. Among them were mens' clubs. Fraternal organizations of varying, but not conflicting, altruistic aims, they were made up of men only, although often the clubs had their female "sisterhoods" as auxiliaries. These organizations became the sponsor of a number of community events. For example, one such group was the Sons of Temperance, the strength of which was increasing across the United States during the 1850s. Clarksville had its own Division of the Sons of Temperance that numbered some 228 strong. At festive events, they would "turn out in very considerable force, with very good music, and the votaries of temperance would make a brave display, with their badges and pure white banners, emblematic of the cause." DeMorse approved of them and the noble work that they did:

> *We are glad to see this order continually gathering strength. It has done an immensity of good here, as elsewhere, and we hope there will be a continued accession to its ranks, until the last drunkard in our country, shall have forsaken the mire and placed upon ground, from whence he can look upon his fellow man with an unblushing confidence, that he is everybody's equal in correctness of deportment, which is the first and greatest quality to be sought for and the acquirement of which cannot be prevented by any adversary, if the inner man of the aspirant is right.* [220]

The ubiquitous "a word from our sponsor" pre-dates television. Whenever the Sons of Temperance sponsored a party, the guests had be prepared to hear a commercial "upon the evil effects of drinking ardent spirits" before they enjoyed the marching, dinner and dancing scheduled for afterwards. The Knights Templars, another fraternal order of Freemasons, claiming descent from the Knights Templar, founded in the 1100s to protect the Holy Land, cooperated with the movement to ban the sale of liquor in Red River county:

Temperance Address

Rev. J. Young addressed our citizens on Tuesday night and Wednesday morning last. The attendance on Wednesday was large, many from the country being present. The Templars had a procession and much interest was excited. The vote in favor of prohibition, we are told, lacked only one or two from being unanimous.[221]

Prohibition of alcohol might have been the Templars principal *objective*, but some of the membership seemed equally interested in having a good time - at least judging by an item from *The Standard,* describing a Templars' dinner that DeMorse could not attend. No problem. The party came to him:

The Templars

On the 8th, the Votaries of cold water had a celebration made up of a march, a speech and a dinner, all of which were excellent in their way, as we are assured, the gastronomic portion of the performance, got up by the sisterhood, not being by any means the least. Indeed, it was, if we were to judge by the somewhat ecstatic eulogy of our Post Master who said in glowing language that he had never been so feted in his entire life. There were some bright eyes and laughing faces there, but [not this editor's] who stuck to his labors, though every member of the printing department left the office and gloated over the jollification until dark.

They marched up abreast our offices and, saying

something about saluting the Star Spangled Banner (the whole of which we did not hear) they gave three jolly cheers to the flag that waved above our Sebastopol and then, turning off churchward, we heard the sounds of their music softening in the distance and heard no more, except as was relayed to us from the fervid lips of the Post Master aforesaid. [222]

Clarksville also had a lodge of the Independent Order of Odd Fellows, an international movement, still active in America. The Clarksville lodge opened in 1853 and DeMorse, in reporting its birth, attached his *imprimatur* to it.

Odd Fellows

Colfax Lodge No.- was organized in our Town of June 3 and the following officers selected:

Hervey Dillahunty,   N.G.

John T. Mills   V.G.

J. H. McLaran   Sec.

G. Ragin   Treas.

We are glad to see this meritorious order, whose objects are of the noblest sort, making a start among us. [223]

In 1855, the Order sponsored a procession, made up of local members and others from surrounding counties, all of whom turned out in full regalia for the grand event. The many citizens who attended "were treated to a talk on the origin and history of the Order, a rapid sketch of its principles, a commentary on some of the objections urged by outsiders against the organization and concluded with a hearty appeal to the vast throng in attendance in behalf of the favorable opinion which the Order merited".[224]

During the winter of 1857, the Jonadab Temple of Honor

No. 14 of the Knights of Templar called for a Grand Temperance Rally in Clarksville. The Program was to include "an address, impromptu speeches, music, vocal and instrumental." It was to conclude with a dinner prepared for the occasion by the Sisters of Eliza Walker Social Temple:

> *All Surrounding Subordinate, Social and Degree Temples and all Templars in good standing are earnestly solicited to attend and take part in the festivities of the occasion.*
>
> *Come One, Come All. Let us have such a grand demonstration as will not only make the Friends of Temperance proud of our great strength, but cause the votaries of old King Alcohol to tremble for the safety and stability of his Kingdom*
>
> *M. H. Partain* [225]

It was a flop, as was another procession, speech and dinner, held two days later by the Odd Fellows to celebrate the Anniversary of Texas Independence. DeMorse knew where the problems lay in the lackluster performances: Fancier dress and better music were needed.

> *Celebrations*
>
> *The Odd Fellows and the Templars, have each had a procession, address etc since our last issue. Both societies made a good appearance with respect to regalia, but both had small processions, compared with the size of the orders. There is a lack of zeal in these public celebrations in our community. We suppose it is not sufficiently aroused by richness of display. Gorgeous dress and appointments and fine music, of which last we are very destitute, would bring out a more imposing display of numbers.* [226]

The Masons, another order that could trace its beginnings to the other side of the Atlantic, also had a presence in Clarksville and the Red River Valley. The following is an advertisement of an upcoming event, followed by a report of how another similar event turned out.

> *Notice for the Masons Friendship Lodge No. 16 of A. F and A.M. design, celebrating the coming anniversary of St John The Baptist on the 24th inst by a procession speech and dinner. All non affiliated Masons in the area in good standing are with their families invited to attend. The brethren of Paris Lodge, Red River Lodge and Jack Titus Lodge have been invited. There will be a barbecue at the conclusion of the ceremonies*
>
> *By Order of the Lodge John Anderson, Secretary*[227]

> *Celebrations on Thursday the 24th*
>
> *The Masons had a turn out and a satisfactory celebration of St John's Day.*
>
> *The procession was the largest and best looking that we remember ever to have seen here. The rich regalia of the Chapter was most decidedly imposing. The greatest deficiency of our public processions is that of a brass band. The attendance of citizens at the church was very large, the ladies being out in full corps. An oration was delivered by Sam Bell Maxey, Esq. of Paris, followed by an impromptu address, upon call, by Rev. J. W P. McKenszie*
>
> *We noticed several masonic members from Paris. The orations were followed by a dinner at the Lodge Room, to which all participated.* [228]

One could socialize in Clarksville without having to be a member of a fraternal order. Clarksville entertainment ranged from the intellectual to the sedate, from the boring to almost "devil may care" conduct. On the least exciting end of the spectrum were the church sermons, the talks on temperance, political oratory and the occasional visiting professor who lectured on the new sciences of biology and psychology.

Musical entertainment was big in Clarksville as well. There were plenty of willing musicians of different performance levels, students, accomplished amateurs and professionals.

In bygone days, the singing and playing a musical instrument were considered integral to the education of women. Clarksville had two girls schools, the Clarksville Female Academy and the Clarksville Female Institute. Both regularly held concerts for parents and friends to show off the their students' progress. The Public was always invited.

Concert

Last night, Mrs. Anderson entertained our citizens and visitors from the country with a concert by her music scholars attached to the Female Institute. The intention was to show the progress of the students generally and, consequently, some were introduced who had only been taking lessons in music for five months. From these, of course, no high artistic performance was to be expected, but, generally, they did well, and those, who had pursued the study longer, made such exhibition of their skill and talent as to draw loud plaudits from the gratified audience. [229]

Demorse advocated the forming of an amateur band. The Clarksville Music Society was a group of musicians and vocalists, who loved music and eagerly promoted and taught it. They held concerts to raise money for new instruments and music books, and volunteered to perform at any civic or religious celebration, without regard to the denomination.

The Concert

The concert given by the Musical Society last week, and in which the ladies of the Town and vicinity figured largely and interestingly, came off at the time appointed. The Presbyterian Church was crowded to its utmost capacity and, we presume, the enterprise paid well.

We got in shortly after it commenced and enjoyed it. The object was a good one and we are glad that it succeeded. Future performances were promised which, we doubt not, will be popular.

On Sunday, the first regular service by the Choir was given in the Baptist Church and certainly assisted the impressiveness of the occasion. [230]

On occasion, professional talent came through town and put on shows. When that happened, DeMorse became *The Standard's* entertainment critic as the three following reviews illustrate. After all, he had lived in New York and had been more exposed to the talent of that city, than had the others in tiny Clarksville!

Music

Our town has been relieved of its accustomed dullness during this dry and sultry season, by the visit of Mr. Tomkins and his two sisters of extraordinary musical talent. They held a concert for three consecutive nights and afforded quite a treat to a considerable audience. They sang solos, duets and trios and were so much applauded in all that we find it hard to say in which they excelled. For ourselves, we admired particularly the comic songs, though the pathetic were beautifully sung, especially the "Snow Storm" and "Death of Ringold." The latter appears to every heart and who shall better commemorate the death of the hero and patriot than the poet, and, when associated with music, and sung by the lips of beauty, it would seem a glorious thing to die for one's country.

We commend these interesting strangers (Mr. T. and his sisters) to all whom they may visit. Their gift of song, although it may not equal Parodi or Jenny Lind, afforded a pure and innocent enjoyment to the many untraveled and unsophisticated citizens of Clarksville. Music has a softening and mellowing influence upon the human heart, and unlike the many devices going through the country, hum bugging and cheating the people, we believe the exhibitions of Mr. T. and his sisters as highly entertaining and moralizing in their tendencies.[231]

Concert by Blind Vocalists

Our citizens were delighted on the evening Saturday and Tuesday with the concerts given by the blind vocalists Mr. Coe and Miss Mary Bush, who were educated at the Institution of the Blind in New York City. We can cordially recommend them to the favor of the public, wherever they may direct their course. [232]

The Carncross Family

These entertainers have passed through the northern line of counties to this point and have given two performance here to the special gratification of the people about town. Tonight they appear again singing dancing etc. Freyer, the violinists who accompanies the troupe, is an excellent performer, good anywhere. The execution of Miss Carncross and Mr Salter upon the guitar is also good. Mr. Henry, who fills the comic role, is a passable low comedy actor. There is nothing very new to people of the world in the range of performances, but they are novel to most of our citizens and afford gratification of a night or two. [233]

In June, 1860, the well acclaimed Peak Family Swiss Bell Ringers bells gave two concerts in Clarksville at the Masonic Hall. DeMorse reported that "music upon bells being quite a novelty here, lead more to attend than are generally wont to do at musical performances. They performed each night to crowded houses and each performance vied in excelling the other."[234]

The Ladies of the Methodist Church in Town had a concert and *"tableaux"* to raise money. A *tableau vivant*, French for "living picture", was the representation of a picture or scene by people properly costumed and posed.

> *A Concert and Tableaux for the Benefit of the Methodist Church*
>
> *Some of the Ladies of our Town have organized an association for the finishing up of the Methodist Church, which lacks all the inner appurtances of a House of Worship. In pursual of their object, they propose to give on Wednesday next, a Supper and a series of Tableaux vivants, to which the admission fee is fifty cents - too little. Of course, we presume that all the beauty of the vicinity will be present and that not a small portion of it will be presented in the shape of scenic pictures, at which the Spectator will have the privilege of staring at intensely without being subject to the charge of rudeness. The object to be carried out is entitled by right to everybody's fifty cents - the supper will be worth fifty cents, the concert a dollar and the tableaux - the value of these is illumitable to each admirer of any one of the beauties who will be placed in view on that occasion. So that any Speculator in rarities can easily see that he will save somewhere from a dollar up to a nameless amount, by paying out a paltry half dollar. It is certainly a great chance to save money by paying out a little. And Franklin has told us that a penny saved is two pennies earned. Consider it in any light you chose. It is a great opportunity. An invitation to attend was left at our offices, during our temporary absence, by some of the*

> *Fraternity. We shall cheerfully do so but shall claim the privilege of paying for it as others do.* [235]

There was evidently an attempt at creating a local theater troupe as well in town. Sadly, we never learn if it got off the ground.

> *The thespians, we understand are on the high tide of success. Great feats are expected of them. The dresses are to be gorgeous and a scenery on as costly scale is to be imported as soon as the financial agent goes to the North.*[236]

Dancing was big in Clarksville a century and a half ago. It was an excellent outlet for the social urge among the Clarksville gallant. DeMorse encouraged the people to learn how to dance and the Town had its own instructor:

> *We call attention to the card of Mr. King. Mr. King has for a short period been teaching dancing in our Town. He is an excellent instructor and parents should not permit the opportunity to pass unimproved. The improvement of personal carriage comes right after the improvement of minds and morals and is of infinite service to all persons, male and female, in passing advantageously through the world. Children should be taught dancing at 8 to 10 years of age if practicable. At this early age, they fall more readily into the graceful movements of the limbs. It matters not that parents prefer their children shall never attend Balls. That is no reason why they should learn to carry themselves gracefully.* [237]

"Balls" were popular among the young and were always held after the dreaded term end school examinations. Young slaves, not invited to the dance, nevertheless swayed to the music in the shadows below:

> *After the examinations closed on Thursday evening, a ball came off at the Star, graced by the attendance of any quantity of the fair, and then again the fete was repeated at the Eagle Hotel. In the upper gallery of that establishment, the youths of the vicinity tripped the merry measure of the dance, while on the ground below, in the bright moonlight, which gleamed upon us, as in one of the boasted nights of Italy, Congos of various hue disported themselves in keeping with the measure of the music above, swaying themselves to and fro in the style of dance peculiar to them.*[238]

Adults enjoyed balls as well. Usually, they were associated with holidays and were held in one of the hotels in town and cost about $2.50 to $3.00 per person. *The Standard* published both the notice of Fourth of July Ball and, afterwards, a review of it.

> *We call the attention of the votaries of Terpsichore to the announcement of a ball at Clarksville Hotel on the evening of the Glorious Fourth. Everybody and his wife is expected:*
> "*Go it while you're young!*
> *For when you're old, you can't.*"[239]

> *The Glorious 4th passed off, hilariously, without any unpleasant event that we are aware of.*
> *At night a Ball, at the Clarksville Hotel numerously attended, held its votaries enchained until the small fours of the morning and was productive of much enjoyment not withstanding the intense heat. The day and night were the hottest of the season, the thermometer at 4 o'clock PM being 98 in the shade.*[240]

There were *impromptu* private dancing parties as well as balls, the participants sometimes having to provide their own fiddler. Charles DeMorse, a widower for a half dozen years, was an eligible bachelor in his forties, affluent, a lawyer, newspaper publisher and a man of some influence and power, who undeniably had a way with words. He must have been in his glory at these affairs. Was he among the "Brave Men" in the following account?

Storm Party

On Yesterday evening, about half past eight o'clock, the worthy hostess of the Eagle hotel was aroused from her reveries by the approach of Fair Women and Brave Men, who upon their arrival, announced their intention to take the house by storm. They had not more than made known their design that the roaring sound of the violin, warned all that they were ready for the charge.

The assemblage was small, but the enjoyment of both sexes were unbounded. About half past one o'clock, the scene closed and the ladies, accompanied by their gallants, were conveyed to their respective homes.[241]

Items in *The Standard* give us, the modern day readers, additional clues as to what the early citizens of rural Clarksville found entertaining. Sometimes, it did not take anything much, just a glimpse of a creature, not native to Texas or the United States:

Our town was thrown into great excitement, that is, the boys about town were greatly excited on Thursday evening last by the arrival of a monkey "a real sure enough monkey." [242]

On rare occasions the citizens of Red River valley were

treated to visits from traveling circuses and troupes of performers.

Washburn's Circus

This establishment got here on Tuesday last and has been performing every night since, generally to good audiences. The performers are better than any that have been here before. The stable of horses is not extensive enough for great displays but the Equestrian, the Herculean and Acrobatic feats, and the witticisms of the clown, Jean Johnson, are excellent. Those who have not seen them would do well to attend tonight and those who have might lend assistance to some worthy men, who have been unfortunate of late. It is the last chance. Go and see them.[243]

Johnson's Southern Minstrels WILL perform at SIMS HOTEL on this Saturday evening and also on Monday evening, the 25th, and will give series of INSTRUMENTAL AND VOCALS

Performances: Juggling and Dancing etc. and conclude with a laughable after piece

Admission: 50 cents - children and servants half price

Front seats reserved for ladies and small children

Doors open at half past six; performances will commence at half past seven o'clock

Will also perform at Paris of Tuesday and Wednesday evening. [244]

The people of Clarksville might not have been an especially sophisticated audience, at least according to DeMorse, but they were not total rubes either. They knew what they did not like and were not hesitant to show their displeasure at having been duped:

Rare Entertainment

Our Town of late has been favored with several exhibitions, lectures, puppet shows, etc., the last of which by professional showmen, perhaps went into the Creek at the instance of the B'hoys who recognize a humbug by demonstrations of that sort. [245]

The Circus

Our citizens, or a portion of them, have been most miserably entertained and gulled out of their money, for the past two days by a band of fellows, professing to be circus performers and traveling under the name of Reynolds & Company. Had we time and space, we should like to give you our opinion of their performance in extenso, but insomuch as the company had busted up, we deem it unnecessary to say more than that it is a miserably poor thing and that is traveling circuses are any of them worthy of encouragement, which is a matter of much doubt with us, this one certainly is not.[246]

Holidays in Clarksville and Red River County

Everyone, not just school children, loves a holiday. It has so much to offer, when approached properly. The rigors of the workplace relieved for a day; the gathering of good companions; themes to celebrate; tables of appetizing food; stirring speeches and dancing; in short, an event, both fondly looked back upon and eagerly awaited. Did the townspeople of Clarksville people celebrate holidays, and, if so, which ones and what did they do?

Today we celebrate religious holidays such as Christmas and Easter, several based on the special events and people of American history, like the 4th of July, Memorial Day and Presidents Day, a few uniquely American ones, Labor Day, Martin Luther King Day, and Thanksgiving, and one- New Year's Day - that is universal, although falling on different dates in different lands. A century and a half ago, a few of these holidays were also observed, together with a handful of others that appear to have forgotten among the populace of today.

The people needed the benefits that socialization brought to a community. Texans of the 1840s and 1850s worked hard. The land was rich but, at times, needed the farmer's undivided attention. In some more settled places, *hard work* may be considered a virtue that should be exercised for its own sake. In Texas in these days, it was a necessity of life. The lazy failed. However, when work was not pressing, there was little reluctance to take holidays and celebrate together.

The Fourth of July is a magnificent holiday. It marked the end of one world order and began a new one, one still encircling the world, spreading the message of Liberty. Sadly, the enthusiastic celebration of the holiday is in decline some places these days. This would have disappointed John Adams, second President of the United States. He had been involved in the Continental Congress in 1776 advancing the resolution of the Colonies to be independent from Great Britain. From the beginning, Adams had exhorted Americans to celebrate it. It part it should be "solemn" as the nation's in "Day of Deliverance, observed with acts of devotion to God. It is also a day of glory which should be "solemnized with Pomp and Parade, with Shows, Games, Sports, Guns, Bells, Bonfires and Illuminations from one End of the Continent to the other from this Time forward forever more." Failure to honor Independence Day would have concerned Charles DeMorse as well: "The day and its memories should never be forgotten and silently passed by, while the Union continues and men remember the priceless blessings which, as countrymen of Washington and John Adams, they enjoyed in the land of the free and the Home of the Brave."[247]

    John Adams would have been proud how Clarksville and Red River county celebrated the Fourth. DeMorse was pleased, most years at least. The townspeople usually did everything up in fine style. Preparations for its celebration began months before. DeMorse would remind, even chide, the citizens into action:

> *What has become of our celebration? Where are the 76 Committees which were appointed to commemorate that memorable era? Where are the Music Committee, and the Ladies Committee, and the gallant Soldiers who were to prove their gallantry, by standing at a respectful distance, while their less patriotic and more carnivorous fellow citizens devoured all the good things provided?* [248]

    The citizens of Clarksville took very seriously their duty to commemorate the Nation's Founding. The senior men of the community sat in formal session to plan the day's events. It was quite special and near to them. In many cases, their grand fathers had fought in the American Revolution. Some of the citizens themselves had fought in the Texas Revolution against Mexico in 1835, which had been patterned on the American Revolution. They knew well the sacrifices made and the peril encountered by our forebears and they were careful that their observance of Independence Day was done properly.

FOURTH OF JULY CELEBRATION

A meeting of the Citizens of Red River County was held in the Courthouse in Clarksville, on Monday the 27th instant, when the following proceedings were had. John A. Bagby was called to the Chair and Frank H. Clark appointed Secretary. Mr. Richard Thompson explained in a few appropriate remarks, the object of the meeting, stating that it was the purpose of celebrating in a suitable national and patriotic manner the approaching 78th anniversary of our National Independence.

On motion of G. H. Wootten, a Committee of five gentlemen, to wit J. W. Russell, Richard Thompson, Charles Dillahunty, Jasper A. Barry and Henry R. Latimer were appointed by the Chairman to devise ways and means for said celebration and required to report to the meeting immediately. The Committee retired to consider of their duty and, after due consideration thereon, reported through their chairman, J. W. Russell, that they deemed it most suitable to celebrate the coming festival with a Public Dinner and that Charles H. Peabody had been selected by them to officiate as Orator of the day and Richard Thompson as reader of the Declaration of Independence and that the place selected for the dinner was the wood near the new Baptist Church.[249]

Today, an ember of past years' celebrations of the Fourth of July can still be seen in some small towns across the nation which celebrate Independence Day with a parade down their Main Street. The marchers are members of the community, veterans of the military, local dignitaries, Little League baseball players, ladies auxiliaries and the like, all representative of the citizens at large, who line the streets, watching as the marchers pass by. Clarksville had about 750 residents in 1846 who would join folks from the outlying farms in the center of the town for the festivities. Often the day began with, or featured, a parade - or procession - that would start or end in the public square. Two more items from *The Standard* in 1853 provide excellent still shots of the Fourth of July celebration that year, from its planning to a recap of it in the next paper after the festivities.

FOURTH OF JULY CELEBRATION

The committee appointed to devise ways and means for celebration the Fourth of July have appointed A. K. Ellett, Chief Marshall, assisted by Col. J. H. Burks and Jno. P. Gaines.

All desiring to take part in the celebrations will meet in front of the new Baptist Church and march to the Anderson School building.

The following order [of march] will be observed:

1. Clarksville Band

2. National Colors

3. Speaker of the Day and Reader of the Declaration of Independence

4. Ladies in sections of two

5. Sabbath schools in sections of two

6. Public schools in sections of two

7. Soldiers of the War of 1812

8. Soldiers of the Texas Revolution

9. Soldiers of the War with Mexico

10. Mayor and Common Council

11. Citizens on foot

By order of
A.K. Ellett, Chief Marshall [250]

The Fourth of July

The Glorious Fourth opened brightly and, save that the rays of the sun were scorching hot, it was a fitting day for the celebration. Early in the morning, people from the country began to come in and, by eleven o'clock, when the procession was formed, there was a larger assemblage in the town than we have ever seen before. The procession was made up, according to the published order, commencing with the Orator and Reader of the day, Mr. Samuel McAnier and Mr. John Montgomery, soldiers of the Revolution of 1776, then Soldiers of the War of 1812, of whom there were four present, Soldiers of 1835 and 1836, the Texas Revolution, then soldiers of 1837 and 38, then Soldiers of the War with Mexico, then Citizens, then boys of the schools, a numerous array of future legislators and Heroes, affording by their number ample proof of the fruitfulness of the Clime. Marching from the Square to the Baptist Church, they received in advance the Young ladies of the Sunday school and a considerable array of maids and matrons generally.

Altogether, the procession was very respectable in number as well as in the beauty and the grace of its leading portion. The Marshall and his deputies went through their duties gallantly. There were also some subordinates on foot who did service keeping the long array in order. One in particular, vastly admired by the ladies for the elegance of his equipment, and the gallantry of his bearing, who halted them every few moments for fear they might get into confusion and then, after glancing up and down the lines, would gracefully give them the word to move onward. On the way to the Church, the whole line saluted the national Flag, flying from the staff over our office by three loud cheers. [251]

A reading of the Declaration of Independence, - the explanation given by the Colonists to the rest of the world as to why they had been compelled to break from the Mother Land - was mandatory, presented by the best speakers in the area. As the two following items illustrate, there also would be orations by local dignitaries selected for the task and the singing of patriotic and religious songs, before adjourning for a public dinner:

> Getting to the Presbyterian church, it was found already crowded, all the aisles where standing room could be got, and all the windows were occupied.
>
> Services being opened by a prayer, by the Rev. Mr. Anderson, "Hail Columbia" was sung by a party of ladies and gentlemen and then the orator of the day Mr. Charles H. Peabody delivered an address replete with eloquent expressions, felicitously uttered, which was received with frequent plaudits. After the address, the National Song, The Star Spangled Banner, then the benediction by the Rev. Mr. Corley and then the procession, reforming, marched to the grove adjacent to the Baptist Church and partook of a Barbecue, well served and bountiful in quantity and variety. [252]

> *Fourth of July*
>
> There was an unusually large turnout of the people on the 4th, on foot, horseback and in carriages, ladies, gentlemen and children streaming past our office, with the sun pouring down upon them a blaze of heat as well as light, to the Presbyterian church where an oration was delivered by Mr B. F. Fuller, the orator of the day appointed by the Templars. Brief addresses were given by J. H. Burks and Dr. Barry. The Declaration of Independence was read by Mr. Jas. W. Thomas and, after all was over, the crowd marched over to the barbecue ground, in the time nearby, and partook of the prepared feast. [253]

The "Grand Barbecue" that followed the speeches and singing was "made up of choice materials with enough to spare." There was no lack of food in Red River County and the cooks "did things up brown" so that the Public Dinner was as generous and tasty as imagination can picture.

> *Ladies Gentlemen Spectators, Odd Fellows Orators, Grand Marshall etc betook themselves to the grove near the Baptist Church and devoured immense quantities of pastries etc and the Negroes feasted on custards, all of which as a apart of the celebration, and which proves conclusively that we are a free people and have good appetites and that is the best evidence that we are a people of sound mind, energy and enterprise.*[254]

During the dinner, there would be toasts made by some of the clergy present and leading citizens. To us, a century and a half later, these toasts and the sentiment they solicit are still worthy of our attention:

> *During the barbecue, the following toasts, which were handed us for publication, were given:*
>
> *By the Rev. John Anderson "May the principles of civil and religious liberty, whose birthday we have just celebrated, receive rapid extension by the sudden overthrow of all despotic power in church and State."*
>
> *By the Rev. Sam Corley: "A free press and liberty of conscience, may they always be dear to Americans!"*
>
> *By J. A. Barry: "This day we celebrate the anniversary of our liberties. May it be the Anniversary of the World's. May it never be forgotten!"*
>
> *By J. W. Russell "The authors of our liberties, may their glorious declaration be indelibly impressed upon the hearts of their progeny!"*
>
> *By Frank Clark, Esq; "The Boy Company joining in today's procession. If ever, at any time, their services should be needed in the field, may their conduct be such that their mothers may exclaim with that Roman Matron, who bore the Gracchi, 'these are my jewels'!"*[255]

Sometimes there were side shows, special interest events,

such as the following presentation to the Sons of Temperance, anti-alcohol civic association, by the ladies of one of Clarksville's two schools for women:

> *The anniversary of American Independence was celebrated on the Fourth by the Sons of Temperance. They formed in procession and marched to the Star Hotel in front of which they were received by the young ladies of the Clarksville Female Academy who presented the Division with a most beautiful flag, the handcrafting of their own delicate fingers. The flag was presented by Miss Francis Cooke of this place, who delivered a very chaste and appropriate address which was responded, on behalf of the Sons of Temperance, by Dr. Wharton in a felicitous manner. The procession then reformed and marched to the Presbyterian Church where the Declaration of Independence was read by Dr. Walker, who was followed by Mr. Joseph J. Dickson in an address advocating the cause of temperance, which he did with earnestness and ability.* [256]

After the Independence Day marching and the eating, speeches and sermons were completed, the townspeople danced!

> *Great excitement*
>
> *Huge efforts are making to celebrate "the glorious fourth" by eloquence, voracity and dancing. The Sunday school led the way followed by the patriotic generally and the way "the light fantastic too" is to be tripped at the Clarksville Hotel and at the Eagle Hotel is to be after the most approved mode, as developed by the two Professors of dancing at present teaching the graces and the German Polka (which we do not include under that head) and to the young representative of Clarksville and vicinage. We expect that the town will be overrun and that Bowie as usual will send up several noble*

representatives to assist in this part of the celebration. [257]

Rain is the dreaded scourge of holidays, parades and cookouts. It cannot be prevented, of course, and must be taken in stride. Following are two accounts of near "rain outs." In the first, in 1847, every one made do and things seemed to have turned out fine. However, two years later, in that horribly rainy year of 1849, DeMorse and his neighbors were not so easy going about it.

In Clarksville, the celebrations were had on the 5th [the 4th was a Sunday]. The day being rainy, until 12 o'clock, the proceedings which were formed under the direction of the Marshall and his deputies, only paraded around the square, and finally halted at the Star Hotel, where the Declaration of Independence was read by A. J. Russell, Esq. and the oration given by B. H. Epperson, Esq. Deterred by the character of the weather, we did not hear the oration, until near the close, but presume it was marked by the orator's usual felicity of expression.

The barbecue followed, served up in the hall of the Star, which was occupied in its full length. There were several hundred persons in Town, who all seemed to enjoy themselves.

At night, there was a Ball at the Star which was graced by a full attendance and, as we learn, everything went off most pleasantly. [258]

The Glorious Fourth

This ever memorable anniversary was passed by our citizens in a mixed manner, first listening to the senatorial address of Col. Clark, then in sheltering themselves from one of the semi daily showers which has greeted us for the first six months, then scouring through the muds to the Presbyterian Church and being edified by the temperance address of Edward McGowan and, then, in receiving another light sprinkle of temperance fluid from the clouds.

It was a glorious day passed between politics, temperance and rain and we have no doubt that all our country friends went home, well impressed with the value of water, mentally and physically.

The night, however, brought on the charms of the dance and at that we are not advised whether water or more pungent fluids were in the ascendant. All we know is that a merry crowd assembled at the Clarksville Hotel and whiled away the hours until midnight and of the niceties of which they were regaled, a specimen was sent to us by the considerate hostess of the house. [259]

DeMorse's new brick printing office had, in front of it, a large flag pole. On it, each Fourth of July, DeMorse would proudly display the American Flag, appreciating how really significant a day it was in the history of the modern world.

The Fourth of July

Before we issue our sheet again the glorious Fourth will have come and gone - the ever memorable day in the annals of the Rights of Man. Having no cannon with which to express our personal appreciation of the anniversary, we cannot usher in the day in the tones of thunder, appropriate or usual. But we do have a tall staff on the observatory of our new office and shall elevate it upon sunrise, the Flag of the Stars and Stripes, and let it float gaily in the breeze - that proud emblem of Freedom and Equality. [260]

Despite the presence everywhere of the Sons of Temperance and the group's almost official status as an organizer of the day's events, Independence Day in Red River county was not an "alcohol free" event. Drinking, however, did not appear to be a problem, even with the crowds from the countryside, immigrants on the way west and visitors from adjoining counties:

> *At the termination of the muster, there was a general invitation to the drinkers, and we may claim credit for our town that, notwithstanding that liquor was furnished as free as water, to a very large number of men, all dispersed quietly. There were no fights, no noise, no drunkenness.* [261]

So venerated was the 4th of July to those only a few generations away from the original participants, that it would be celebrated wherever even a few Americans clustered together. For example, tiny settlements throughout Red River County observed the day:

> *At Millville, on Pine Creek, an oration was delivered by John R. Bedford, Esq. The Declaration of Independence was read by Capt. T.G. Wright. The barbecue followed, in accordance with the arrangement previously published by us, and finally, they did the thing up "brown" by having an excellent supper. We are told that Wine and Pastry were plentiful. It strikes us that we would like to have been at Millville.*
>
> *We have not heard from Fannin and Lamar but suppose they did about right up there.* [262]

> *Fourth of July*
>
> *The celebration of our National Anniversary took place in Savannah in this county on the 2nd, the object for selecting that day was to prevent the ball that night from interfering with the Sabbath.*
>
> *The ceremonies were opened by the reading of the Declaration of Independence by Thomas Scurry, Esq., which was done in an audible voice and in an impressive manner*

Then followed an oration by B.B. Smith, Esq., of which the public will probably have opportunity to judge for themselves. We can say of it that the manner of delivery was excellent.

There followed a barbecue which was decidedly the most orderly we have ever witnessed, being entirely so. The meats were cooked in excellent style under the supervision of our old friend Jas. Atkinson, Esq., who fully complied with his promises that they should be better cooked than any barbecue we ever saw. All the arrangements of the festivities, as far as we witnessed them, were of the best sort and there was "enough and to spare" as the Committee said there would be.

The claims upon our times did not permit us to witness the Ball which closed the enjoyments of the day.[263]

While the Fourth of July was the most intensely celebrated holiday in Texas, it was not the only one. Texas, of course, had its own Day of Independence, March 2, commemorating that day in 1835 when Texas had declared her independence from Mexico. For the first generation Texans, like DeMorse, who had participated in the war and who had been citizens of the Republic of Texas for the decade of her existence, there was, naturally enough, a deeper feeling for the day that newcomers could appreciate:

The 2d Day of March

Yesterday was the anniversary of the Declaration of Independence of the heroic little Republic of Texas. We marked its recurrence by raising the flag over our office, the only demonstration in our power to make for our respect at the Natal Day of our Nation, whose chronicles for the brief time of its existence are filled with records of its gallantry, never surpassed. Few probably of our present population thought much of the incoming and the passage of the day, but there were some within the borders of Texas, who were in at the birth, who still recur the moment with a thrill of emotion, to the olden times, to the remembrance of a new and wild country with a charm in its newness and beauty, with its scant population of reckless daring pioneers, no one of whom ever thought of an instance, even while the advancing columns of well appointed army was pushing the band of patriots before them - never so much as once thought about abandoning the soil or of being beaten, men of iron nerve and heroic daring who asked no better equality of numbers than not more of the five of the enemy to their one - who all the inspirations of founders of a nation and felt the eminent enthrall of agency in a great work.

The Country has improved since then. Its National Government is a absorbed in the great Confederacy of States. We are more comfortable now in domestic appointments. We find everywhere, as we look around, the stamp of the foot of progress and the evidences of industry in the tillings of the earth and raising products for profit. The Country is as beautiful as it ever was, but the charm that enrobed it as a garment in its primal days of brilliance, scarcely lingers about it now in such brilliancy as it then had - at least in our eyes.[264]

The day was observed in much the same way that the Fourth of July was: speeches, parades and dinners. DeMorse urged that the holiday be regularly celebrated. How long it was we do not know, but it is rarely commemorated today in Texas.

The 2nd of March

The Natal day of Texas Independence came on Sunday and the flag raised over our office was the only recognition here. On Monday, however, the Society of Odd Fellows made an imposing demonstration.

> *After a march around the Square, arrayed in really elegant attire, they filed in the Court House and were addressed by Judge Mills and Dr. J. A. Barry. We did not hear the speeches but were told they were both excellent. Following the speeches, came a very fine dinner at the Sims Clarksville Hotel, said to be the best dinner ever set in Town.*
>
> *We hope to see the annual recurrences of this day observed hereafter. The several societies could not chose a better festival day and citizens en masse should honor the birth of Texas Independence.*[265]

May 1, May Day, is an ancient holiday, once celebrated with dancing around ribboned May poles and the crowning of "Queens of the May" to preside over the festivities. It is rarely observed these days. Instead, the Communists adopted the day as one of displays of military power and America countered by making it Law Day. Clarksville had its own way of celebrating it, not unlike the New Year Day Bowl Parades of today, a lot of pageantry and a sponsor selling something. It might not have been how May Day had been celebrated on the Village Green in Merry Old England some centuries before, with maidens dancing around a high May Pole, but there were some still telltale similarities. Maidens still figured prominently in the celebration. They were provided by the two well reputed girls schools in town. The sponsor seemed to change from year to year. For example, in 1850, the Clarksville Division of the Sons of Temperance, some 228 strong, organized the event, including providing the sponsoring message "say no to alcohol". It was a serious day, no doubt as fit the subject matter.

> *May Day*
>
> *This pleasant Anniversary was celebrated in our Town by the Sons of Temperance, who seized upon the fine associations connected with the commemoration, to have a procession and an address from one of the order.*

> Turning out in very considerable force, with very good music, and gathering to their column of March votaries of temperance from other localities, they made a brave display, with their badges and pure white banners, emblematic of the cause. And it certainly was no disparagement of the imposing effect of the array, that the young ladies of our Female institutions added their fair forms to the long line of the procession.
>
> The address of Dr. Ellliot was chaste and appropriate. Altogether the ceremonial was appropriate and credible. We are glad to see this order continually gathering strength. It has done an immensity of good here, as elsewhere, and we hope there will be a continued accession to its ranks, until the last drunkard in our country, shall have forsaken the mire and placed upon ground, from whence he can look upon his fellow man with an unblushing confidence, that he is everybody's equal in correctness of deportment, which is the first and greatest quality to be sought for and the acquirement of which cannot be prevented by any adversary, if the inner man of the aspirant is right.[266]

In 1855, however, the Order of Odd Fellows were the sponsors and the events of the day were decidedly more upbeat: big crowds, parades, lots of out of town visitors, flashy uniforms, some pomp, music, events for women, dinners, dancing and an all around good time, with only a brief "message from the sponsor."

> *May Day*
>
> Our town on Tuesday last presented quite a pleasant aspect and our citizens genuinely seemed to enjoy themselves in the festivities of the day. How many little hearts beat in the buoyant excitement of juvenile amusement and, of them, not a few may, ere the return of another May Day, be called from among us and their joyful countenances may not grace another festival.

According to previous arrangements, the lodge of the Independent Order of Odd Fellows, made its first public appearance in procession. The novelty of this to the celebration brought into our Town a large concourse of citizens, not only of our own, but from some of the neighboring counties. Members of the Order from other counties also were in attendance and the Order turned out in considerable force. The officers and many of the private members turned out in full regalia, which really was very beautiful and, had all the members been in full regalia, the Order would have presented a spectacle never before equaled in this part of the country.

According to a time honored practice, the young ladies of the various schools enjoyed "holiday" and really seemed to enjoy themselves and the situation in which they were placed, with a zest that may be imagined, but not described. By previous arrangement, the Odd Fellows dispatched an escort to each of the schools, who conducted them from their respective school rooms to the Public Square, opposite Mrs. Donoho's hotel, where they formed in procession immediately in the rear of the Odd Fellows, who proceeded them with banners waving and music, to the Presbyterian church. When arrived at the Church, the Odd Fellows halted and opened file, and the Ladies of the Rebecca Degree first entered the church, they were followed by the young ladies of the various schools, when the Odd Fellow marched into the church in the reverse order in which they came. A very large concourse of ladies and gentlemen also joined the procession and the church was quite sufficient to accommodate the members in attendance.

As soon as the order had taken their place in the church, prayer was offered by the Acting Chaplain, the Rev. Mr. Porter, after which an ode was sung by some ladies requested to do so. The orator of the day, Joseph J. Dickson, Esq., was then introduced by the senior Marshall of the day who delivered in handsome and chaste style an admirable address in which he took a cursory glance and the origin and history of the Order, gave a rapid sketch of their principles, commented on with happy affection on some of the objections urged by outsiders against the organization and concluded with a hearty appeal to the vast throng in attendance in behalf of the favorable opinion which the Order justly merits.

At the conclusion of the address the procession was reformed, and, when it reached the Public Square, the Odd Fellows opened up, and the young ladies of the school having passed through, the schools were severally conducted by an escort to their respective school rooms.

The young ladies of the Female Institute, having, according to an old custom, prepared supper at the Academy for such as of the parents and their female friends as they cared to invite, entertained at half past six, a very large circle of their most intimate friends. After supper which was laid out with much taste and which reflected great credit on the committee of arrangements, the young ladies came into the class room from where for about an hour they entertained each other and their visitors with some excellent vocal and instrumental music. At about 9 o'clock the pianoforte was closed and all returned highly delighted with their day's pastime. The King and Queen, who with the attendants were finely decked out, laid down the ensigns of their authority and next morning in their places in the various classes, it could not have been known that they personated such characters, so lately.

The Odd Fellows concluded their celebrations by a splendid ball and supper at C.P. Thomson's, Esq. which was very largely attended. The members of the Odd Fellows Lodge in attendance wore their regalia during the evening. Dancing was kept up to late, or rather an early hour of the morning of the 2nd, when all departed, highly pleased with the whole proceedings of the day. [267]

In 1856, the maidens from the school seemed to celebrate

the day without the need for a sponsor like the Sons of Temperance or the Odd Fellows and, from all we read, with great success

May Day

Our town was on Thursday the theater of festivity and joyousness. The young ladies of the Institute and Seminary kept up the time honored custom of celebrating May Day. The young ladies of the seminary, under the charge of Mrs. Gibson, crowned their Queen in a grove adjacent to Town, after which they returned to their Academy where they had prepared for the entertainment of themselves and their guests a sumptuous dinner, after partaking of which the company separated, many of them to join with the young ladies of the Institute. Long before the appointed time for the ceremony of the crowning of the Queen had arrived, the town was filled to overflowing, by strangers from a distance - the friends and relatives of the pupils - and those of our citizens who wished to feast their eyes, ears and inner man. The young Ladies had prepared an elegant dinner, of which all who were present, were invited to partake. The young ladies who took part in the ceremony of crowning the Queen, performed their parts with a gracefulness of ease and dignity rarely to be equaled, but never to be surpassed. As for the favorite on whom the choice of the ladies centered to presided on the occasion, she looked "every inch a Queen." We would not be surprised if not the hearts of many a young man as well as some of the old bachelors, will remain in a kind of tremor for some time to come. It would be invidious to mention names, but we who were among outsiders, heard many a well mentioned compliment passed on individuals, and were we not already satisfied that those on whom they were passed, were already sufficiently conscious of their fascinations, we would particularize. On the whole, the day went off with great eclat and the citizens of our town and the surrounding districts were highly delighted with *the celebrations of both schools. Long may their young hearts have nothing more to trouble them than on May Day. We have heard but congratulations to those young ladies who acted as managers on behalf of their fellow students.*

In the evening, we understand, that a party was given at Mrs Donoho's at which those who wished to join in the festivities of the dance had an opportunity of indulging. Our town during the day presented quite a lively and animated appearance and delight and satisfaction seemed to reign in every bosom. [268]

Thanksgiving, of course, can be traced back to the Pilgrims in 1621 and has been celebrated regularly since then. It was not, however, officially celebrated as a national holiday on the third (then the last) Thursday, until 1863. Before then, customarily, the Governor would declare a day to be one of general Thanksgiving for the blessings the people had received and urge the citizens and clergy to observe it as such. You can see that custom in the following proclamation. You can also see the evolution of a common date, the last Thursday in November.

Thanksgiving

Gov. Pease has issued his proclamation recommending the people of the state to observe Thursday, the 27th, as a day of Thanksgiving and Prayer to Almighty God for the numerous blessings he has bestowed upon us as People and in soliciting a continuance of his Divine Power and Protection. He invites the clergy through out the state to observe the day in an appropriate manner. [269]

It seems increasingly popular for folks in the business world, to view the week between Christmas and New Year's as one long holiday. African Americans celebrate the period also as one of holiday. It is not a new idea, not for Texas: "The Christmas holidays come but once a year and there is a general disposition in this land (where necessity does not drive men like beasts of prey) to enjoy them." [270] In fact, DeMorse, calling it "the annual week of leisure and recreation", would shut down *The Standard* for the last week of December to give himself and his staff a week of rest. Instead of work, the towns people, "especially the juvenile portion", would enjoy public balls and private social gatherings.

> *The Holy Days.*
>
> *The period between Christmas and New Year having been from time immemorial devoted to leisure and enjoyment, by all Christian people, no paper will be issued from this office next week.* [271]

The week long holiday began with Christmas, but was not particularly celebrated in any religious way or with the images we associate with the day now, be it of a Baby in the Manger or the jolly face of Santa Claus. However, as with most celebrations in Clarksville, the citizens were ready to parade, dine and dance without much prodding, and Christmas seemed a good excuse for one of the associations in the Town to get up a Procession and Dinner. For example, the Masons organized the festivities in 1849

> *The holy week passed off in our quiet town without any misfortune, more lamentable than a cock fight or two and the eating of sundry hearty dinners, not so good by half as they might have been in more favored*

regions, but still better than common and eaten with peculiar gusto, from the fact that dinners are presumed to be good at Christmas time. Our friends at the Masonic fraternity undertook to get up an excitement in the way of a procession, but the mud was mighty and prevailed. But the ancient fraternity had to content themselves, like the King of France, who marched his army up the hill and then down again, not making much of a march. They found pavement for about 2000 feet and marched on that to Dr. Look's house, then marched up the stairs, listened to an oration, and then marched down again, and betaking themselves to the Star Hotel, did their best to eat up all the dinners prepared for them. This finished the day's achievements as far as they were concerned, but in the evening the votaries of music and motion assembled at the Star and, to the music of a part of the Band from Fort Towson managed to pass the hours right gaily. Although the weather was most inclement, the attendance was large, including persons from Bowie and Doaksville and some of the officers from Fort Towson.[272]

The Sons of Temperance were in charge of the Christmas celebrations in 1851 and their efforts in the crusade against alcohol were applauded by DeMorse.

Sons of Temperance

As announced in our papers, the member of this Order made procession through the streets of our town, on Christmas Day and were addressed, at the Baptist Church, by Mr. Smith Ragsdale. The procession was quite respectable in both appearance and number, although, as we understand, the divisions generally throughout the state are broken up. We trust to see the *ones here long maintain their organization and go on increasing in number and in spirit. Its establishment has been a palpable benefit to the community, withdrawing some brands from the burning that were fast consuming. Its objects are pure and beneficent. We trust that it may long throw its light over the region hereabout and its members never tire in their efforts for the good of their fellow man.* [273]

Today, holidays mean sales. That was not usually the case in Clarksville 150 years ago. However, at least one year, the week between Christmas and New Year's ended in a Big Liquidation Sale at Peabody's Jewelry store. Everything had to go. The store's proprietor, Mr. Peabody, who had read the Declaration of Independence in the 1853 Fourth of July celebrations had been murdered in the public square some months back. The sale attracted young ladies who in turn drew young gentlemen.

The New Year--

The holidays have been occupied by those who comprehend that something pleasant to look upon conduces to the substantial happiness of life, by a daily attendance at the sales of the jewelry shop of the late S.H. Peabody. There were congregated "from early morn to dewy eve", a large portion of the beauty of the vicinage and what hard hearted male could resist the temptation to be present. The attendance of both sexes, we are very pleased to say, was quite regular, the Ladies drawn thither to gaze upon the flashing ornaments, with which they were presented, and the gents only too happy to get a daily view of their sweet faces on any terms. The sale went off finely. The ladies looked beautiful, interested and interesting and the

Christmas week enlivened by dancing parties at night, has been the most pleasant week we have passed this many a day. But it is all over now. The jewelry is gone. So are ladies or, at least, they are not so congregated and we can only dwell with pleasure on the happiness that has passed - hoping that it may return again, some other bright week in our life time.

A very joyous gathering on Monday Night last at the upper room at the establishment of the Rhines, continued on Tuesday night by a party of dancers, closed the Christmas festivities. Now, as we write (Friday) it is drizzling rain and somewhat cold and we may anticipate, ere long, long unpleasant weather, for we have had a a bright time so far and rain, which is unpleasant in winter, must come some time. [274]

 The Sporting Life

Attendance at balls and parading through Town "in full regalia" were about the most exciting things to do within Clarksville town limits. Outside of town, however, there were less tame recreations available. Not surprisingly for an agricultural region, horse racing was a favorite past time. In fact, some of the sporting gentlemen in Town had formed a club for *afficionados* of this Sport of Kings

GREAT EXCITEMENT!

ALL those who have subscribed to the Clarksville subscription club are notified to come forward and pay one-half of their subscriptions, as the races are just at hand, and the money I must have. Let no gentleman fail to comply. [275]

J.C. Hart, Secretary and Ex-officio collector

The Club sponsored races and underwrote the purses that would be awarded the winning horses.

CLARKSVILLE COURSE.

THE Fall Races will commence on the 7th day of October next.

There will be offered, by the directors of the Clarksville subscription club of Red River County, the following purses, to-wit:

First Day - Mile heats, Purse worth $75.

Second Day - Two mile heats, Purse worth $125.

Third Day - Mile heats, best three in five, Purse $100.

The entrance money will also be added to each purse.

The community at large are invited to attend, and more especially the sporting world.

The proprietors of said track will also give $25, which will be run for on the 5th of the same month, a dash of one mile, free for any untrained saddle horse - three or more to make a race. Ten dollars entrance, which will also be added to the purse.[276]

J. C. Hart, Sect'y

The *Standard* reported on the outcome of some of these matches:

CLARKSVILLE JOCKEY CLUB RACES.-*Tuesday, First Day.-Purse $300, Two mile heats-Two entries: Benj. Johnson's br. filly, Purity, and Johnson & Aik's John Ridge. Won by Purity in two heats, easily.*

TIME - *5:04 - 4:59.*

The heavy rains of the preceding day had rendered the track excessively heavy, being most of the way over the hock in mud, and in some places nearly knee deep.[277]

Wintertime brought its own amusements. The colder winters in 1855, 1856 and 1858, and some foresight on DeMorse's part, provided the residents of Clarksville with winter sports, for the first time since the town's beginnings.

Imagine the scene. Charles DeMorse, with never before seen ice skates on his shoulders, leading, like the Pied Piper of Hamlin, all the young boys (and some of the adults) of the town to the frozen Delaware Creek and to a large puddle nearby, which had been christened Lake Shannahan, probably after the cabinet maker nearby. It is a wonderful, if long winded, picture.

> *A New Era of Amusement in Clarksville*
>
> *During some winters past, we have noticed occasionally, once, twice or thrice of a winter, when skating may be done in the vicinity of the town, if one only had been in possession of skates. But, in this climate, merchants do not bring such articles in for sale and so the occasion, yearning of one of the most exciting sports of our boyhood, had to pass ungratified. Last Spring, however, we thought of this and, when we ordered our Spring supply of paper from Philadelphia, we sent for three pairs, one for myself, one for the legitimate representative of our name and line and one pair for companionship.*
>
> *On Monday last, the weather was freezing cold, accurately speaking, and we thought of skating, but had forgotten about it before morning and were in the office at ten o'clock, preparing to go to our usual labors, when an Arkansas gentleman, temporarily resident, and a North Carolina emigrant called to borrow our skates. Inquiring the prospect of their use, we brought out three pairs, put on our overcoat and gloves and headed for Lake Shannahan, a remarkable sheet of water, not far from the center of town. Lake Shannahan is about 50 feet long and 20 wide and during the summer months, the frogs make music and disport themselves gaily there; the male of that beautiful species chanting amorous ditties to his mate until the water dries out of*

entirely, when they have to seek more genial residences. Lake Shannahan now, after receiving the flood of the first winter rains, is about 12 or 14 inches deep. There is one point of character about the lake then which in part offsets its lack of extended circumference. If it is not very large, it is not very deep and there is no probability of any loss of life from venturing upon the treacherous ice, with which the winter's cold may gloss over its surface.

It is usual in the description of great events to give a preparatory conception to the reader of the locality. This however is enough we imagine to permit an understanding of the first field of operations. Sallying down to the lake aforesaid in the most gallant manner, the ice was tested by the writer of this who concluded that the ice would not bear pressure. The Arkansas man put on his skates and sidled about and the Carolina man sought a log away off on dry land to put on his skates and try the ground first, before getting on the slippery surface of the lake. It was concluded however from the continual cracking of the ice that three getting on it would break it in. Consequently, we sought the woods for a spot sheltered from the sun and wandered down the Delaware in search of a pond, or a hard place in the creek. The pond we sought was dry. The creek was tried by the boys who followed in train, and having never seen skating, were anxious for a sight but everywhere they tested the ice, in they went and, if we did not have exactly what, we sought we had a great fun, in seeing the surprised boys clamber out somewhat in a hurry. In our passage through town, we had attracted quite a crowd to whom our skates were curiosities and the gathering really looked like something of a skating party from olden times. We pursued the Creek to the writer of this was satisfied and turned back to the Lake with the determination to have some type of skating anyhow and we got to make the round of the lake a few times, going under several times but persisting until there was no sound space to turn upon and so, for the first time in twenty years, we have had skating. The Arkansas man and the Carolina went down the Delaware to a lake of some size and the Carolina man, who put on his skates on the dry ground, went on - and in -up to his middle. The Arkansas man has not lived in the woods for nothing, kept out. Tonight, we anticipate a freeze and by taking an earlier start, we think we shall find ice. So we live in hopes of the morrow.

On Wednesday morning and every morning since we have found in the Delaware small skating places, on which various persons have enjoyed themselves. Those who could skate, by skating, those who could not by trying and satisfying themselves, while they more than satisfied the spectators. Really, we have continuous sport nearly all this week in a way we had hardly ever expected to have for so long of a time near Clarksville, and yet it has been so warm all the time, except at night, that gloves and overcoats are thrown aside and in perfect comfort we have the amusement of a Northern Winter. This has resulted from the fact that, after the first cold weather, the ice that formed there has remained in beds in the creek extending north and south, where the banks were high and the sun could not shine on it very long at a time. [278]

A snowstorm in 1856, followed by a week's worth of cold weather, gave another opportunity for winter frolic. Even DeMorse had not procured sleds in advance, but the townspeople nevertheless improvised as best they could.

During Saturday last one to two jumpers or slides were hastily put up and put in requisition and, if good sleighs had been in command during Saturday and Sunday, the sleighing would have been as good as it is anywhere. Seven and a half to eight and a half inches was the general depth of snow on Saturday last. The weather has been cold ever since until yesterday. [279]

When the snow came of 1856, so did another winter sport - snow ball fights. Two items from *The Standard* depict the timeless play of boys, both grown up ones, like Widower DeMorse, and young pranksters.

Apropos to the season, we have just received a challenge by a special messenger, from four ladies to meet them across the Delaware, in dangerous combat with snowballs. The missive is accompanied by our well made hard snow balls, carefully wrapped up in two newspapers. Our heart beats for the fray, but hard fate compels us to attend to The Standard, until late in the evening, when we shall storm the hill and expect to have a desperate encounter with a probability of being made to leave the ground to the enemy or to remain upon it only by courtesy. [280]

To DeMorse's surprise, the women were worthy foes and the youngsters could not resist the chance to throw a snowball or two at passing gentlemen.

Rare times the boys have had of it, since our last, including the old boys, for the venerable editor of this paper was nearly snowballed all day last Sunday by a fair array of females, who could not "pretermit' the unusual opportunity and pelted him occasionally, until after night fall. Commencing on Saturday, the boys took the town and filled the ears, and knocked the hats off, of nearly all the men who made themselves visible about the Square, and they had it all their own way, for the unlucky individual who showed signs of resistance or threatened vengeance had no chance against their numbers.

As to our case, we were formally challenged, as we reported last week, and had to go through a most desperate contest with numerous foes from which, however, we emerged satisfactorily, after a hard conflict in which the enemy as may be presumed displayed a great deal of tactical skill and perseverance.[281]

Texas is noted for its devotion to football and whole towns follow their high school squads on Friday nights to towns, scores of miles away, to root on the team. Clarksville is no exception. Something like it has excited fans for more than a century and a half ago, if not longer.[282] The first game, college or otherwise, was Princeton against Rutgers, played in New Jersey in 1869. A full decade before, however, the citizens of Clarksville cheered at something remarkably similar to it, called Choctaw Indian Ball Play. The rules of the game are not clear, but there is an uncanny resemblance to football, including cheerleaders and coaches.

Such a Choctaw Ball Play was held at Roland, Clarksville's landing on the Red River, fifteen miles north of Town. The Red River separated Texas from the Indian Nation to the North. The Choctaws, one of the Five Civilized Tribes, lived across the way and were peaceful farmers and hunters, moved there from Mississippi some thirty years before. The Ball play was some type of ritualistic battle, as is football today, played competitively, but within their own tribe, not against enemies. Their white skinned neighbors in Red River county were invited to attend and DeMorse hyped it during the weeks before, not unlike the sports media of today:

BALL PLAY

Ball Play - Fun Ahead.

There will be a Choctaw Ball play at Roland 15 miles from Town on the 8th of July. The Public is invited to attend. Much sport is anticipated. [283]

The Ball Play to come off at Rowland on the 8th instant is attracting much attention. Betters are already backing their favorite tubbees. [284]

At last the big day came, and it was well attended. Read the report on the game and ask yourself whether the differences between it and football are not really cosmetic.

The Indian Ball Play

Friday, the 8th, was a brisk day in our sister town of Rowland and her usually quiet streets and lanes presented a gay and animated appearance not often to be seen in that quiet adjunct to our town. The long talked about Ball Play was to come off at 12 noon and great excitement was caused thereby. Early in the morning quite a number of the citizens left our town to witness the sport. They returned in the evening highly elated at the fun they had witnessed and from them we glean our items of the play. There were 54 Indians engaged in the play, 27 on a side. Captain Sautuska had charge of one party and Captain Jones the other side. Before the play opened, a party of well dressed gay looking squaws, about 25 in number, proceeded to chant and dance the "Conjure Dance" after the music of a tin plate beaten with a stick in hand of one of the parties. This display of the "poetry of motion" was for the success of the Sautuska party. When the red skinned nymphs of the Sautuska had closed, a like number of squaws decked in the gayest trinkets went through the same salutary evolutions for the benefit of the Jones faction. Each party was attended by his own medicine man who performed several offices of conjuration and invoked the Great Spirit to give their respective captains the victory. The medicine man of the Jones party was a venerable, pinched back looking a little savage, well stricken in years, whereas the medicine man of the Sautuska party was a pale robust athletic looking fellow of not over 25, and to appear venerable and grave looking, despite his youth, had recourse to a long beard of sheep skin, with the wool of which he wore under his chin. At 12 noon, the ball was thrown up and the play began.

The game was 12 marks. The Jones party took the lead and made the first three scores and their friends "came down with their dust upon them" at great odds. The blood of all the Sautuska was up, however, and they made the next two scores and. at the eighth score, were a score in the lead of their competitors and continued to lead to the 12th score closed the game which stood thus:

Sautuska   12 scores

Jones   6 scores

The game was about two hours in being played. General good order and harmless hilarity prevailed throughout the day, although we are pained to add, that in a brawl that took place between some Indians the *night previous, three of them were severely stabbed. We learn that the next play between the same parties, of which due notice will be given, is to come off in this town.* [285]

Today, sports resorts and health spas are all the rage, golf, tennis, water, weight watching, whatever. Again, however, this was nothing new for Clarksville, which was well ahead of its time. A century and a half ago, it had its own sports and health resort to sneak off to in the summer time, Dalby Springs in neighboring Bowie county. Dalby Springs were sulphur hot springs considered therapeutic by the populace. They became popular, as a summer meeting place, for some of the upper crust of Northern Texas. DeMorse, in a familiar refrain, praised the spa but then claimed that the press of business, no pun intended, kept him from participating. In the following series of items from *The Standard*, covering a two week period in August, 1856, we see the Editor DeMorse's dramatic struggle with his conscience, beginning with protestations about staying at home, followed by the fall to temptation "on the outside of a sorrel horse" and ending with the dashing Major DeMorse, the eligible man about town, reporting on the fun he had at Dalby's Springs and the ladies who were there. Characteristically, he added his two cents, giving the owner some advice as to how to make it better and more profitable.

Dalby Springs

Our readers will see a notice of this place for resort among our communications. At present the spring is the retreat of a gay company of Ladies and gents from our town and from sundry other localities not far distant. We had hoped to be with them at one time, but who ever knew an editor to have any spare time for recreation. The best part of us, our heart, is down there now, and, in dreams our heart is down there too. Perhaps, we do just as well, for there are few joys in life the reality of which is equal to the anticipation. Nevertheless, those who have time and , with it, retain the capacity for pure heartfelt enjoyments, might do worse than to while a few days away at Dalby's. [286]

Dalby's Springs

We learn that there is quite a crowd of visitors at this summer resort. Several of our townspeople have taken themselves thither within the past few months, among them the Editor of this Paper who left for the locality on the outside of a sorrel horse, on Sunday night last . [287]

Dalby Springs

We passed some three days and nights most delightfully at Dalby's, in drinking the amber water, dancing, promenades to the Spring with Music and sunning ourselves generally. We found there pleasant spirits that had thrown off for a little time the cares of life. Some were angelic and spirituelle and scarcely touched the earth with their dainty feet; others were not so much so, but they looked of the earth, and had a solid substantiality which made a sensible impression upon the sand as they pressed upon it, yet they were light hearted and most entertaining. As to the male bi-peds, there were some of them there too, agreeable gentlemen but we can not waste ink and space upon them. Quite a number of ladies and gentlemen came in from about Boston, while we were there and more were expected.

We found the atmosphere surprisingly cool and

the accommodations, though plain, quite comfortable. Various amusements varied by the occasional walk to the Springs, varied the occupation of the day and at night the dance was unfailing and ever fresh. Charlie Leigh's violin was worth its weight in gold.

The amber colored water of the springs is the richest looking fluid we ever saw and has a vivacity of appearance that approaches sparkling. It has a healthful, though not rapid, action upon the stomach and bowels.

There is a sour spring at this place which has gone dry during the drought or affords so little water as to be useless.

The locality is pleasant looking, somewhat broken, sandy and presents large rocks that have undergone volcanic action. If a little money was judiciously expended in improving and clearing up the place, with the advantages of its waters, and the fish and game adjacent, it may be made a regular and most pleasant summer resort. [288]

By 1858, Dalby Springs was part of DeMorse's summer routine, especially since he had received reports that the ladies gathered there to escape the heat of the summer. There was plenty of social activity and the waters indeed might be as healthy as advertised:

On my way from Clarksville, I spent a night at Dalby Springs. On my arrival there I found the house crowded almost to the point of suffocation, notwithstanding, the visitors seemed to be enjoying themselves finely. Riding on horseback and driving in carriages, seemed to be the chief amusements of the day, and immediately after supper, the merry dancers usurped the place of all other past times, until late at night. When dancing concluded, what a scramble among gentlemen to get hold of a blanket, a pair of saddle bags or a saddle for a pillow and room enough to spread the blanket for the night. Shady trees and carriages were in requisition for shelter and as the rule "first come, first served" was carried out to the fullest extent towards the "wee small hours of the morning" you may see some unlucky wight wandering around in search of a place to pitch his tent for the night.

I must state that I have heard of several whose state of health has improved from the time they left home. I have no doubt that "the Springs" under their present management afford the best summer retreat in the state for dyspoptics. The food is so admirably adapted to their condition that some who are more robust of health have occasionally been found among the class called grumblers and discontents.[289]

No Man is an Island:

The World outside Red River County

John Donne's realization that each of us is part of a larger picture was equally true for the citizens of Clarksville and Red River County. While they did not have the internet or phones, they were still connected to the outside word because of Charles DeMorse and *The Standard.*

Nothing happens in a vacuum. Clarksville might have been somewhat isolated but it was part of - and felt the influence of - what happening contemporaneously in the rest of Texas, United States and even internationally.

The press had been a powerful institution in America since Colonial times. An informed citizenry was considered beneficial and preferential treatment was given the journals to encourage them to disseminate local and national news. For example, newspapers were permitted to "exchange" their papers, postage free, with other publishers across the nation, thereby creating a primitive national news network. Locally, papers could be sent postage free to patrons who lived within thirty miles of the newspaper office.

In 1846, there were almost as many newspapers published in United States as there were in the rest of the world[290], and, despite its being only recently settled, Texas had thirty one of them, including two religious [291] in nature and one published in the German language.[292]

The Standard was one of the premier papers - second in the state in circulation - and Charles DeMorse was considered the Father of Journalism in Texas. What was it like to be a newspaperman? It can be gleaned from remarks made by DeMorse about an old friend, John W. Swindells. Swindells was DeMorse's counterpart at the *Dallas Herald*.[293] DeMorse thought him "an excellent specimen of the typographic fraternity, intelligent, without pretension and feeling that interest in the *Art Preservative*, which is a feature of [journalists] and is continued through life undiminished, a sort of affection for a hard, un paying, but mind improving, profession." [294]

Running a weekly newspaper had its difficulties. DeMorse often had to barter subscriptions for his own necessities. Beef, corn, wheat, flour, wood, bacon and lard, all were acceptable methods of making payment for the paper. Some years, a low river forced the cancellation of the papers for weeks at a time. Once, DeMorse went temporarily blind[295] and another time he was sued - and lost - for libel.[296] Newspaper delivery was effected by the U.S. Mail, sometimes an uncertain proposition. DeMorse was especially irritated at the postal service. Subscribers do not pay for newspapers they do not receive. DeMorse claimed to need his "dimes", as he called them, to keep the paper going, "our outlay being heavy and continual."

Despite irritations like these, DeMorse was obviously addicted to the newspaper business. He had even opened another office of *The Standard* in Bonham, Fannin County (later closed) and purchased the state of the art printing presses.[297] Except when the river was down and the paper supply exhausted, *The Standard* published weekly on Saturday. The paper consisted first of four pages, then of six and then seven columns each. It was the first page and sometimes part of the second that kept the reader in touch with news outside Red River, featuring news of the rest of Texas, the United States and the world, reprinted from his exchange papers.

The Rest of Texas

(i) East Texas

The Citizen of Clarksville could observe Clarksville and Red River County first hand. He also knew a fair bit about some of the surrounding counties, an awareness supplemented by Attorney DeMorse's reports of his visiting a number of counties in northern Texas: Bowie, Cass, Titus, Hopkins, Kaufman, Fannin, Lamar, Grayson, Cooke, Tarrant, Collin, Hunt, Denton, Dallas, Wise and the frontier counties of Parker, Johnson, Ellis Jack, Upshur and Montague (the subjects of the volume two companion to this work). However, the citizen of Clarksville needed *The Standard.* to learn what was happening in the rest of Texas, the wider United States or even the world. It was during the first two decades of *The Standard* that the different regions of Texas were beginning to be settled. DeMorse reported on all of them, usually from items from exchange papers or notes that friends sent him.

East Texas was long populated by Texas standards, prospering both in commerce and in agriculture. Yet, it was still young enough to allow DeMorse to engage in debate with the editor of the *Houston Telegraph*, as to which city would become East Texas' dominant city. DeMorse predicted that "the City of Galveston is destined to be a place of great commercial importance and in Galveston, the clink of the hammer and the sound of the forge is ever in your ears, the busy hum of labor, the rattling of wagons and the smoke of steamboats."[298] On another occasion, he wrote Galveston "was destined ere long to absorb nearly all the trade of Houston, and which, a few years hence, will be a great Commercial Mart when Houston will be "no whar." If he had not made his point, he added " Let us predict for you: In ten years, Clarksville will be a much more considerable place than Houston, for Houston will then be deprived of all its trade. It bears no comparison with Clarksville. " [299] As sometimes happens, DeMorse was wrong. Recent population figures put Houston at about 2,000,000, Galveston at 57,000 and Clarksville at fewer than 5,000.

Houston grew quickly, despite DeMorse's pessimism

Houston

[Wagons] arrive daily from the interior with cotton and the business of the city is steadily increasing. Four or five new stores have been opened here with in the past month, and we are informed that several merchants are prepared to open stores as soon as annexation is consummated. Several new buildings are being constructed and the hotels are literally crowded with boarders. The value of real estate in this city has expanded by one hundred per cent in the last two months. The favorable position which Houston enjoys, will necessarily render it the depot of the most fertile and productive of the upper Brazos and Trinity and the intermediate regions. It is quite probable the whole trade of the vast and fertile region, extending from the Trinity above Cincinnati to the Colorado, above La Grange, including an area of 20,000 square miles, will be diverted to this city. The tide of immigrants now settling that fertile land will, ere long, bear to this city treasures more valuable than the mines of Chihuahua."[300]

Cities that become large encounter growing pains. Some of them are no worse than traffic problems, a continuing problem in Houston. *The Houston Telegraph* reported, as copied in *The Standard*:

> *For the first time since Houston was founded, complaints have been made before the recorder that the immense number of cotton teams in our principal streets obstructed them so that the drays and a carriages could not pass. The city marshal has actually been compelled to keep continually at work, to open a passage through the long file of teams to enable drays to convey goods from the landing to the stores. When it is recollected that our streets are 80 feet wide, some idea may be formed of the quantity of teams that are daily arriving. It is estimated that at least 200 teams are daily arriving and as many departing from the City.* [301]

Crime is another problem that accompanies the busy life of a city and Houston was no exception, judging by the following items:

> *Wm Jones, a Justice of the Peace, was shot in Houston on Wednesday by David Allen, who is known to many persons here as a sporting character and violin player. The circumstances, as near as we can gather them, are briefly as follows. Allen had a pair of pistols deposited at a public house. He called for and received them. One was loaded and he loaded the other. He gave one to Jones and told him to hand it to Boyce, which Jones declined doing, as he seemed to apprehend that Allen contemplated violence. Allen cocked the other pistol and laid it on the table, with his hand on the trigger and called for some liquor. Jones took hold of the pistol with the muzzle toward him, and in attempting to get possession of it the gun went off and killed him. Allen was immediately arrested but denies, we understand, having fired the pistol voluntarily and that*

seem probably to be the fact."[302]

An affray occurred in Houston on the 9th instant between Henry G. Runnels and W. S. Hansbrough, both of Brazoria county, which resulted in the death of Hansbrough having been shot through the heart. The difficulty is said to have grown out of an insult offered the wife of Runnells by Hansbrough. Runnells was examined and gave bail for his appearance at the next term of Harris District Court."[303]

Harris county

On Monday the criminal docket was taken up. Austin Burnett was indicted for cattle stealing. The jury found him guilty of petit larceny, the penalty of which is confinement in the state penitentiary for a period of one year. John K. Hyde, the murderer of Charles Butler, received the sentence of death yesterday. When the sentence was pronounced on him, the Judge, together with nearly the whole assembly, were deeply affected - some to tears - but the prisoner evinced little emotion. He has a haggard and emaciated condition and is very weak from sickness and long confinement. On Friday the 11th of July, he will suffer the penalty of late under the gallows."[304]

Residents of the towns of southeast Texas, living along the coast, had an additional risk - yellow fever. No one knew the cause of the scourge, that it was transmitted by mosquitoes. Yellow fever was reported in Port LaVaca[305], Houston[306], Galveston[307] and at Victoria, where "the alarm was so great that it was difficult to get persons to bury the body of the deceased."[308] Cholera was a danger too, killing one hundred and forty at Indianola and Victoria.³⁰⁹ Ships arriving from Europe with immigrant settlers brought it.

Despite these difficulties of life, the settlers in southeast Texas also enjoyed great blessings in the fertility of the soil and the almost tropical climate that allowed a longer season and greater range of crops than the counties to the north and west. "Texas Oranges [were] as fine as any we have seen imported from Havana."³¹⁰ So were lemons. "The largest we have seen were grown this season in the garden of H. B. Martin, measuring eleven and a half inches over the smallest circumference", the circumference lengthwise being about one inch larger.³¹¹ Sugar too was raised in the Southeast; "We were highly pleased with some beautiful specimen of sugar,[from] the plantation of Messrs Mercer and Menfree, on the Colorado and Mr. Sweeney on the Brazos. These specimens are better than the best imported sugar that we have seen this year in our market. The grains are large clear and well formed and the sugar has a delicious flavor."³¹² There were even vineyards in Galveston.³¹³

(ii) Central Texas

Central Texas, more or less from Dallas to Corpus Christi, was being settled from 1848 through 1860. Settlers were pouring in. Yet, it was still sometimes a dangerous place, a frontier as illustrated by the frequent clashes with wild Indian

Any view of the central part of Texas must include the Trinity River as it runs through it like a zipper. Today, the river serves little, if any, commercial use. However, a hundred and fifty years ago, it was considered one of the natural benefits of the region that made it attractive to immigrants. The easier and more economic the ability to get crops to market³¹⁴ and to import supplies for the next season, the more prosperous and popular a region became. The steam and flatboats of the Trinity opened central Texas to immigration, just as the Red River had to the north. At high water, during the rainy seasons, the Trinity would be navigable 650 miles from its mouth.

Towns sprung up along the river which DeMorse visited, thought highly of and, even in one instance, invested in. Many began as ferries across the Trinity. One was Buffalo which DeMorse claimed –again incorrectly[315] -was "the most important port on the Trinity River, surrounded by a country unrivaled in beauty and fertility by any other. Nothing can deprive it of its agricultural and commercial advantages and who can prevent or retard its ultimate prosperity and importance." [316]

Another town of interest was Porter's Bluff – also called Taos. It had started as was a ferry crossing and shipping point on the Trinity River. It was becoming a major town between Austin and Dallas and many thought it would outrival both of them. Apparently, it was a "fun" town and widower DeMorse especially enjoyed its all night dances.[317]

When DeMorse visited it, Porter's Bluff was thriving with a blacksmith shop, several stores, and a sawmill. It was also a port for small steamboats, known as packets, which before the Civil War sailed up the Trinity bringing supplies and down it, loaded with cotton. DeMorse thought so much of Porter s Bluff/ Taos' future that he decided to invest in it by purchasing some of the town lots of Taos.[318] Porters Bluff did have good prospects. If the Trinity River could be navigated that far north, then Porters Bluff/Taos would become a commercial hub. Cotton crops could be transported down river to the coast for shipment around the world. Needed supplies for the planters could be brought up. Best of all, there were several military posts that needed to be supplied and Porters Bluff was ideally situated to serve as a depot.

Were one to look for either Porters Bluff or Taos on the map today, he would find nothing. Today the town - including

DeMorse's investments in it - does not exist, not a building, not a wall, not a stone. It had been the victim in the early 1870s, when the Houston and Texas Central Railroad extended its line to Corsicana, about seventeen miles upriver. It could not take the competition. River traffic came to an end and with Porter's Bluff. Even the ferry was discontinued in the 1880s, replaced by a bridge.[319]

Crossing the Trinity, DeMorse would head southwest towards Austin. En route he would stop in Limestone county at Tehuacana Springs, another town destined for greatness, or so it seemed at the time. Some lobbied that it become the State capital and it received a number of votes in a statewide election, but unfortunately not nearly enough to win.[320] Today the town has a population of approximately three hundred. It had been the site of an old Tawakoni Indian village. DeMorse's description of his approach to the town suggests an answer to why this had been named Limestone county. It should also appeal to those interested in geology[321], fossils[322] and botany.[323]

About seventy miles south of Dallas, was Waco, where the Brazos and Bosque rivers join. On the site of what had been a Waco Indian village for centuries. In 1849, Jacob DeCordova, an early day entrepreneur and real estate mogul, developed a new town, he intended to call Lamartine, but which ended up being called Waco Village instead. The first town lots went for five dollars each and farming properties at two or three dollars an acre. DeMorse, en route to Austin, visited it in that first year. He was not impressed. The town "comprises an unfinished tavern of Capt. Ross, formerly of the Rangers, a grocery with a backroom and perhaps a half a dozen log cabins scattered over the prairie" and its citizens were "the class of persons usually known 'as sporting characters' [who] had extended their operations to old Waco and run several races there of late." [324]

From Waco DeMorse would ride through Williamson County and its county seat Georgetown. [325] It was not the place to tarry. Georgetown and Williamson county sometimes had Indian problems. A news item reported "that a large body of Comanche Indians had appeared within the immediate neighborhood of the place [Georgetown] and has manifested signs of hostility by killing cattle etc." A band of nineteen calvary men from their Station in Austin went after the marauders.[326]

South of Williamson county was the quickly developing Austin, the State Capital. *The Austin Gazette*, reprinted by DeMorse, described those first days:

> *"Our City is daily improving. Every house is occupied and a considerable number of families are encamped in the vicinity, being unable to procure houses. Several new buildings are going up and many contemplate improving their town lots in the course of the present season. At least 50 private dwellings could, at present, be advantageously rented and sold in this city and we are informed that several new stores would be immediately opened, if suitable houses could be obtained for the purposes. There are, at this time, nine full dry goods and grocery stores and six retail groceries or coffee houses in Austin and every one of them is doing a profitable business. There are also 7 or 8 public or private boarding houses, with an average of ten to fifteen boarders each, besides the numerous hosts of transient persons who are daily coming and going out of the city. Our streets are thronged with strangers and hardly a day goes by without the appearance of newly arrived emigrants' wagons, some stopping in or about the city and others going through to the west. We do not remember to have seen such an influx of emigration to any new country as is now pouring into Texas from all quarters of the United States and portions of Europe.*[327]

Barton Springs in Austin is known as a picnic, camping and swimming spot. The pure water gushing up from the limestone strata below is crystal clear. One Sunday morning during DeMorse's 1849 trip to Austin, he was tempted away from attending church to make "an exploration for natural curiosities and for a look at the scenery of the surrounding country."[328] The fossils[329], flora[330] and fauna[331], ancient and modern, were breathtaking to behold as DeMorse's confession home tells: "For a long time, we stood upon our rocky prominence and admired the beauty of the prospect, now watching the fishes, now looking at the rocks and trees." [332]

If one, unlike DeMorse, did not want to spend all his day watching the grass grow, there were other things to do in the area as diverse as going to the circus[333] or hunting for gold in the nearby hills.[334]

As idyllic as the region around Austin might appear in DeMorse's descriptions, it was still frontier in many aspects. Life was difficult. Drought could wipe out crops.[335] Pests were also destructive. Grasshoppers, for example, "which covered the ground thick with them and when disturbed they fly up as thick as swarms of bees. They came from a northern direction and during the heat of the day, they fill the air as high as the eye can reach, and the reflection of the suns on their wings makes them look like snowflakes." [336] Illness -inflammatory dysentery and influenza - was a scourge as was lawlessness.[337]

South and west of Austin, before reaching San Antonio, were the settlements of German farmer and mechanic emigrants in the Texas Hill Country. The colonies had been organized and financed abroad by Prince Carl of Sohm-Braunfels.[338] The German settlers were welcomed to Texas with praise and optimism.

The German Immigrants brought over in the Steamer Globe two weeks since are the finest looking set

> *of emigrants we have ever seen. They are said to be wealthy and of the best classes of the German population. They are well educated and many of them speak the English language fluently. We learn it is their intention to engage in agricultural employment and stock raising on the Guadalupe river above this place. We trust that they may lead a prosperous and happy life and that we shall have the pleasure of welcoming large accessions of such emigrants to our new and beautiful country.*[339]

Prince Carl had purchased a well watered and wooded tract on the intersection of the Comal River with the Guadalupe, north of San Antonio. It was settled on March 21, 1845 by about 300 German immigrants. They were the survivors of three shiploads who had landed barely three months before at Indianola, wintered outside on the beach without shelter and then trekked from Indianola to what would be called New Braunfels by Prince Carl, after his province in Germany.

The task of settling New Braunfels had been entrusted to John O. Meusebauch, formerly Baron Meusebach. He was the agent of the German Emigration and Railroad Company and commander general of the German colonies in America. Located on a tract of three leagues purchased by the German Association of the estate of Hernando, the former Governor, New Braunfels was "handsomely laid out on the banks of the Comal and the Guadalupe."[340]

> *Its streets are broad and regularly laid off nearly with the cardinal points. Sequin and San Antonio streets (being in the direction of these towns generally) intersect each other at the public squares, in the center of the town where there is a town bell which assembles the people together on all public occasions. There are*

already about 300 frame buildings and the people appear to be busily engaged in constructing more. The present population is estimated at 1500. The lumber is at present hand cut but the Comal affords some of the fairest mill locations and the Agent is making preparations for a mill by next season. The buildings of the future will probably be of stone as the material is of great abundance and of the best quality.

There is now in New Braunfels one good variety store by Messrs Ferguson and Heater, six groceries, one silversmith shop, one copper smith, one saddler, six shoemakers, one printer, three tailor shops, one wagon maker shop, one lock maker, two tan yards, three cigar manufactures and one baker. Besides these, there are other mechanics who are intended for the upper settlements. The company has two engineers. The present prosperity and rapid growth of this colony must equally surprise and delight every person who visits it. The Director Baron Meusebach offers encouragement to all people, especially Americans to settle in the colony and enter into unrestricted intercourse with the emigrants. The enlightened and republican liberality is in remarkable contrast to the policy of the predecessor and deservedly recommends the colony to the favorable consideration of their future government. [341]

New Braunfels was only the first of several communities planned. The next was to be eighty miles to the northwest in the beautiful Hill country. It was to be named Fredrickburg, in honor of prince Frederick of Prussia. The erection of the town is a fine example of German organization and building skills:

An expedition under Lieut. Bine of the colony and Capt Murchinson is now about starting for the

Pedernales, with mechanics and the necessary materials and means for putting up buildings. The company will consist of about 50 men and four wagons. They will construct a road 40 feet wide across the mountains to the north prong of the Pedernales in a direction about northwest, the distance being about 25 miles. A town is to be laid out by the name of Fredericksburg in a delightful valley, 15 miles in width, with numerous springs and rivulets and supplied with an abundance of timber for building. Here Lieut Wilcke, the engineer and surveyor for the colony, will lay off the town in lots, while Captain Murchinson will return to New Braunfels for 1000 colonists, who are expected soon to arrive. [342]

Fredericksburg is mentioned most often in *The Standard* in connection with Indian attacks on the German settlers there: 'In its vicinity, a German girl was shot through the arm with an arrow which caused a severe, but not a fatal, wound. [Another] German who had been engaged in bringing hay to a military post had his horses stolen from his encampment and one of his oxen killed by an arrow."[343] A third German, working an Indian trading post thirty miles from Fredericksburg was murdered by a small party of four or five Comanches "who had been trading with their usual friendship." [344]

A 1855 item reports "that, unless some assistance is furnished that this settlement will be entirely broken up. Already several had to leave and come further into the settlements. The Indians have stolen several horses lately and killed others in the stables, which were locked up. The Indians have been several times seen lately and that they came very close to catching an old man's little boys who were working in his fields, near the house but the little fellows escaped by out running them. All of this happened within plain view of the house. The people of Fredericksburg are, at this time, afraid to travel from there down here unless several are together." [345]

Baron Meusebach was a competent leader. To protect his colonists, he successfully engaged in peace negotiations with the tribes of the region. The Indians promised "to refrain from all hostile contact towards the settlers and to notify the colonists of the approach of any hostile bands of other tribes." The Germans gave in exchange "presents and provisions to the amount of 2,000 dollars, were guaranteed to the Indians. most of which have already been distributed."[346]

South of the German colonies was San Antonio. San Antonio was already old when the Republic of Texas was born in 1835. It had developed in 1718 in association with some Indian missions in San Antonio and East Texas. The missions were secularized in 1783 and 1784. Thus, in 1846, when this visitor saw the Missions of San Antonio, they were already ancient by American standards and beginning to deteriorate, so much that the visitor wishes his artist friend was there, so that he could sketch and save it for posterity. One of the missions – the Alamo – was already venerated.

> *Let a person imagine a town two or three miles in circumference, situated on a level rocky plain, more than two centuries old, composed of large grotesque walls of rock with perfectly flat roofs and dirt floors with the ravages of a hundred battles still imprinted upon it with one of the prettiest rivers in the world running through the center, and he can perhaps form a faint idea of the appearance of the ancient town. There is much romantic feeling associated with the appearance and history of San Antonio, but the Alamo alone is enough to make me look at it with solemn reverence upon the scene of the heroic bravery of its dauntless defenders. I had always a lingering curiosity to see the Alamo. Now I have seen it. I have stood at the spot where the Lion Hearted Crockett fell, bravely battling for liberty. The whole building covers an area of about two acres and*

looks older than the town itself. [347]

Visitors found the citizens of San Antonio "as usual gay and happy. The same hilarity among its denizens - an insatiable love of music and dancing and cock fighting - and the same love of ease and 'busy idleness', which has ever characterized its indolent, luxurious and care killing, cigar smoking people."[348]

They liked bull fights as well:

On Sunday July 16th, with the consent of the city officials, there was exhibited publically a Bull Fight - after the ancient manners and customs done years ago on Sunday in Spain and said to be practiced even now in Mexico. There were several hundred spectators present of both sexes. In fact, the arena was even crowded. Poor taurus, after making sport for the assembly a long time, was stabbed some six or eight times, by four or five champions of the pit and alas he died. Dulce et decorum est pro patria mori [it is sweet and fitting to die for one's country]. [349]

San Antonio may have been among the oldest settlements in Texas, but it bustled like a boom town when Texas joined the Union[350] and, two years later, DeMorse reported that " very few Mexican families have immigrated to that town during the last four or five months. The American population is rapidly increasing and several new houses are in the process of erection."[351]

Beauty can be deceiving and the "beautiful" river, the Guadalupe, that ran through San Antonio and from which the citizens took their drinking water turned fatal in late Spring, 1849 when there was an out break of cholera. "The citizens were falling at the rate of 50 a day."[352] Science had not yet traced the spread of the disease to contaminated water

Reports had it that San Antonio could be dangerous for reasons other than cholera.

> *The Editor of The Victoria Advocate learned from several gentlemen in San Antonio that a set of desperate men in that place - gamblers and discharged soldiers - had collected together, to the number of about 70, on pretense of fighting Indians, but with the real object of robbing the Quartermaster's safe and stores, but were prevented by the death of their leader, a man named Sears, who was shot by Mr. Wallace, whose store he rode into with a cocked pistol, intending to kill him. Some of the party after the death of their leader, revealed the plot.* [353]

The outskirts of San Antonio could be dangerous too. Wild animals still roamed there.

> *A Texas Hunt*
>
> *A short time since, Capt W. G. Crump and five or other citizens of San Antonio, made a hunt on the Medina, a small stream 14 miles west of San Antonio and returned after two days having killed a large panther, eight bears, seven deer and partridges too numerous to count. The largest of the bears weighted over 400 pounds. The panther was nearly 10 feet in length, measuring from the tip of the nose of the animal to the tip of his tail.* [354]

San Antonio was not the only town in the south central region of Texas that seemed out of place - on the wrong continent! Castroville, named after its benevolent French founder, Henri Castro, appeared more a French - Alsatian village that should sit on the border of France and Germany, not on the Medina river, 25 miles west of San Antonio on the frontier of the Republic of Texas. The spot was so much on the frontier that, when the first settlers arrived in 1844, they were escorted by the legendary Ranger and Indian Fighter Jack Hays and five of his men. A visitor, seemingly a foreigner himself, describes Castroville two years later. Among his interests were the women and the wine of the area. There was no reference to music.

>   *The town of Castroville is surpassingly beautiful and even now in its infancy, is quite flourishing. It is settled with French and German emigrants.*
>
>   *We found shelter in Castroville with one of the Agents of the Colony, in a small tenement that was appropriated, as a home and magazine. We slept in the magazine adjoining the bed chamber of the proprietor and his wife, who was a chatty little French woman, and who did all in her power, as woman usually do, to make one comfortable. And, here, let me remark as worthy of mention, that in all our wanderings in Texas, we have never met with a female who seemed unhappy or discontented with her condition, while the men are too often grumblers.*
>
>   *Fortunately for my spiritual comfort I early discovered in to Castroville a cask of the richest Rhonish wine which by some magic or other had found its way here from the Banks of old Father Rhine. This wine was probably brought here as a sample and another year we might expect the vintage of Texas to produce a similar kind. The country abounds with the richest kinds of grapes.* [355]

But make no mistake about it. This was not Old Europe.

> *We learn from The San Antonio Texian of the 3rd instant, that five persons were murdered by a party of Indians supposed to be Comanches, near Castroville, while engaged in opening a farm. On the 25th, a Mr. Forat of Castroville, had a horse stolen from his very door, says the Texian; three more were taken from a neighbor of his and one killed. It is stated on good authority that the Indians have of lately killed many cattle and committed many other depredations on Cow House bayou.*[356]

Below San Antonio, south to the Gulf of Mexico, the central corridor of Texas was thinly settled. There were only a few towns, but they were distinguished ones. Take a town like Goliad, for example. Goliad, sacred because of the massacre there of 342 Texans during the War for Independence, was founded in 1749, as a mission to the Indians and a fort, called *La Bahia*. When the missions were abandoned and the settlement secularized, its settlers were principally Mexican and Indian. After the Revolution, it was in large part deserted, many of those of Mexican ancestry finding it prudent to return to Mexico. Anglos started moving in the 1840s, but its Spanish culture was not erased. [357]

Goliad had Indian problems. A band of between twenty and thirty "visited the neighborhood of Goliad, plundered a house and stole several horses." The citizens fought back.

> *Mr. Isaac W. Johnson, with eight young men and lads, went out immediately in pursuit and came up upon the Indians, at about 11:00 o'clock at night. Mr. Johnson ordered a charge and it was so promptly executed that only a few Indians could mount and escape*

> on their horses, while the others fled on foot. The Indians fired several guns and many arrows, as they fled, but without effect, although there was imminent peril... In the morning, the little company gathered its spoils - nine horses and mules, saddles, bridles, ropes, buffalo ropes, blankets, a shield and many other objects.[358]

A couple of years later, Lieutenant King of Capt. H.E. McCulloch's Ranger company, with seven men, at nightfall encountered eleven Lipan ApachesIndians and "a considerable number of horses, which they were driving off." A fight ensued and King was slightly wounded. Next morning, Capt. McCulloch chased after them and at about twelve o'clock came in sight of the Indians, then only seven in number, from which it is supposed that four were killed in the fight of the night previous". Capt. McCulloch chased them about 15 miles. For the sake of speed, the Indians abandoned the horses and other things they had stolen. "The horses, which were afterwards ascertained to have been stolen from the neighborhood of Goliad, were recovered and a considerable amount of booty thrown away by the Indians in their flight." [359]

Refugio is another town that traces itself back to Mexican rule, when its population was half Mexican and half Irish. Like Goliad, it too played an important role in Texas' quest for independence, the scene of the Battle of Refugio, when many of its Texas defenders were captured and executed by the Mexicans. History repeated itself, a half dozen years later. In 1842, the town was again captured by the Mexicans in an offensive against Texas. All but two of Town's men were taken prisoners and sent to Mexico.

Nor was Refugio immune from Indians. In April, 1851, the fourteen year old son of a Mr. Hart who lived in Refugio, rode out of town and a few hours later "his horse returned without his rider, with Indian arrows sticking in his body." They searched for the boy but did not find him, leading the Rangers to conclude "The boy was probably made prisoner or else his body would have been discovered."[360] Four months later, the boy was recovered from the Comanches who had in fact captured him. The youngster described how "his horse was at first shot by the Indians and thus being on foot, they seized him, mounted him on another horse and bore him off. The next night after taking him he says they seized and rode away with Col. Lott's horses, riding them up into the mountains and, as is their custom, setting them loose." He also gave a glimpse of what life was like as an Indian prisoner. "He speaks of his being compelled to subsist on horse meat, as a hardship he was exceedingly loathe to endure. It constitutes the principal food of these savages. The lad seemed to be rejoiced at his escape from a captivity so cheerless and happy, almost beyond measure we assume, at the prospect of soon returning to a father's fireside, to endearments of home and a civilized life."[361]

San Patricio Hibernia - St. Patrick of Ireland - was founded in 1828, even earlier than Refugio. Most of its first colonists were from Ireland and they numbered almost 500, mostly cattle raisers, at the time of the Texas Revolution. The streets of San Patracio also became a battle ground, with nearly a dozen of its defenders killed and double taken prisoner, to be carried off to Mexico.

After annexation to the United States and the War with Mexico that resulted, Texans no longer needed to fear their neighbor to the south. But that did not mean that they had nothing to worry about. Indians and bandits were frequent visitors.

Indian depredations

During the past months, the town of San Patracio has been several times visited by thieving Indians.

> *[Once] they were discovered in the moonlight and pursued by several young men who fired among them, and, it is believed, wounded some of them. [On] their last visit on the night of Saturday, the 30th of May, they took every horse belonging to the town and within three miles of it. Col. Lovemore, who resides more than three miles below town is the only man who has a horse left to ride upon in San Patricio county. The stocks of these people are scattered about the prairies. Their corn is suffering for tillage and they are left without the animals necessary for taking care of the one or cultivating the other. They were conjectured to have been Tonkewas."*[362]

But were they? Another report from San Patricio suggested that the horse thieves had conducted "their exploits under the cover of night and dropping arrows at suitable places, they have heretofore succeeded in leading many to believe that the robberies were committed by Indians. It is now believed that there are a number of Mexicans, and some Americans, engaged in this lawless pursuit."[363]

Finally, at the southern end of the central corridor of Texas was the town of Corpus Christi, which lies on the Gulf of Mexico. Its origin can be traced back to 1832 when Henry L. Kinney, an adventurer/promoter, who was to become a powerful figure in south Texas through annexation, set up a trading post there. He reportedly hired forty men to protect it. Upon annexation, Corpus Christi showed great promise as a seaport to the world as well as an entranceway to south central Texas, and was "now vying almost with Galveston, in life and importance."[364] But before the town could develop too much, something had to be done about the Indians.

> *We learned from a gentleman who lately arrived from Corpus Christi that the business of that place is almost entirely destroyed. Scarcely any traders have visited it for several months. Only ten or a dozen families remain in the place, and if it were the not the County seat of Nueces county, it would probably be entirely abandoned. The trade has all been diverted to settlements along the Rio Grande and the Mexican traders prefer to purchase at those settlements rather than to venture across the wild country between the River and Corpus Christi. Hostile Indians and thieving Mexicans are almost constantly lying in wait at Sel Colorado and other streams to intercept the traders.* [365]

Another report added:

> *The continued depredations of the Indians with impunity at Corpus Christi and its vicinity has almost destroyed that fair portion of the State, depopulating neighborhoods and settlements that were just springing into existence. Near Corpus Christi, they have murdered citizens within gunshot of that place and driven away large quantities of stock besides destroying other property for a considerable amount. The loss of Col. Kinney alone is several thousand dollars. At one ranch belonging to that gentleman they drove off 120 head of gentle horses, besides killing and driving away a great number of cattle.*[366]

The State Gazette reported that from April 1, 1849 and the end of that year, twenty eight persons had been killed by the Indians, many others wounded, and $28,000 worth of property destroyed near Corpus Christi.[367]

Plans were made in 1848, however, to cut a road to Corpus Christi from San Antonio, 120 miles to the north, and, by 1851, things were looking up for the town:

> *The country around Corpus Christi is also improving. New settlements have been opened all around this thriving town. No Indians have visited this section for several months and the inhabitants are beginning to feel quite secure from Indian depredations.*[368]

West Texas

In 1848, West Texas encompassed anything west of the frontier, which lay along a line of Forts in a north - south orientation, running from the Red River to the Gulf of Mexico. Modern day Fort Worth was one of these forts, marking the beginning of the frontier. Over the course of the next decade, as more and more settlers arrived and pushed the frontier back, new forts were erected in the Nueces and Pecos River regions as protection against the Indians. On the other side of the retreating frontier lay the Rio Grande River and another string of American forts earlier erected in the War against Mexico. The land between the moving line of frontier forts and those westward on the Rio Grande was treacherous, occupied entirely by hostile Indians, who were becoming increasing aggressive as their hunting lands were reduced and their conflicts with whites multiplied.

For years, Texans had envied the trade between the towns of St. Louis and Independence, Missouri, with Santa Fe and other Mexican towns.[369] The famous Jack Hays, Texas Ranger, hero in the War against Mexico and unequaled Indian fighter, was commissioned by the citizens of San Antonio to find the best route across the hostile frontier.[370]

El Paso had been Hays destination. The westernmost city in Texas, it sits on the Rio Grande River. It was near a pass through the mountains, through which the Spaniards could travel north to Santa Fe and even farther to the Missions in California. While modern El Paso can trace its history to the 1820s, its surge forward came when gold was discovered in California and it became a stop of the overland route to the Pacific. DeMorse, was there, if only in print, at the birth of El Paso county in 1850. It was by then already an active place

> *The people of Texas will be gratified to hear that the county of El Paso had been duly organized. The election went off in fine style, on the 4th day of March, and at several of the precincts, especially at this town, we had splendid balls in honor of the extension of civil law. This is a fine country and has 5,000 inhabitants.* [371]

Not only was El Paso the gateway to the west, it also held promise as a first class agricultural region, if it were not for Indians, Indians and more Indians

> *"If this valley were cultivated by an energetic American population, it could yield ten times the quantity of wine and fruit at present procured. Pears, peaches, quinces, figs and apples are produced in the greatest profusion. The climate of this country is most salubrious and healthful. The inhabitants here suffer more from the attacks of the Apaches than from any other cause. They are frequently robbed of all they possess in one night by the incursions of these lawless plunders. Ten companies of dragoons, however, would*

drive them from their hiding places in the mountains and put an end to all their depredations." [372]

No doubt about it. El Paso, like the rest of West Texas, was plagued by Indians. *The Standard* had scores of items about "great depredations committed by the Apache and Comanche Indians" including killings[373], thefts[374], attacks on the mail riders[375], and kidnapings [376]

There were other settlements south along the Rio Grande, below El Paso, such as Praesidio and Eagle pass. Two thirds way down the River was the town of Laredo. Founded by the Spanish in 1755, it had a population of 1,700 at the commencement of Texas Revolution. In the 1846 War against Mexico, it was captured by the Americans.

The town of Brownsville, lay on the north side of the Rio Grande, about 22 miles from it empties into the Gulf of Mexico. The town developed in association with nearby Fort Brown, built in 1846 at the time of the conflict with Mexico. It was baptized quickly and sharply by being bombarded later that year by the Mexicans in the Battles of Palo Alto, Resaca de la Palma and Palmito.

After the war, the citizens of the town that grew around the Fort soon realized that Brownsville was well situated from a commercial standpoint. Across the Rio Grande River was Matamoros, a Mexican trading town of some substance. Brownsville, lying along the coast, itself was ideally situated for ocean trade with American and European. Moreover, its steamers could make their way up the Rio Grande in the proper season all the way to Laredo and even farther to Praesidio. By combining with Matamoros, it could also be the gateway to the many towns of Mexico.

By 1853, Brownsville was indeed flourishing and its trade routes expanding. The large Mexican American population in Matamoros was beginning to have its effect upon the citizenry of Brownsville as well. All in all, Brownsville seemed to be a diverse and tolerant community.

> *The City of Brownsville is situated opposite the Mexican town of Matamoros on the left bank of the Rio Grande, or Rio Bravo del Norte, 25 miles south from its mouth in a direct line, and was named after the gallant Major Brown, who was killed during the bombardment of the fort, which also bears his name, situated in the immediate vicinity of the city. Brownsville is to be considered at present as the great emporium of the south western frontier. Perhaps the most novel feature, considered with the city is the character of the trade which is almost exclusively foreign. In this respect, she probably differs from every other town in the Union. Of the amount of this trade, we have no statistical information, but it cannot be less than 4 or 5 million dollars the past year.*
>
> *The commercial marine employed in the business of Brownsville consists of several sea and river steamers, besides lines of packets to New York and New Orleans. Of a population of the same size numbering a little over 4,000, there is perhaps no city in the country wielding a capital so large as this. Brownsville is advantageously situated with respect to communications with the interior of Mexico. There is a fine river and vegetation of 300 miles to the Rio Grande and Roma, and good roads from thence to Monterey, Saltillo, Durango, Zacatecas, San Luis Potosi, Guanajuato and the city of Mexico, besides being the near the route to Chihuahua and our own province of Santa Fe. There are several fine steamers plying on the river to the ports above and connecting Point Isabel and Brazos harbors with the city, and two lines of stages and a train of several hundred wagons connecting them by land. In*

point of situation, there is nothing very attractive to the eye. The country above is flat and covered with eternal chaparral, but the climate is the most healthy and desirable in the world. It is true that the days are hot, but the nights are magnificent and more than compensate for dust and sultry days and the slight inconvenience of a new city. es. A fine market house has already been erected having and several public buildings are shortly to be commenced. In approaching the city, from the river, for the first time, one is struck with the number and style of the buildings in a city where less than three years ago, the Indians raised their war whoops in defiance at the still larger city of Matamoros.

Brownsville like most American cities numbers several churches and public schools and is becoming almost as moral as a New England village. Social intercourse between the cities is fast wearing away the mutual prejudices of the different races and the beautiful Spanish language is beginning to be spoken in our streets and drawing rooms. In exchange, our style of dress is the only commodity not considered contraband - our language is decidedly so and probably will never be admitted. Upon all national and festive days, there has been an almost completed fraternization among all classes, civil and military, of both countries. [377]

The treaty with Mexico, ending the war, provided that the United States would prevent the Indians, north of the Rio grande, from raiding Mexican villages along the river. The following item describes the Texas Calvary in an engagement with the Comanches. As the following item reprinted in *The Standard* illustrates, it was not an easy task.

FROM THE RIO GRANDE

Latest accounts from Saltillo represent that the Comanches have made a descent in large force upon the Mexican settlements of Parras and Saltillo, robbing and murdering in every direction. Major Lane of the Texas Calvary, with 60 men of his command, had a fight with them and a large force has been sent to his assistance, to enable him to drive them back to their homes in the mountains. The following is an extract of a letter written by Major Lane to a friend in Saltillo, describing the engagement:

We had a fight yesterday with 120 Comanches. The red devils got wind of our approach and were formed in battle order and bold array to receive us. I ordered a charge and we dashed into them in gallant style. They received us in good order but were soon put to flight and we kept up a running fight with them for two miles or more, killing thirty and wounding many others. We pressed upon their mountain ponies so much that they finally dismounted and took to the mountains on foot and the pursuit was given up. Our poor friend W. H. Bell was killed in the charge and McNurty and two others wounded. The men fought well and can whip Comanches on any ground. I start for Parras tomorrow with my whole command, again in pursuit of the Indians who, we understand, are in a large force in that neighborhood, some say 900 strong. They have been devastating the settlements, killing the Mexican hombres and carrying off the women. This you know is unchristian like and we go to show our gallantry in defense of the fair. Mount and come with us. [378]

While, upon annexation, the frontier forces of Texas Rangers were replaced by U.S. soldiers in central Texas, the

Rangers remained on duty along the Rio Grande for most of another decade. Rangers were used to patrol along the river and were effective. A series of forts in West Texas in an effort to control the Indians and protect the settlers built. One of the earlier ones, constructed in 1849 and named after a fallen officer in the War with Mexico, was Fort Inge. It sat on the east bank of the Leona River in what is now Uvalde county. Due west of San Antonio, the fort lay almost midway on the road to the Rio Grande. Garrisoned with two companies of the 1st Infantry, the post consisted of a dozen buildings, including a hospital, all white washed and shaded. A parade ground sat in the middle. Fort Ewell was another frontier outpost, this one on the Nueces river in La Salle county and meant to protect the road from San Antonio to Laredo. It had been built in 1852 and garrisoned with mounted riflemen. Fort Ringold, built in 1848, was up the Rio Grande River from Brownsville. Rio Grande City grew next to it.

Indians were certainly a problem to the settlements along the Rio Grande, but they were not the only one. Another came in the form of Mexican bandits and patriots, who continued to view the Anglos as intruders. *The Standard* was full of tales of these *banditti*, who attacked travelers en route from or to Mexico. When caught by the Rangers, their punishment was quick and final. "Shot while trying to escape" was often the official report. [379]

Outbreaks of cholera were all too frequent and a report from Brownsville indicates. "It has been very bad here. For the first two days, there was an average of 23 deaths and then a great number of citizens left for the mouth of the Rio Grande River and up the river. For the last 11 days, there has been an average of eight deaths per day in a population of about 700. Among the deaths, were P. Violette, S. Smith and some 10 or 12 Galveston and Houston folk. Louis P. Cooke and wife died within 8 hours of each other." [380]

Indians were not immune from the disease which first

make its appearance in a party of Comanches on the San Gabriel. "Several of the chiefs have fallen victim to the disease. The Indians were flying in every direction, completely panic stricken." [381]

In addition to all the other dangers faced by the traveler or settler in West Texas was criminal violence. There was law on the frontier, to be sure, but there were also many rough characters, some of whom had come to the West as men on the run. Justice was dispensed quickly in West Texas, sometimes after formal legal proceedings[382], sometimes in the Court room of "Judge Lynch."[383]

As forbidding as the land beyond the frontier was, the possibility of amassing great wealth, either in its natural state as gold or its modern age currency, trade dollars, compelled some to cross West Texas. The hardships of a wagon train from Lamar county during its two month trip across the wilderness, en route to the gold of California, was described in a report to *The Standard*.

> *For a distance of about 200 miles, we have had bad grass and water. This made it necessary to delay a great while on this part of our trip. The grass is entirely dried up and there is a distance of 70 miles where not a drop of water is to be had. It lies on the east side of the Puerco, a dirty little stream about 25 yards wide with perpendicular banks, it runs with great rapidity. Some fish were caught in it. Cat fish only. Between the Puerco and the Rio Grande is a mountainous country, though which we succeeded with the aid of an Indian pilot to get good passes for our train.*
>
> *I am now fully aware of [the peril] of an undertaking of this size, situated as we were encumbered with families, the uncertainty of water, the exposure to the stampede by Indians in the Pass through the*

mountains, the dreadful sand hills and drifts etc, any of which could have proved destructive, especially to the feeble and sick, the tender female and the child.[384]

The International Scene

The Citizen of Clarksville, sitting on a bench on the square and reading *The Standard* could learn not only what was happening in town, around the county and the region and even throughout Texas, but, with *The Standard* as his magic carpet, he could see the whole world. The New York papers carried the news of Europe and beyond and DeMorse passed some of it on to his readers.

Internationally, the world of the 1850s might be mistaken for today, although the players have changed from time to time. The English were fighting the Shikhs in India. France and England together declared war against Russia. Persia [Iran] was induced to declare war against Turkey by a direct promise from the Emperor of Russia, to remit the debt due by Persia. There was cholera across Europe and the Far East. Earthquakes in Turkey. The May 28, 1853 issue of *The Standard* reported a fight at the Church of Holy Sepulchre in Palestine between Armenians and Greeks on Easter Sunday. In Prussia, there was reference to "the Jewish question" and " a petition to restore rights to Jews."

Most, of course, of this news from faraway places was read and quickly forgotten. Sometimes, however, what was happening abroad was recognized in Clarksville.

For example, one of the two major events in Europe during this period were the so called Revolutions of 1848. All across Europe there was unrest. Crops had been bad for the prior three years and a liberal, politically frustrated middle class stirred the pot.³⁸⁵ The roots of those revolutions was our own American Revolution and the revolutions in France, Mexico and Texas that followed it. For the first time, a self governed society had been established that was built on the concept that, unlike serfs or slaves, no man was subjugated by nature to any other man.³⁸⁶ Texans were aware of these struggles over seas. "America" wrote DeMorse "applauds the French revolutions and the advent 'of liberal principles in the eastern world', recognizing that they are 'but an echo of the same great principles on which are founded the prosperity and advancement of our own Republic.'" ³⁸⁷ Regarding the Town's Fourth of July celebrations, DeMorse noted that "The memory of the era is hollowed in these times, by the imitations it has induced among our struggling bondsmen of Europe."³⁸⁸

The second event in Europe of interest to America was the Potato Famine in Ireland. It was to kill two million Irish.³⁸⁹ Another two million of the suffering souls fled Ireland, mostly to America, to begin a new life.³⁹⁰

The May 6, 1847 edition of the *Standard* contained an item about the horrible famine in Ireland and the sympathy it engendered in the town of Doaksville, part of the Indian Territory, in what is now Oklahoma, not far north of the Red River and Clarksville. The benefactors were refugees themselves, having been forced by the Indian Removal Act of 1830 to emigrate westward.

> *Relief for the Irish -- A meeting of the citizens of Doaksville, Choctaw Nation, was held a few days since and one hundred and fifty three dollars, immediately subscribed for the benefit of the starving Irish. Considering how far in the wilderness Doaksville is situated, its small population, the fact that nothing but unprompted sympathy for distress elicited their aid, and its very great distance from the scene of the famine and*

from all active efforts in its behalf, induced the subscription, we consider it very credible to the citizens of that little place. [391]

Within the United States

Domestically, there was a revolution underway in America also, but not of blood or violence as in Europe. In the 1830s, the Industrial Revolution had been an equally dramatic upheaval. Many aspects of American life changed - some for good, some for worse - with its onset. It introduced to America machines and manufacturing processes that yielded standard, uniform products and, in doing so, changed the country from a collection of more or less independent, rural, agricultural communities into a nation dominated by the cities and the manufacturers. [392] Now *The Standard's* classified could offer "ready made" clothes and machine made farm implements, among other modern miracles.

There were miracles in communications too. The telegraph, invented in 1845, made messages almost instantaneous and opened up all sorts of opportunities from trans Atlantic cables to a the weather forecasting business[393]. By 1852, there were 14,000 miles of telegraph wire laid, mostly in the northeastern United States.

The railroad was to transportation as the telegraph had been to communications. By 1852, there were 12,500 miles of track in the United States. The demand across the nation for building railroads was huge, but the supply was limited and the price expensive. [394] It would be well after the Civil War that either the railroad or the telegraph would have much impact on Texas.

Agriculture had its own leaps forward. First among them[395] was the McCormick wheat reaper could cut 15 acres a day with three horses. Before, a farmer could not get enough workers to cut wheat. Now he could do it with his sons. Another invention that would change life in America for a dozen decades to come was that of the sewing machine. One person with a sewing machine could replace three or four hand seamstresses, maybe more. Bradshaw's Telegraphic Sewing Machine bragged it could do the work of 8 and could be worked by a child.[396]

Improvements in weapon making also would affect the settling of the west. There were "Jennings repeating rifles", the Sharp patent rifle, used by the mail guard from San Antonio to El Paso and a new pistol -"90 rounds a minute, carrying a ball 40 yards farther th any pistol now in use, and that it is also much lighter and is in every respect superior to Colt's celebrated pistols."[397]

The Californians' shouts of "gold" were heard across the nation. Everywhere, the fever possessed the adventuresome and thousands upon thousands of ordinary citizens dropped what they were doing and went west to find their fortune. The great rush began in 1849 and continued for several years. California's population grew from about 14,000 in 1848 to 100,000 in 1850, to 250,000 by late 1852. Many came from America's established eastern regions. The *Memorial,* a newspaper in Plymouth Massachusetts, the landing place of the Pilgrims in 1620, reported: "We doubt that any town in New England will send a greater portion of its male inhabitants to California than Plymouth. The number of our townsmen destined thither will not fall short of 75 or nearly one fifth of the entire voting population of the place."[398]

A good number of the adventurers came from Clarksville -15 of them - and another 104 from the counties adjoining Red River County.[399] The journey across Texas and into California was very dangerous. There was no food en route. The temperature could soar to well over a hundred and there was no shade. Water and grass for the horses were scarce and hard to find. It was easy to get lost, broken down and disheartened. The worst threat, however, were the Indians, the Comanche who would swoop down on horseback or the Lipan Apache who would lay in ambush. At least two Clarksville parties were attacked by Indians en route to California. Others from Clarksville found profit - as much as $100,000 - in driving Texas cattle to California to resell.

The right to vote is essential to a free society. It had been won in the Revolution against England of 1776. During the first decade of statehood, the citizens of Texas participated in three Presidential elections, those of 1848, 1852 and 1856.

Before annexation, DeMorse described himself and his newspaper as without a political agenda. In the beginning of statehood, he maintained the paper's political neutrality. However, a year or so later, a second newspaper, *The Western Star*, moved into Clarksville. Unabashedly pro Whig in its political preference[400], the entry of the *Western Star* compelled *The Standard* to surrender the pretense of objectivity it had previously assumed. Its appearance "renders unnecessary, if not improper, a continuance of neutrality upon our part, believing, as we do, in the truth and justice of principles and systems to which the party our neighbor represents is bitterly opposed."[401] DeMorse revealed he followed the Democratic banner[402] and why, then dramatically unveiling a new slogan for *The Standard's* masthead:

> *Believing that the Democratic Republican party, is the one of the present day which combines most of the elements of pure Republicanism; believing that the Whig party is the party of the privileged class, or of those who would make themselves such and that by its success, the few would be advanced at the expenses of the interests of*

the many; believing that money would always have the attendant privileges and influence increased and that the struggle between Whigs and Democrats in at last, minor questions aside, is the struggle between capital and the masses, we proclaim our self, now and forever, a Democratic Republican and upon our Standard we inscribe our motto

"EQUAL RIGHTS PRINCIPLE BEFORE MEN, OPPOSITION TO CHARTERED MONOPOLIES"[403]

The first U.S. election in which the people in Texas participated was that of 1848. At the time, Texas had 20,748 eligible voters, among its white population of 100,508.[404] DeMorse became intrigued with the process whereby Americans rule themselves and *The Standard* spoke of little else it seemed from May 1848 until the final tally was published in December.

The Democrat Polk had used his four year term, beginning in 1844, to protect American borders by obtaining California and the American southwest in a combination of conquest and purchase. He chose not run in 1848. A three-way contest among Democrat Lewis Cass, Whig Zachary Taylor and Free Soiler Martin Van Buren, emerged.

The Whig candidate General Taylor, had been a hero of the just successfully completed War against Mexico.[405] DeMorse and *The Standard* clearly favored the candidate put forth by the Democrats, Lewis Cass and disliked his opponent.[406]

In the coming contest for the Presidency, we hope to make the Northern Standard one of the most efficient of the advocates of the rights and interests of the Great Masses of the People and shall advocate the election of the candidate selected by the Democratic National Convention without regard to our personal preferences, because, with us, the success of the cause is first, of the candidate, second. Still, we trust to see our choice LEWIS CASS, the choice of the Convention and we think the chances of his nomination better than any of the others."[407]

Each week, *The Standard* carried a big advertisement for Cass, gave enthusiastic notices of Democratic "Meetings" and applauded all things *pro* Cass.

Raise the Tall Poles

Our fellow citizen J. C. Hart, raised on yesterday morning, by his grocery at the corner of the Public Square, a tall spire of the forest, at which about 70 feet from the ground, dances a white banner upon which the words are displayed

"Liberty & Democracy
Cass & Butler"

There should be raised in every village in Texas, these lofty evidences of the grateful recollection which Texans maintain for their friends.[408]

The rallies and barbeques of the period have their counterparts in today's election regalia. But it is not all "hype" and was not then either. There were serious issues involved in the 1848 election, not the least of which was the increasing friction between Northern and Southern sections of the country over the arguably related issues of slavery and the right of a "general" or federal government to decide issues that states had traditionally tended to themselves. Taylor pledged to leave the question of the extension of slavery "to the unbiased action of Congress." Cass, on the other hand, pledged to veto any bill embodying the principle.

As their first election day approached came, DeMorse reminded those who "from the lapse of years, to have forgotten the mode "of voting for certain electors, who then vote in the Electoral College, for a candidate." He passed along from a paper in Georgia that the results of the election might be "projected" as early as the following morning:

Presidential Elections. A Busy Day. The day on which the next presidential election will take place, the 7th of November, will be a busy one. Two million of voters over the country record their choice for a national ruler, and, as the telegraph communications would extend by that date over near the whole country, enough returns in the election may be known and telegraphed by the next morning to indicate with tolerable certainty whom the Nation has chosen. [409]

Texas was not connected to any telegraph and the votes in Clarksville would not be relayed to Washington D.C. soon enough to be part of any projection. Nonetheless, it had what DeMorse stated to be a "full vote", Red River County had 554 vote out of an eligible 571. Cass received 369 of them and 185 for Taylor and Van Buren of the Free Soilers none.[410] But, sadly for Editor DeMorse and the Democrats, Taylor narrowly won the national vote. DeMorse broke the news in a somewhat less than gracious manner:

The Battle and the Defeat

It becomes our duty as a faithful chronicle of events to record the destruction of the fair hopes which our friends have entertained of the election of the standard bearers of the faith and another defeat of democracy, similar to, if not fully as desolating, as that of 1840. Again has the plain banner of principle been pressed out of the field by the followers of military glory, and by the man worshipers, money changers and fanatics.[411]

Despite his intensity in the 1848 election, DeMorse seems to have lost some of his interest in the national scene. There was so much in which to be involved in locally. Texas was growing by leaps and bounds. [412] Taylor died in office. His vice president, Millard Fillmore of New York was never a true Whig. He modified many of Taylor's objectionable positions and persuaded the Northern Whigs to support the Compromise of 1850, which postponed, but did not resolve, the increasing division between the North and the South on several issues, principally slavery.

In 1852, the Democrats and Whigs both nominated moderates for the presidency. The Democrats selected New Hampshire politician Franklin Pierce. The Whigs, abandoning Fillmore, chose military hero General Winfield Scott, a man with undefined political views. This was appropriate. The Whig party was breaking up. Many of the anti slavery Northerners of the party, upset at the acceptance of the Compromise of 1850 which continued slavery in Washington D.C. and enacted a Fugitive Slave Law to return runaways, had defected from the ranks of the Whig Party, joining the Free Soil party instead.

The Standard was, of course, a Democratic newspaper and endorsed its slate. It carried that endorsement every week.

But while in 1848, DeMorse had devoted a substantial part of *The Standard* to election news and reports as early as the beginning of summer. The election in 1852 was different. Pierce had good credentials. [413] It was only until a few weeks before the election that DeMorse began to actively promote the Democratic candidate:

> *Let every good Democrat remember that the Ides of November are approaching rapidly. Now is the time to be up and doing for Pierce and King. Every vote cast for them is so much gained for Southern principles, Southern rights and the Union.*
>
> *The Union! Untouched and hallowed as when first recorded as such by our venerated sires of the Revolution, may it long remain!*
>
> *Pierce's grand sire battled at Bunker hill. Can we believe his off spring to be less of a patriot? No, no he has served his country in the Council and on the field. In her legislative halls, he lifted up his voice for the Constitution his grand sire had fought for and he has spilt his blood for her honor on the plains of Mexico.*
>
> *Let us then boldly do battle for the Northern man with the Southern principles, who has repeatedly vowed his horror at abolition, Free Soilism and kindred errors, who has even declared that his dead body should be trampled, upon before they should triumph.*
>
> *Vote all of you, both Whigs and Democrats, for the man who sustains the Constitution.*[414]

The Standard waited to the last issue to tell his readers why this was such an important election, citing the "dark cloud" of abolitionism ever ready to obscure the Republic's horizon:

> *This will be our last issue before the Presidential election Tuesday next will be decided and, with it, the momentous questions bearing upon our future destiny among the nations of the earth. Perhaps, no other election has ever been so important in its results as this one must prove. Our very existence as one undivided and glorious Republic may depend upon the choice of the people for the next Presidential term. Does it not behoove us then to look well at the present aspects of affairs?*
>
> *As Southerners, we must recollect that there is a dark cloud ever ready to obscure our horizon, originating and existing only among fanatics and corrupt politicians, it is true, but they have assured too much importance to be longer disregarded.*
>
> *Let us ask whether Scott or Pierce will best combat against this deadly foe for the peace and harmony of the entire Union. Who will best sustain the principles of Union and Democracy, the Seward and abolition candidate or the man who has battled for the Constitution and Southern Rights?*[415]

Although a "dark horse" candidate, who secured the nomination because the three leading candidates were deadlocked, Pierce carried the "Banner", taking all but four states and receiving received 254 electoral votes to Scott's 42. The final tally of the popular vote in Texas had 13,530 for Pierce and 4,988 Scott . In El Paso county, it was a perfect victory - 650 for Pierce and no votes for Scott.

In the election of 1856, it was neither the neophyte Republican party that worried DeMorse nor the expiring Whigs. The former would be a foe for future, the latter was one of the past. Instead, the enemy was a familiar one that appears every so often on the American political stage, excites the attention of the electorate for a couple years and then dies out amid public disgust. It was termed Nativism - anti-foreign sentiment. A couple of years earlier, a new, secret version of it, had appeared on the scene, called Know Nothingism. Cloaked in secrecy it was anti immigrant and anti Catholic. [416]

There had been considerable unhappiness among the native born citizens of English /Scotch Irish/Dutch descent with the influx of Irish and other Catholic foreigners. [417] DeMorse was not among them. While no one could accuse him of being fond of "Popery", he detested their persecutors. *The Standard* reprinted accounts from its eastern exchanges of the mob conduct of the party's members - church burnings in Boston, Massachusetts and in Bath, Maine; a Catholic priest tarred and feathered at Ellsworth, Maine pursuant to a vote taken at town meeting; riots in Newark, Philadelphia, and St Louis, among them. Soon he mob moved from the street to the polls.

DeMorse was fond of his "dimes" as he called the money he earned from selling his papers. But he even bragged about not caring about losing them because he alienated Know Nothing readers.

> *The "15 Know Nothings" [from Grayson] addressed a letter to the editor of this newspaper and who, in conclusion, very politely said to us: "You will do us the favor not to send your newspaper to us any longer. You will please send your accounts to your agent here (if you have any here) and we will [pay him] what we respectively owe you" had very much raised our hopes of making a tolerable collection in Grayson but [did not] .Whether in politics or payments, we fear their characters are very unreliable. They are gay deceivers.*[418]

Know Nothingism did not survive. But, although it had dimmed by 1856, it nevertheless had an effect as one of several agents that shaped the election of that year and the birth of the Republican party.

The battle lines had been drawn. The Democrats, defending popular sovereignty on the question of the extension of slavery in new territories, nominated James Buchanan of Pennsylvania. The Republicans, in their first presidential contest, denounced the expansion of slavery and advocated a program of internal improvements. They nominated John C. Fremont, an explorer of the Far West with no political record. The Native American, or Know-Nothing, party, beginning to crumble, nominated former President Millard Fillmore. The few remaining Whigs endorsed him also.

Perhaps, not recalling that he had the same thing about the 1852 election, DeMorse rallied *The Standard's* readers in support of Democrat Buchanan. The continuation of the Union required it.

Presidential Election

Never, since we became a nation, has a more important election taken place than that which is to come off on the 4th of November. The permanency of our glorious Union is involved in the contest. Should Fremont be the successful candidate, we have no other notion but that this would be the death knell of the Union. The position of the South would be that she could not in justice to herself, her interests, her institutions, submit to the licentious domination of Northern fanaticism and the aggressions of Abolitionist and black Republicans must be met either by separation or civil war.[419]

If one could read the election results, as a gypsy reads tea leaves, to predict the future, the conflict to begin five years later could be clearly seen. Nineteen states were for Democrat Buchanan with 174 electoral votes. They were all southern and western. Republican Fremont won 10 states, receiving 110 votes. All of New England, New York, Ohio, Michigan and Wisconsin went for him. Fillmore won only in Maryland. Buchanan had polled 1,833,000 of the popular votes to 1,340,000 for Fremont and 872,000 for Fillmore. In the North, Fremont received more votes than the other two candidates combined. In Red River County, however, he received not a single one, 388 having been polled for Buchanan and 235 for Fillmore.

While the strength of the showing by the Republican Party and the marked division between North and South should have been cause for fear as to what the future had in store for the Union, it did not seem to affect the victory celebration in Clarksville.

DEMOCRATIC JOLLIFICATION

The Democrats of Red River county have postponed their grand jollification until next Wednesday, December 3. All are invited to attend who rejoice in the elections of Buchanan and Breckenridge to the highest offices in the gift of the American People. We expect many Democrats from surrounding areas.

Come one and come all and let us rejoice together, for our country is saved from those who would tear down our great temple of Liberty. [420]

On the Horizon

By the end of the 1850s, there was an undeniable gulf between the peoples of the North and the South. Each side was convinced that it was following the course set out by their ancestors in 1776. Many in the North proclaimed the right of all citizens to own property, to work for whomever they please and at the wage to which they agree as fundamental rights in a democracy. There was a lot going on in the North at the time. The Industrial Revolution had come. Telegraphs made communication instantaneous. Railroads were being built. Factories and mills, filled with farm girls and immigrants from Europe with their work ethic, were producing products for the rest of the nation and abroad. To such busy people, the slow moving, agricultural society of the South with its large slave population, planter "aristocracy" and the poor white slaveless tenant farmers seemed to be lazy, backward and almost decadent.

The South, of course saw things much differently. Since DeMorse, although Yankee born, was now a Southerner and *The Standard* was a southern journal, he tended to give the Southern slant on things. A great part of the growing conflict between North and South, they claimed, was, quite simply, the offensive attitude that the North had adopted in its strident "holier than thou" preaching about the Southern society's sins. Abolitionist writings had been antagonizing white Southerners for years, but *Uncle Tom's Cabin* especially enraged them. They felt the object of an attack of lies, glibly accepted as the truth. Take, for example, the item that *The Standard* reprinted from one of his exchange papers, *The New York Tribune.*

> *Southern newspapers are continually publishing advertisements like this: I keep dogs trained to hunt runaway Negroes. They are of the best breed and are*

> *sure to catch the game if the scent is not too cold * * **
> *Stop the runaway. My boy Bill has run off again. He*
> *may be known by a buckshot wound in the face, received*
> *when he was caught the last time. $50 will be paid for*
> *his recovery, dead or alive.* [421]

DeMorse's response would not have been unlike those of his readers in Texas.

> *This is a positive falsehood, fabricated for the*
> *base purpose of lessening the people of one grand*
> *division of the Union in the estimation of the others. The*
> *scoundrel who can slander one half of his countrymen*
> *deserves to be hung up on a lamp post, which, we trust,*
> *will be his fate yet, unless he mends his courses. The*
> *heartless wretches that make use of these positions to*
> *stir up ill will between brethren, have a day of reckoning*
> *in the future. It will be a terrible one to some of them*
> *yet- we earnestly hope- it will not be for all.* [422]

The truth was that the North suffered from many social shortcomings as did the South. Throughout the 1850s, *The Standard* printed a number of items that illustrated the hypocrisy of the North. For example, it pointed out that the righteous people of Connecticut voted 4 to 1 (19,148 to 5,353), to deny the free Negroes of that State the vote. Or that the Pennsylvania Senate did the same by vote of 16 to 10. Wisconsin would not give it either. That was better treatment than Blacks received in Indiana. There, as well as in Delaware and Illinois, Negroes, it was said, were not even allowed to enter into contracts or own property. *The Standard* also printed pieces about how the Northern Chapter of the Sons of Temperance would not admit black members and how at their convention in New York, the Episcopal Church refused to accept the colored churches into the Episcopal Union or admit their delegates to the Convention. DeMorse advised the North not to waste its sympathy on the slaves in the South but to turn its attention to slaves in New York City where 35 immigrant laborers from Ireland died in a single day from heat exhaustion. What an outcry there would have been if 35 slaves had been worked to death. Slave owners do not kill valuable property. DeMorse concluded that "it is only the free laborer, working for his daily bread, that can happen to."

Make no mistake about it. Slavery was an ugly institution. Older than the Bible, it had been practiced continuously through the 1700s in every place in the world. Undeniably profitable[423] and necessary to harvest cotton[424], slavery was widespread in the United States.[425] The slave population in America was valued at a billion dollars in 1850 dollars. Some could justify to themselves that slavery was not immoral.[426]

However, by the 1850s, increasingly more citizens recognized the inconsistency between the institution of slavery and the aspirations behind the revolutions in America in 1776, France in 1789 and those across Europe in 1848. England prohibited slavery and the United States had declared illegal trading in slaves from Africa.[427] Some Northern states were abolishing slavery within their borders. The abolitionist movement was growing strong and *Uncle Tom's Cabin* sold in unimaginable numbers here and abroad.

Abolitionists, however sincere in their mission to free all men, were viewed in the South as dangerous trouble makers who were encouraging slaves to runaway and even revolt. *The Standard* warned against some "abolitionists disguised as missionaries" in the Indian Territory, north of Red River.

Choctaw Missionaries
We are not opposed to Missionaries being sent to

> *Indians on our borders as long as they know and tend solely to their business as such. But we are opposed to the plan of sending avowed abolitionists among them, who are disposed to meddle with the institutions of the South, particularly slavery. It is a well known fact that all the runaway Negroes from this place always fly to the Indian Nation and it is equally well known that they are being encouraged and harbored by reason of the influence propagated by these Reverend Northern Gentlemen, and, in truth, it is difficult for a master to recover his slave once he has gotten among them.*[428]

Positions polarized. Soon some Southerners, Texans among them, were past the issue of slavery and into underlying issues as to whose way of life - North or South - was really "American" and that the South, until now victimized by the evil North, did not need to deal with Yankees to survive, but vice versa.[429]

A group, DeMorse among them, were neither abolitionists nor Southern ultras, or Nullifiers, as they became known. Instead they stood for preserving the Union:

> *There are some I know who talk lightly of what would happen the destruction of our national Union. But I cannot. I believe it would be the abasement and ruin of our national life, of our central supporting principle of strength and glory as a free people. It is my sincere conviction that the dissolution of the union with civil and servile wars, dogging after, would be a calamity second only to the expulsion of the Christian religion from the continent. If we speak of such an event without inward terror, we know not what we say.*[430]

At the beginning of the decade of the 1850s, DeMorse was "proud to say that there are as many Union men in Red River country as there are in any county in the state. Nullifiers and ultra southern men are as scarce as hen's teeth. They stand no show at all."[431] However, ten years later, he could not say that. There were more and more Nullifiers about. The presidential election in 1860 would turn out to be the pivotal DeMorse had been predicting the prior two would be. The Democratic Convention in Charleston in the springtime of 1860 was deeply divided. Stephen Douglas was the favorite of Democrats from the North, but would not yield to Southern insistence on a platform defending slavery. The Democrats nominated Stephen Douglas and the Southern Democrats, who called themselves National Democrats, nominated John Breckinridge. In addition, John Bell was nominated by the Constitutional Union party. At their convention, however, a united Republican party nominated Abraham Lincoln.

Although as events would prove, the Civil War was but months off, there was no sign of animosity in DeMorse as he encouraged the citizens to prepare for the upcoming July 4.

Eighty four years ago the independence of the United States was declared. On that day a nation was born, destined to outvie any of antiquity in the form of government, the dispensation of its laws, and the fruits of its resources. Everywhere is felt the power of these United States, the strength of its institutions and the stability of its government. Over every quarter of the globe floats the star spangled banner waves and the American citizens in foreign lands were beneath its folds, conscious of its protection. Throughout the Union, in every little village and hamlet in every state, the influence of the day will be felt. For one day at least internal dissension and political wrangling should be forgotten and all unite in celebrating our nation's birth day.[432]

The split between the Northern and Southern Democrats would prove fatal in the election. Stephen Douglas received about 30% of the vote, John Breckinridge about 18% and Bell about the 12%. The clear winner, but with only 40% of the popular vote, was Abraham Lincoln.

The election results triggered mass meetings like the one held in neighboring Lamar county in the Baptist church "which was filled to overflowing" yielded a report by more than a third of those in attendance:

> *Whereas for the last 30 years there has been gradually organizing at the North a great sectional party, whose sole object is the abolition of slavery in the southern states; and*
>
> *Whereas the recent election in the United States for President and Vice President has resulted in the election of Lincoln and Hamlin, the candidates for those offices proposed by the abolition party; and*
>
> *Whereas, we the citizens of Lamar county regarding said election as a clear and unerring indication of public sentiment at the north in reference to our constitutions; and*
>
> *Whereas, the firsts law of nature is self preservation*

> *RESOLVED*
>
> *First that we regard the election of Abraham Lincoln and Hannibal Hamlin as a declaration of hostility on the part of the north against the institutions of the south and so regarding their principles; we are in*

favor of resisting by the best and most effective means which can be adopted by the states to be injured

Second, to form as convention of Southern States to negotiate and reach a compromise with the [Free states];

Third, that we regard the so called "Personal Liberty Bills" which most of the Northern States have enacted as a direct nullification of the Fugitive Slave Laws and the Constitution and as such an outrageous aggression upon our rights as cannot and will not be tolerated; that we are in favor of requiring of our northern brethren an unconditional repeal of these obnoxious acts, also our just and equal rights in the common territories of the United States and in short to all the rights to which we are entitled under a strict and literal interpretation of the Constitution. Should they agree with these, we will remain in the union and support and cherish it as heretofore; but should they refuse these guarantees, then in our judgment we should form a separate Confederacy of such states as will unite in the movement.[433]

The die was cast. Soon fighting would break out in the War Between the States and Texas would join the Confederacy. Neither Clarksville nor Red River county would ever be the same again. Nor would the rest of Texas, the Unites States or the world .

END NOTES

1. America was news hungry. In the year Texas joined the Union, there were 1,855 newspapers published in the United States and only 1,891 in the rest of the world! In America, a program of "exchanging" papers had developed whereby a paper, like *The Standard,* each week would send a copy of its paper free of charge to, for example, the *San Antonio Western Texian* or *The New York Tribune*, each of which would reciprocate by sending a copy of its paper to *The Standard*. In this manner, the New York paper would obtain its news about the Texas frontier from *The Standard*, (which itself might have gotten it from *The Western Texian* which was closer to the frontier). In exchange, *The Standard* and, ultimately, *The Western Texian* would receive the New York and even foreign news it needed for its readers. To encourage the process of news dissemination across the nation, the Federal government allowed these newspaper exchanges to be postage free.

2. July 24, 1851

3. Indeed, this population was huge when contrasted to the size of the population a dozen years earlier upon its Independence from Mexico. In 1836, the entire population of Texas was barely 52,670. Of this number, 30,000 were Anglos from the United States and western Europe, 3,470 Mexican, 14,200 Indians and 5,000 slaves of African descent.

4. March 26, 1853

5. It was not much of a court house, a two room log cabin built in the center of the square. It would stand for two decades, until 1855, when a new one would be erected.

6. Clarksville had not been the first commercial hub in the region. Jonesborough, which lay 25 miles northeast of Clarksville on the Red River, had that honor. Sam Houston first set foot on Texas soil there on December 2, 1832. So did Davy

Crockett three years later. Jonesborough, named for the ferry owner Henry Jones, was heavily used as crossing from 1817. Reportedly, it had a population of 2,350 people by 1834. In 1843, it fell victim to the flooding of the "great freshet" of that year. It wiped out the buldings and shifted the course of river channel a mile away. Jonesborough declined rapidly after that and a proclivity to malaria. Many of its merchants and citizens moved to Clarksville.

Nor was Clarksville the original county seat for Red River. La Grange, known as Madras today and located a few miles northeast of Clarksville had that distinction.

7. May 13, 1846

8. December 5, 1846

9. June 8, 1850

10. September 10, 1853

11. February 18, 1854

12. May 28, 1859

13. January 29, 1859

14. *We see that a call has been made by the citizens interested in the welfare, prosperity and orderly conduct of the town, for the purposes of electing a mayor, Town Constables and Board of Alderman and enforcing our corporate laws and we say God speed them in their work for we have long felt the necessity for such a body. Every night can be held the reports of firearms upon the streets and the whooping or halloing of drunken men and to strangers and persons visiting the place, such operations are not calculated to make a favorable impression or give character abroad. We have a good jail for the purposes of keeping those transgress the laws and bid defiance to peace officers and a little bit more expense for improvements upon our streets collected for corporate Texas would not be a useless expenditure.* December 3, 1859

15. January 11, 1851

16. March 13, 1847

17. The grave of James Clark's father, Benjamin, is there as well. A sergeant major in the American Revolution and a Methodist preacher, he had accompanied his son James to Texas in connection with a contract he had to feed the Indians of the Five Civilized Tribes, who were being relocated, across the Red River, in what today is Oklahoma. Reportedly, Benjamin's slave, Uncle George, is buried at his feet. The "Hanging Tree" was also said to be in the northwest corner of the cemetery on Washington Street. It was high post oak tree estimated to be over 200 years old. Also called "Page's oak", it is said that several men were hung there in 1837 for murder.

18. November 26, 1846

19. December 24, 1846. Clarksville had its own "house and sign painter", G. B. Brem.

20. There was another fire in 1859 at the blacksmith shop connected with the carriage making and painting establishment of G.B. Brem and Sons. Fortunately, there had been a lot of rain the days before and no breeze, the fire was confined to the building where it originated. However, "so rapidly did the fire extend over the building but that little of the contents was saved. Several persons lost portions of carriages and wagons which were undergoing repairs. Some guns and pistols were also destroyed. We have not heard the loss estimated but we should suppose not less than from 600 to 800 dollars." April 30, 1859.

21. October 4, 1851

22. November 1, 1856

23. June 16, 1847

24. March 11, 1846

25. August 8, 1858

26. March 5, 1859

27. November 1, 1856
28. October 7, 1846
29. August 5, 1854
30. September 10, 1853
31. May 17, 1851
32. October 11, 1851
33. September 15, 1849
34. June 16, 1847
35. June 16, 1847
36. July 17, 1847
37. July 12, 1851
38. March 11, 1846
39. January 1, 1859
40. February 5, 1859. In the same issue was the report that Mr. Gill of Red River County sold his Jonesborough plantation of about 4,000 acres - for $50,000. It cost him a dollar an acre twelve years before. In other words, he made a $11.50 profit per acre.
41. November 4, 1854
42. October 18, 1851
43. DeMorse saw agriculture in more than just in economic terms or as of personal relaxation. He believed, as a Jeffersonian Democrat, that farm life was essential to the American value system. *The Standard* would often reprint the wisdom expressed by others regarding it. For example, "The Plow - its one share in the bank of earth is worth ten in the bank of paper." Or "He who encourages young men in the pursuit of agriculture is doing a good work for the morals of a society a hundred years hence. The brightness of the plowshare will prove to be as better security to our republican institutions than

all the long windy speeches in Congress." August 13, 1853.

44. October 12, 1850
45. June 23, 1847
46. November 1, 1856
47. November 15, 1851
48. June 23, 1847
49. May 31, 1851
50. June 2, 1855
51. DeMorse grew fruits of all kinds at his home not far from the public square:

> *We have been for some years looking for toward the time when the fruits of the larger region shall be plentiful here, but so far the attention given to apple orchards has been general as we could wish, considering the unquestionable fact that good apples can be raised here. We have the apple, pear, peach, cherry and plum trees growing upon our own lot, some of each of which have commenced bearing. All of them that are in favorable situations, are thrifty in appearance and growth, and, yet while only a few have borne and those only begun, the promise is good.* June 9, 1849

52. January 3, 1852
53. August 15, 1846
54. November 7, 1846
55. November 21, 1846
56. August 14, 1847
57. January 6, 1849
58. August 23, 1851
59. December 11, 1852

60. August 12, 1854

61. November 5, 1859

62. December 2, 1848

63. *We have always believed that tobacco may be successfully raised here but have been told that the climate was not sufficiently humid enough in the summer. In Jasper county, we have been informed that a very fine quality of Cuba smoking tobacco has been raised. In 1843, we think it was the late Dr. Smith of Bowie brought from Cuba some seed, which his brother Judge Smith tried the cultivation of, but that did not come up. Year before last, some fine Cuban tobacco seed was sent to us by the patent office and was divided among several old tobacco raisers who took much care in planting but did not get them to germinate.*

We are probably too far north for the successful cultivation of Cuban tobacco but the quality raised in Kentucky and Virginia it seems to us should grow here. February 28, 1857

64. February 28, 1857

65. February 15, 1851

66. March 11, 1854

67. September 5, 1857

68. March 25, 1854

69. August 5, 1854

70. December 6, 1851

71. July 31, 1852

72. June 4, 1853

73. October 22, 1853

74. June 24, 1848

75. May 12, 1849

76. May 8 1858

77. August 5, 1854
78. June 10, 1848
79. April 12, 1851
80. July 2, 1853
81. December 31, 1853
82. January 1, 1859
83. October 21, 1854
84. January 19, 1856
85. March 30, 1850
86. November 29, 1856
87. April 22, 1848
88. March 17, 1849
89. April 14, 1849
90. April 14, 1855
91. April 19, 1856
92. May 3, 1856
93. May 3, 1851
94. February 4, 1854
95. November 25, 1848
96. January 3, 1852
97. December 25, 1852
98. July 1, 1848
99. October 8, 1853
100. March 20, 1852
101. January 26, 1856
102. that is, the county by its Commissioners.
103. October 1, 1853

104. September 13, 1851

105. October 8, 1853

106. July 10, 1852

107. November 1, 1856

108. December 12, 1846

109. December 6, 1851

110. Charles DeMorse and Texas could not be blamed for dreaming of a railroad. Railroads were all the rage in the United States, since Peter Cooper introduced Tom Thumb in 1830. By 1852, there were 12,500 miles of track in the United States. Massachusetts had expended $40 million on railways and, even before it had been completed, it was operating at a profit. The demand across the nation for building railroads was huge, but the supply was limited and the price expensive. For example, the 800 workers of Rogers & Co. of Patterson, New Jersey were turning out just seven locomotives a month. More than 3,000 days work were needed for a single locomotive. At that rate, the expansion of a rail system as far west as Texas would take a decade. Yet, the finished product - that locomotive that required 3,000 days of work to build - could travel at 80 miles an hour, a unheard of speed, and one that fueled the fervor even further. Advocates for proposed rail lines crisscrossed Texas, just as the train tracks would a decade or so later. Meetings would be held in county seats during court week where promoters would offer stock in contemplated lines in exchange for pledges of land. Proposals abounded. Northern capitalists offered financing of rail road from Vicksburg, Mississippi to the Texas line. It would cost, from track to engines to station houses, $17,000 a mile and they thought the work could be done in 3 years. Another railroad was to go from Houston to Austin, and cost $8,000 a mile. DeMorse rationalized his support of these ventures, even though he knew they were not realistic at the moment.

> *Railway Movements... Meetings have been held and addresses given in at Paris and Bonham relative to the proposed road and the donations for it. Our impression is that moderate donations will be obtained in both counties.*
>
> *We have resolved the matter in our head and have come to the conclusion that, notwithstanding all objections raised to the plan as now developed, it is better to assist in its promotion that to allow it to fail and pass a few more years in inadvertness, leaving the richness of our section of the country underdeveloped and withholding from ourselves that prosperity which must follow the completion of the road. If the donations are made and the road built, the donors lose nothing, for the contingency, upon which the lands are to be given, are to vest in the company in the putting of the road in operation, from Galveston to Red River. This is expressed in the deed specifically.*
>
> *So taking all things into consideration, we believe it is best that our citizens should act energetically, give generously and immediately.* October 7, 1848

111. April 30, 1853
112. November 6, 1847
113. May 21, 1853
114. April 3, 1852
115. January 28, 1843
116. February 4, 1843
117. August 7, 1844
118. September 4, 1844
119. The recently completed War with Mexico and battlefields of chapparal grass were the origin of his analogy.
120. December 9, 1848

121. May 12, 1849

122. June 30, 1849

123. July 7, 1849

124. July 21, 1849

125. July 28, 1849

126. The first two weeks of August 1850 was the only period over a dozen year span that reported temperatures in the range of 98 - 100 . One might wonder, whether it was regularly as warm in the 1840s and 1850s as it is now, when the century mark is reached a number of times each summer in Northern Texas.

127. May 3, 1856

128. January 12, 1856

129. August 23, 1856

130. January 15, 1859

131. February 12, 1859

132. March 5, 1859

133. March 5, 1859

134. April 2, 1859

135. November 12, 1859

136. December 31, 1859

137. January 7, 1860

138. October 8, 1853

139. December 22, 1849

140. March 3,1849

141. Women , of course, could not vote and, in many jurisdictions, married women could not own property in their own names.

142. December 25, 1847

143. June 30, 1847
144. July 16, 1859
145. August 4, 1849
146. July 30, 1853
147. July 14, 1855
148. October 8, 1853

149. It would six years later. *The Standard* reported in its March 5, 1859 that "from our office building we see the large frame of the new Presbyterian Church, in its commanding position overlooking the eastern part of the town."

150. April 5, 1856
151. November 20, 1852
152. April 16, 1853
153. April 23, 1853
154. December 3, 1853
155. June 15, 1850
156. September 16, 1854
157. February 17, 1855
158. January 12, 1850
159. January 12, 1850
160. October 8, 1853
161. June 5, 1858
162. June 19, 1857
163. December 25, 1847
164 . June 16, 1847
165. December 25, 1847
166. December 25, 1847

167. March 3, 1849

168. February17, 1849

169. September 18, 1852

170. Few Americans today know much about the disease of cholera. It is an infectious disease, usually caused by the drinking of water, contaminated with the bacterium *vibrio cholerae*. The first symptom is profuse diarrhea, often accompanied by vomiting, then, a rapid loss of fluid and salts, severe muscle cramps and thirst and cold wrinkled skin. If lost fluids are not replaced, coma and death may follow in 24 hours. It is endemic to India and periodically spreads westward to other countries. It is not a new disease and it is thought to have carried off 70,000 in Israel during the time of King David.

171. May 12, 1849

172. September 15, 1849

173. November 19, 1855

174. October 8, 1853

175. October 8, 1853

176. February 21, 1857

177. February 10, 1849

178. August 15, 1846

179. December 22, 1849

180. July 2, 1853

181. July 2, 1853

182. Six years later, DeMorse, commented that the new courthouse in Sherman was "to be a copy in size and arrangement as that in Clarksville." He complained that the Clarksville one should have been larger, at least 50 by 75 feet. He also warned that in the Sherman courthouse, "if it follows closely the Clarksville pattern, the space below will be foolishly wasted and the offices made far too small for immediate use and the shape of the roof will give the courthouse an almost

unprepossessing appearance." He concluded, however, that "the Clarksville courthouse is better than any other near it, but it is far from being architecturally in good taste or conveniently divided within the first story." May 8, 1858

183. February 28, 1852

184. March 29, 1856

185. September 30, 1854

186. March 29, 1856

187. January 30, 1847

188. April 6, 1843

189. August 27, 1842

190 . December 3, 1859

191. September 3, 1842

192. *Charles DeMorse:, Pioneer Editor and Statesman*, by Ernest Wallace, at p. 13.

193. October 25, 1856

194. *The Undersigned commissioners appointed by the County Court of Red River county will receive until the first Saturday in August, the 7th day of the month, proposals for the erection of the walls of a brick jail to be built in the town of Clarksville. The size of the building is to be 25 by 36 feet, two stories of ten feet each, wall 18 inches thick, one partition wall of brick to each story. The undertaker to provide his own materials and submit his proposition by the thousand of brick. The work to be done by the 25th of December, ready to receive the roof. A specific plan will be ready in a few days and can be seen at the offices of J. C. Hart. The building must be of the very best material and put up in the most substantial and workman like.*

J. C. HART   EDWARD WEST   D. K JAMISON

July 10, 1858

195. March 20, 1852

196. August 28, 1852

197. Con artists are not recent creations as evidenced by the following item:

> *Two men named Flynt and Mullens were arrested in Town on the first day of Court last week, upon suspicion of Negro stealing and dealing in counterfeit coins. The two men are residents of Harrison County and on their way home from Arkansas, having a Negro man with them as they passed through here. The circumstances connected with the transaction are of a most suspicious character. The Negro had made an appointment with a Negro of Mr. William Donoho, to meet him the night of the day they had left town. Mr. Donoho's Negro suspected and, at night, at the appointed time, the Negro of Mullens came for him and was arrested and confined; and, on being searched, was found in possession of $320 of counterfeit American gold.*
>
> *The Negro stated several things against the men Flynt and Mullens, and among others, said that he had been sold several times (giving the names of the purchasers) and then run off again by Flynt.*
>
> *In the morning, Mullens came in looking for his Negro and was arrested. At night, a party of citizens pursued Flynt, who was found on the other side of the Sulphur. Mullens and Flynt are under a bond to appear at the next term of the District Court. The Negro has escaped.* October 16, 1844

198. Coins were usually not counterfeited and paper money was not yet in circulation in the United States. Rather, bank notes, issued on out of state banks – Texas law did not allow banks at the time – were usually the instruments altered.

COUNTERFEITERS

Counterfeiters have been in operation in St.

> *Francisville. Spurious notes of the Louisiana State Bank and the State Bank of Indiana were set afoot. An individual who passed some of the money was pursued as far as Waterloo where he was arrested and brought back.* March 16, 1843

199.   *Smuggling-We understand that goods to a large amount have recently been smuggled into the Country near the mouth of the Sabine River. This has been effected by clearing small vessels to New Orleans for some point in the southwest corner of Louisiana, which instead of stopping at their ostensible destination, proceeded to uninhabited spots on our own coast between the mouths of the Sabine and Trinity Rivers and there discharged their cargoes which, from there, were hauled into the interior.* June 22, 1843

200. DeMorse was quick to warn the community of risks like this. For example:

> *FRAUDULENT LAND TITLES.--We would advise our friends, and the public to be on their guard in respect, to the Land titles of De Leon's colony, as we learn from a respectable gentleman of Western Texas, that the late commissioner of that colony, who has been residing in Mexico since the revolution, has lately returned to Victoria, and has brought with him many titles to Lands granted to members of his family, the originals of which are not and never have been filed in the General Land Office of the Republic of Texas, as by law required. Some of them are now offered for sale, and we understand that a number of titles have found their way to New Orleans for Market, where every exertion will be made to dispose of them to the innocent purchaser.* June 21, 1845

However, it is likely that, if a law were broken here, it was the claimant under the Spanish land grant that was being treated illegally, not the Texans who now claimed title to those lands. Before the Revolution, the Colony of DeLeon was comprised almost entirely of Mexican colonists, although some Irish and Italian settlers had also been recruited to the Colony. All the townspeople, including the Mexican settlers fought on behalf of the Republic of Texas against Mexico. But, after the battle of Goliad, white Texans attacked the Mexican population of DeLeon and attempted to drive them from their land, with some success. The titles in dispute here may well have been those of the Mexicans driven off their land.

201. Usually, the theft was the work of professionals. Sometimes, they would work on their own, like the one, reported by DeMorse, who, after arriving in town on foot and, reserving a room for the evening cooly in broad daylight "stepped up to a rack at the public square and unhitched a horse belonging to a young man named Arnold and left for parts unknown."

202. An interesting glimpse of the both operations of a gang of horse thieves and the criminal justice system, which exchanged a light sentence with one defendant for a list of the other gang members:

The large number of horses stolen from our citizens in Texas has become the most alarming evil and led in some cases to the summary vengeance of the Lynch law.

We lay before our readers a confession of a horse thief at a late term of the Court of Burleson County. We and trust that it may lead to the breaking up of the horse thievery gang declared to be in existence in this state and well organized

"When he [Hugh Allen] first came to Texas, he met with Tom Middleton at Buck Horn in Austin. The accused was drunk at that place. Tom Middleton employed him to work for him. They immediately left Buck Horn for the town of Bastrop and, at the direction of Middleton, the accused stole a horse; then they started

for the town of LaGrange and, on their way, stole two horses, one a paint. Middleton, up until this point, never told the accused that he was engaged in the regular employment of horse stealing. They then stole two on the Colorado River and, then on their way back to the town of Chappell Hill, Washington County, they stole three, a little black, a bay, a sorrel. They then stole two, a bay and a brown at the White's, near Colonel Kirby's. Accused said that they often stole horses in the day as well as in the night. They then went to Col. Wm. Sledge's plantation, where they stole an old black mule.
Middleton then went up the country to Mr Griffiths for the purposes of stealing a fine horse. He did not succeed, but stole two others on his return. The accused stated that he had been engaged in stealing horses with the following named persons, to wit: Nat Berry, Bill Berry, both killed at San Antonio; three of the Samuels, who live down the county; three Batton boys, who live on Lost Creek; Hillard Putnam and Vandy Putnam; he, does not know where they live as they are young men having no wives; old Jim Cox, Burleson county, William Hutton, Reuben Dean, Washington County; Thomas Taylor of Eastern Texas, John Ake, a large raw boned man with sandy hair who lives in Arkansas and visits Texas for the purpose of stealing horses,

The accused says he has been shot at since he was in jail and thinks that Middleton did it, as he sent word that he intended to kill him for telling on the party. The accused was raised in the state of Alabama and came to Texas in July 1856. The name of his mother is Little; he is an illegitimate. The name of the man who raised him s Joe Allen and lives in Benton county, Alabama.

Accused stated that Tom Middleton had informed him that he [Middleton] had killed a Jew pedlar and took from him all his valuable property; this occurred in one

> *of the lower counties,*
>
> *The Jury then received the charge of the Judge and retired to consider verdict.*
>
> *They returned in ten minutes with the verdict of guilty, assessing the penalty as two years at hard labor in the penitentiary* December 12, 1857

203. In an August 17, 1861 item, DeMorse argued for a more drastic penalty.

> *We know of no work more efficacious for checking this work, as the immediate administration of Hemp, whenever the thief is found with the horse and the case is clear. We have always thought that the old law of the Republic was the best extant on this subject. That statute punished horse stealing with death. It is an offense so easy of accomplishment in this state, that Penitentiary punishment is not adequate to its prevention.*

204. October 7, 1854

205. September 5, 1857

206. February 24, 1855

207. October 12, 1850

208. January 31, 1852

209. Latin for "mine" and "yours".

210. November 7, 1857

211. April 9, 1853

212. June 4, 1853

213. June 11, 1853

214. June 18, 1853

215. July 8, 1854. The prime suspect in the case, Westerns, absconded on his bail and fled the jurisdiction, never to be heard from again. G. W. Frazer, indicted as an accessory, was tried, a

whole day used in getting a jury, seventy being summoned before the requisite number of competent jurors could be empaneled. He was acquitted after a two day trial. Miles Husband was also acquitted, a week later, after a separate trial. It was an evidentiary ruling that saved him. The jury could not find "a conspiracy" between Miles and Western so that, earlier statements Miles had made about poor Peabody, could not be introduced as evidence of intent.

216. June 19, 1857
217. July 29, 1854
218. March 3, 1855
219. February 13, 1847
220. May 4, 1850
221. March 3, 1855
222. January 12, 1856
223. July 9, 1853
224 July 14, 1855
225. February 21, 1857
226. March 7, 1857
227. June 19, 1857
228. June 28, 1858
229. March 10, 1855
230. June 11, 1853
231. September 13, 1851
232. May 10, 1856
233. May 24, 1856
234. June 9, 1860
235. October 4, 1856

236. January 21, 1854
237. July 9, 1853
238. August 4, 1849
239. June 28, 1856
240. July 5, 1856
241. April 5, 1856
242. April 9, 1853
243. September 26, 1857
244. October 23, 1858
245. October 23, 1858
246. July 22, 1854
247. June 28, 1858
248. June 24, 1846
249. July 2, 1853
250. July 2, 1853
251. July 9, 1853
252. July 9, 1853
253. July 7, 1855
254. July 10, 1858
255. July 9, 1853
256. July 6, 1850
257. July 2, 1853
258. July 10, 1847
259. July 7, 1849
260. July 1, 1854
261. July 8, 1848
262. July 8, 1846

263. July 10, 1847
264. March 3, 1855
265. March 8, 1856
266. May 4, 1850
267. June 2, 1855
268. May 3, 1856
269. November 17, 1855
270. January 1, 1853
271. December 25, 1847
272. January 6, 1849
273. January 3, 1852
274. January 6, 1855
275. October 2, 1847
276. October 2, 1847
277. May 6, 1846
278. February 3, 1855
279. January 19, 1856
280. January 12, 1856
281. January 19, 1856
282. Classicists believe the ancient Greeks played a game like football, called *harpaston*, the aim of which was to move a ball across a goal line by kicking, throwing, or running with it. It included ferocious tackling. Others claim that football originated in 12th century England and that, over time, divided, evolving into soccer and rugby, and then, in America, reunited to become what we, in America, call football.
283. June 18, 1853
284. July 2, 1853

285. July 16, 1853

286. August 16, 1856

287. August 23, 1856

288. August 23, 1856

289. September 4, 1858

290. By 1853, the United States had 1800 newspapers, more than three times the number in England and 400 more than the rest of the world combined, including England. Some of the American papers were quite large. For example, *The New York Herald* claimed a weekly circulation of 103,000, spread out over seven morning, twelve evening and one weekly edition, an average of 5,150 copies for each edition. *The New York Sun* claimed 330,000 copies per week, which divided among six editions, gives an average of 55,000 copies per day.

291. By 1854, there were nine newspapers in Texas devoted to religion, temperance or education

292. Six years later, there were even more papers, many with specialized interests. For example, 750 Whig and 850 Democratic newspapers were published in the United States. There were also seventy anti-slave papers, twenty relating to agricultural, forty six to the Temperance fight, two hundred with religious themes, and eight hundred and seven neutral and miscellaneous. New York led the nation with 433 newspapers, Pennsylvania 328 and Ohio 300.

293. *The Dallas Herald* was owned at first by James W. Latimer and William Wallace, who purchased the Paris (Texas) *Times* in the summer of 1849 and moved it to Dallas in the fall. John W. Swindells became co-owner in 1854 and, in 1859, owner and editor of the paper.

294. July 3, 1858

295. In 1853, without any sort of explanation, came the statement: "The editor of this paper has been substantially blind

for a week and cannot now see to read, nor does he now perceive the line with which the pen traces. Correspondents, who are not answered, will understand the cause. He hopes to be better next week." October 15, 1853. Next week's issue contained a plea for forgiveness of typographical errors because of his blindness as well a belief that the condition was "improving."

296. DeMorse had published an article describing the disbarment of a local lawyer, the facts of which he had received from another lawyer. He lost the case but the plaintiff was happy with the vindication and did not seek damages. This led DeMorse to proclaim that he was not giving any more reports, and, if the reader wants to know, he can "do it in the primitive way in which it was done before the Flood - come by and hear for yourself." Despite his outcry, DeMorse did not appear to have changed his style.

297. In 1853, DeMorse announced his new "Power Press", specially manufactured for him which would materially enlarge - adding a column to each page - the size of the paper without a price increase. DeMorse bragged that the new press made twenty two "impressions" or copies a minute, more than was needed at present, but "with the way subscriptions are pouring in from North Texas, we might be needing it within two years."

298. January 11, 1846

299. March 13, 1847

300. February. 11, 1846

301. December 18, 1852

302. December 18, 1852

303. August 7, 1852

304. July 26, 1856

305. "The hotels were all closed, stores shut up, the paper had stopped and many of the citizens had left." October 22, 1853

306. January20, 1849

307. September 2, 1854

308. October 8, 1853

309. October 9, 1852

310. December 16, 1848

311. January 12, 1850

312. December 24, 1846

313. The vineyard was scaffolded with trellises, seven feet high and hundred feet long and ten feet apart. Half an acre would be covered by ten trellises. "The produce of half an acre will be 530 bushels of grapes, which at $5 a bushel will give $2,650. If made into wine, the result will be 1950 gallons of wines at $1 per gallon, 60 gallons of brandy at $2 per gallon, at total of $2,050." February 15, 1851

314. The Trinity unlocked the agricultural potential of central Texas and changed existing market patterns. Cotton would be sent by River to Galveston, not overland to Houston or Shreveport, Louisiana. Traffic on the river was encouraged. Special vessels were designed and built with "subscriptions" from the planters and merchants on the river. The cost of getting the cotton crop to market directly affected the planter's profit. The worse that could happen to the farmer, if he also owned a piece of the steamboat, was that any high freights paid by him would only go from one pocket to another.

315. In 1848, the legislature reduced the size of Henderson county and at the same timed moved the county seat from Buffalo. The town's promise withered but it survived. Today it has a population of about 1800.

316. October 2, 1847. Buffalo, organized in1846, was on the eastern bank of the Trinity, high on a bluff.

317. His report on a marathon dance he attended there gives us today a glimpse of what was considered "a good time" more than a century and a half ago.

Dear Sir - Left Kaufman, on Thursday last, for Porters Bluff and arrived there on Friday morning. We stopped at the house built by Major Porter, now kept by Col Hodge, who has improved very much the character of its larder. One object of our travel to the Bluff was that there was to be a grand ball, assembling all the belles and the beaux of the country twenty miles around. As the evening advanced, in they came, in troops, and long before the night, the violins commenced and the more ardent of the dancers opened the fete. The majority, however, reserved themselves till beauty should become more lustrous in the glare of concentrated light. After dark, the work commenced in earnest. About 50 ladies were present and a large number of gentlemen, I cannot say how many. The music was excellent and the prompting clear and in good time. Cotillions were the order of the night exclusively. In new counties, of all others, dancing is done with a zest and at the Bluff it was especially so. Until eleven o'clock, next morning, the sound of the violin never ceased for more than three minutes at a time. I went to bed about Midnight but all night the violins sounded in my ears and, after breakfast in the morning, I went up to take a look at the dancers. The femines all seem exhausted and they hopped through the measure of the dance, but the men, either through better power of endurance or because they had occasionally withdrawn and recruited their energies, trod the floor with undiminished vigor. After breakfast, however, the number began to decrease. In couples and, in half dozens, they mounted up and rode off home, some to go twenty miles after dancing all night. May 14, 1853

318. *Having some lots to select at Taos, I concluded to stay until next morning. During the night, a heavy snow fell and the next day it was cold and the river being from hill to hill and no other traveler to cross, I had to wait till next morning. Taos (despite*

its name which would kill any other locality being identical with a little, mean sheep stealing village in the county of Santa Fe) is a growing place and will make a town. Col. Porter had a circular saw mill which furnished cedar lumber of which the town is building. The houses are all small, except for the hotel put up by the Colonel, which is a rather large, two story house, which is not quite finished, and not by any means well kept. This was apologized by the absence of the Colonel who was in New Orleans purchasing for the house. He has since died and I fear the town will feel the want of his enterprise and activity. I was informed that, upon his return, he would build a plank road, through the narrow bottom opposite the town, which would make a splendid crossing of it. As it is, it is probably the best crossing on the river and the only one that is passable at all times.
February 16, 1850

319. Although their births were not nearly so heralded, other river towns, like Bezzata and Pine Bluffs, suffered the same sad end.

320. When it lost the election to become Capital of Texas, there were some hard feelings, probably by speculators who had bought up valuable town lots and adjoining lands in the hope of great profit when the capital was moved there from Austin. The author of the following letter to DeMorse and published by him is one such fellow crying "foul" at the election. He too must have been a speculator for the article turns from complaint to sales pitch, suggesting that, if it is not to be the capital, then this beautiful site should be university center for Texas.

> *Tawakanah springs. It was not long since that this locality was voted by a large portion of the people of Texas to be their seat of government. By popular vote no choice was made, the number of localities in nomination, defeating the election of any one of them. By fraud and by the failure of the mail to carry the returns of the election to their destination, or perhaps, more correctly speaking, the determination of some interested that they*

should not get there, the voice of the people was set at naught and a locality not chosen by them and having no likelihood of having been chosen by them, has been determined to be the seat of government against their will.

It is indeed a beautiful place, helpful and in every way inviting, central too for the territory for which it was proposed as capital and for which had the returns for the first election been received, it would, at the next trial, have been selected by at least a 5,000 majority. It would have been at the center too of a land of plenty, with navigation within 30 miles and a dense population surrounding it. The people have been defeated but the beauty of the place and its natural advantages of locality still remain. The traveler who views it in his passage from east to west or west to east, never fails to look upon it with an admiring eye and with enthusiasm record the impression it makes upon him. Its destiny may be yet worthy of its natural advantages. The cedars, the rock, the limpid waters will still remain, and perhaps some day not far distant the beautiful hill of Tawakanah may become the seat of an institution of learning for the Lone Star State and Minerva preside where Ceres was not allowed to seat herself. January 10, 1852

321. *Some rocks standing up, like Druid's monuments, appear to be natural pillars standing as if the God or nature of some convulsion of the earth has placed them. They were none of them higher than perhaps 5 feet, but had an abrupt bold look, partially in consequence of the rapid decline of the hills behind them.* February 9, 1850

322. *I found the ground closely studded with large gray limestone rocks, rather flat and weather beatened and showing throughout a formation or rather an agglomeration of shells, the shape of which was still distinctly preserved, occasionally the hollow of the shell being outward on the surface of the rock,*

retaining all its original indentations. February 9, 1850

323. *Among these rocks the prickly pear and the species of the cactus known at the Turk's head were growing. At the northern end of the hill, I saw where rock was pried for bulding purposes and found that it came up in ledges with two flat surfaces in good size and shape for building.* February 9, 1850

324. December 22, 1849

325. The county was established on March 13, 1848. According to the census of 1850, the county had a population of 1,379 whites and 155 slaves living either in agricultural communities on Brushy Creek and the San Gabriel or in Georgetown, the county seat, was laid out during the summer of 1848.

326. July 6, 1850

327. January 23,1847

328. February 20, 1850

329. *We commenced operations by examining the banks of the ravine, which opened into the creek between the spring and the house. In the perpendicular soft limestone banks of the ravine, we found a number of shells and bones of fishes etc. which we readily disengaged, some with our fingers.* February 20, 1850

330. *After getting up the creek a mile or so, we found abrupt cliffs of limestone covered with the dwarf cedar peculiar to this region and in the spaces of the rock, midway between the top and the bottom, grew laurel and prickly pear.. . . I found among the cedars a few shrubs of the mountain laurel I had never ever before found them except in the mountains and from these I obtained some beans and for the third time I well try them back in our town. We also came across the specimens of the shrub or bush cactus which I had never seen but once before and then up at Bryant's Station, upon the Little River. I procured a spade and dug up some roots of this, which I will take to Clarksville with some other varieties. . . Before us, on the opposite side of the creek, the hill rose gently and the cedars was interspersed*

between the bare Elms and Pecans. A little below us, upon the opposite side, was another high cliff of rocks, surmounting which the autumn leaves were rich in their dyes. February 20, 1850

331. *The water was remarkably clear. We got to a place where the crags rose higher and the scenery presented itself in an arrangement of peculiar beauty. Below us, some 25 feet, was a basin of water, perhaps four or six feet deep, through which the mountain trout, the cat and the sucker swam along swiftly and were clearly visible as if they had been in a clear vessel on our table before us.* February 20, 1850

332. February 20, 1850

333. *The Company of Reynolds and Lok have exhibited two nights in this city. The performances were rather good and some of the feats well executed. Mademoiselle Josephine and other ladies are attracted to the company. The bright eyes of the lady equestrians would bring good houses were there no other inducement to attract the gay and the gallant. The attendance has been quite general, notwithstanding the scarcity of money.* September 23, 1854

334. *A new El Dorado is now being found in our own beautiful state. Rumors are rife of large finds of gold being found throughout the western portion of the country. We understand there is great excitement prevailing in Austin, San Antonio, Seguin, Gonzalez up the country and that several companies have left those points within a few days past in search of the hidden treasure and others are making ready to travel. These mines are found in the Upper Colorado, Hamilton's Valley and various other places and are said to be very rich, supposed by some to equal the best California mines. One person sold a piece of quartz in San Antonio for $25.* May 7, 1853

335. DeMorse's correspondent in Austin wrote him that "our early corn in this section is an average crop, all late corn is utterly destroyed. No rain having fallen in town for months, the creeks have dried up and the prairie looks like a nipping frost had

fallen upon it. A few more dry days and it will be a vast field of hay." August 23, 1856

336. November 24, 1855

337. *Increase in Crime - Scarcely an exchange reaches us that does not contain an account of daring robberies or murders. The State Times of the first instant says that, on 26th ultimo, a body was found in Waller Creek, near the residence of General Harney. Circumstances indicate that he had been murdered for his money. The remedy, and the only one, for this growing is a more rigid enforcement of the criminal law. Although indictments, we might say, almost by the hundreds are found by the different courts of the state every year, yet a conviction is scarce ever heard of. Many of the deaths by violence that take place in this state take place from affrays and the survivor is usually acquitted on the ground of self defense. In many instances, the acquittal is just and the accused is entitled to the sympathy of the community, but frequently his claim to such sympathy is more than doubtful. It is time that the men who constitute the juries of our country should begin to act upon the principle that "a just severity is mercy in the end." Men should be taught that it is safer and more honorable to avoid getting into difficulties and that a good character and gentlemanly deportment are a surer defense than a Bowie knife and a six shooter. But in all cases where such extenuations cannot be pleaded, the death penalty should be inflicted with infallible certainty. Those who have once tasted "of human blood", like certain wild beasts, ever afterwards have an appetite for the same and are continually seeking an opportunity to indulge their propensity.* July 29, 1854

338. In the 1800s, the German states, like Prussia, which were not unified into a single nation yet, were suffering from an overpopulation. As early as 1818, Texas had been promoted as an ideal spot for Prussian settlements, and many came, prospered and sent glowing reports home. The *Adelsverein* or Association of Noblemen of these German states, was organized in 1842 for

the purpose of purchasing land in Texas and relocating German citizens there. Before it went bankrupt in 1847, the group had brought 7,380 immigrants to Texas from Germany and the Low Land countries. Refinanced, the work was taken over by Prince Carl of Sohm-Braunfels (first cousin of Queen Victoria of England) who, as Commissioner General of the *Adelsverein,* spent a great deal of time in Texas, first purchasing suitable tracts for settlement, then preparing for the immigrant settlers and finally, assisting in settling them. He bought land on Lavaca Bay as a landing stage -first named Carlshafen, now Indianola - where the newcomers to America would be prepared for a journey inland to lands he had purchased for them on the frontier.

339. January 27, 1849

340. February 25, 1846

341. February 25, 1846

342. February 25, 1846

343 November 23, 1850

344. October 12, 1850

345. April 28, 1855

346 July 3, 1847. Interestingly, the contract "also stipulated that all future intercourse, trade etc shall be carried on under the Supervision of the United States Indian Agents." Under the Non Intercourse Act of 1789, only the U.S. government could make treaties with foreign nations, which the Indian tribes were considered to be.

347. August 15, 1846

348. June 4, 1846

349. August 5, 1854

350. *Business is brisk there, more so than it has been in the last 7 years. The price of prosperity is on the increase, a great influx of strangers, some coming in to make permanent settlements in the country, others on the lookout for suitable locations and*

some generated by curiosity alone. February 4, 1846

351. November 25, 1848
352. June 2, 1849
353. December 2, 1848
354. January 4, 1851
355. June 4, 1846
356. February 16, 1850
357. February 3, 1855
358. July 14, 1849
359. February 15, 1851
360. April 19, 1851
361. August 9, 1851
362. July 24, 1847
363. September 30, 1854
364. February 4, 1846
365. October 30, 1847
366. July 14, 1849
367. February 16, 1850
368. July 26, 1851
369. In fact, the ill fated Santa Fe Expedition of 1841 had been an attempt to wrest that trade away from Missouri to the Republic of Texas. It failed. The Mexican government took prisoner the caravan of more than three hundred Americans and $200,000 of trade goods.
370. new route to Chihuahua
371. June 1, 1850
372. March 17, 1849

373. *Indian Depredations on the Rio Grande*

On Thursday last our town [Brownsville] was thrown into a great excitement by the arrival of an express from Palo Alto announcing the startling intelligence that a numerous and formidable band of Indians had just made a descent upon that place and have already committed many acts of startling and savage barbarity. The stage from Port Isabel had been intercepted and the proprietor Mr. Bangs and Mr. Lombardo, a passenger, were taken prisoners. A train of transport wagons had already been taken between Brownsville and Port Isabel, containing much valuable merchandise.

Partial accounts have reached us about the acts of these savage marauders. Doreteo Zamora, a most estimable citizen, we regret to learn, was among the slain. Mr. Zamora had just elected under the treaty to become an American citizen. One of Mr. Zamora's sons was killed off at the same time, another badly wounded and his daughter, a girl of about 14 years of age carried into captivity. At the ranch Santa Olaya, two men were killed and a women and two children taken into captivity. From the Rancho delos Indois, Mrs. Willsey, the wife of Capt. Benjamin Willsey, his brother and sister in law were carried off captives. The aged mother of Mrs. Willsey persisted in following her children and did so for some distance, regardless of savage menace, when the Indians seizing her, tied her hands behind her, pierced her with their lances and arrows and left on the ground weltering in her blood, as they supposed dead. This poor woman, however, succeeded in reaching a neighboring rancho in a most shocking and mutilated condition and is now we understand a maniac. The destruction of property of this river has been immense. We learn today of the loss of 70 horses by one gentleman. June 16, 1849

374. *We have learned from Mr. Womble, the mail carrier from this place (San Antonio) to Laredo that, about the 10th of October, a party of Indians, about 30 in number, took from the neighborhood of the Rio Grande about 140 head of horses and*

mules- the property of Major Durst and others. The Indians were pursued by Durst, Walker and others but escaped, the rain stopping the progress of the pursuit. In their retreat, the Indians passed two mustang pens, killed several Mexicans

375. The usual semi monthly mail from Laredo to San Antonio did not arrive last week and there fears were entertained that the mail rider, Mr. Vestell, had fallen into the hands of the Indians, which proved to be too well founded. June 1, 1850

376. A gentleman of this town [Corpus Christi] has received a letter from a Mexican friend at Laredo, which gives an account of recontre with the Indians near that place. He said a party of 15 Comanches arrived at the Rancho Capitaneo and carried off a girl of about 12 years old whose father and other relations immediately called together the inhabitants of the other ranchos and pursued them but, being badly equipped, the force gradually diminished until only eight of their men were left, who being friends of the unfortunate captive and excited by a feeling of anger, resolved to pursue and punish them severely. On the 7th they overtook them at a place near the old Rancho de Dolores, near Laredo, and after a fight of more than an hour, rescued the prisoner. The Indians had three killed and the Mexicans three wounded, the former losing all their plunder and horses. Since that day, the Indians have returned in force and now range the line with perfect freedom, robbing the ranchos and destroying everything they can lay their hands on. July 14, 1849

377. November 8, 1851

378. January 15, 1848

379. A party of Texans was dispatched by the Commandant at Comargo to arrest the murderers. They were arrested, but escaped from their captors before reaching Comargo, after the manner in which Texans always allow such men to escape." June 9, 1847

380. April 7, 1849

381. July 21, 1849

382. *Howard Slaughter and the two Mexicans, who were severally convicted of murder at the last session of the District Court, and sentenced to be hung on Friday last, were accordingly executed. They all confessed their guilt at the scaffold and repented of the crime they had committed. The Mr. Rev. Chamberlain of the Presbyterian Church, at the request of Slaughter, made an impressive prayer in behalf of the prisoner, and the official priest of the Roman Catholic Church addressed those assembled in Spanish and English, expressing the deep sorrow and regret of the culprits against the laws of the country. The last words of Howard Slaughter were "Beware of liquor, because it has brought me to this."* February 15, 1851

383. *The trial of the offenders, though prosecuted we have seen in an informal manner, is said to have had a most salutary influence on those persons, of which there is said to be many in the county, who are disposed to be riotous and quarrelsome.* April 12, 1851

384. September 1, 1849

385. To a greater or lesser degree, the revolutionary movements, arose again in France and in Poland, Switzerland, Italy, Germany, Denmark Russia.

386. The American Revolution, as they say, "turned the world upside down." It created a Republic in which the common men (who up until now had no say) became the recipients of the absolute power to govern themselves. They elected representatives from among their number (Congress) to assist the President (a shadow of the former king) to govern

387. June 3, 1848

388. June 10, 1848

389. *The Dublin Nation,* quoted in *The Standard* of March 6, 1847, gave some idea of the horror:

> *In many counties of the south and west, hunger*

rages unalleviated, as it would in any country where there was no government at all. Stark multitudes stagger through the public faces with famine in their faces, thousands crowd to the poor houses - now become pest houses more of fever and are refused admission. Many even of the middle class live on one meal a day and are gladdened. Many more of the poorer classes eat once in every two days or in three and, which is stranger, live; and some lie in the ditches by the side of the road, turning their livid faces to God and others howl on men the curses which are evoked by despair. And all this is among a people with a government, an Executive and laws, and Boards of Works and a machinery and poor laws and everything but home grown food, which is stored in the graneries of the foreigner [England.]

390. In his February 6, 1847, issue of *The Standard*, DeMorse quoted an Irish Newspaper, the *Sligo Champion*, to describe the emigration:

The county people are still emigrating; hundreds of them take their departure from this port on every steamer that leaves for Liverpool. A few days ago the Richard Watson left our quays with her full number of passengers bound for New York. Such a thing was never heard of before in this part of the kingdom. Nothing could have induced these people to venture across the Atlantic in the depth of winter" DeMorse quoted *"except for the convincing idea that if they remained in this country, they would be exposed to the horrors of famine more appalling than the dangers of the deep.*

The May 6, 1847 edition of *The Standard* contained an item about the horrible famine in Ireland and the sympathy it engendered in the town of Doaksville, part of the Indian Territory, in what is now Oklahoma, not far north of the Red River and Clarksville. The benefactors were refugees themselves, having been forced by the Indian Relocation Act of to emigrate westward.

391. May 5, 1847

392. The factories, especially those in New England where the natural resources, including the soils, had become depleted, were, fed, via the new railroad, the raw materials of the rest of the nation. Using immigrants and girls from the over populated countryside, whom the agricultural society no longer could support, the factories sent back, on the return trains, manufactured goods of all kinds, consumer and industrial, for the rest of the country to buy.

393. *The Standard* passed on the clever idea employed by the Astor Hotel in New York City of using the telegraph and advising departing guests of the weather they might expect on their return trip home - the beginning of the weather forecasting industry.

394. For example, the 800 workers of Rogers & Co. of Patterson, New Jersey were turning out just seven locomotives a month. More than 3,000 days work were needed for a single locomotive.

395. Others included an improved cotton gin, a potato gathering machine that "digs the potato, separates it from the earth and loads them into the wagon" and one which would husk and shell corn at one operation.

396. Sadly, sewing machines lead to child labor. *The New York National Democrat* reported that in New York City there were no fewer than "50 sewing machines, powered by steam, which turn out an enormous number of pants each day, besides fine coats and other articles of appeal. One girl with the aid of a machine can turn out as much work as six girls can with the needle used by hand. The profits of the machine labor are enormous but it is the capitalist who owns the machine who realizes the gains." December 13, 1851

397. October 18, 1856

398. March 3, 1849

399. *The main company, which rendezvoused at Paris, was organized after reaching Cross Timbers. Captain Griffin of Lamar county was elected commander; Captain Edward Hunter of Red River county 1st Lieut.; Mr. Stewart of Hempstead county, Arkansas, 2nd Lieut; and Wm. H. Winlock of Red river county, 3rd Lieut. They numbered in all 104 men and had seven families and 40 wagons along with them.*

The pack mule company which started from Preston in Grayson county, had some 70 members.

Another considerable company, at last advice, was said to be assembling at Bonham. They were from various points below. April 28, 1849

400. The Republican Party, had not yet formed, although some of the Whig Party would be among the founders of that new party a dozen years later and would put Abraham Lincoln in the White House.

401. August 14, 1847

402. DeMorse endorsed the Democratic Party and its platform with such fervor that, years later, he came to be known as the Father of the Democratic Press in Texas. The Democratic Party is the same Democratic Party as exists today and which traces its principles to Thomas Jefferson.

403. August 14, 1847

404. Of course, none of its 35,038 slaves, 229 free blacks or women of any color could vote.

405. The Whig party, a major political force within the United States between 1834 and 1856. had been formed to oppose Andrew Jackson and the Democratic party. Its leaders included the famous Henry Clay and Daniel Webster of Massachusetts. They advocated an active federal role in the nation's economic

development such as programs for federally sponsored roads and canals, a high tariff to protect American manufacturers, a powerful national bank, and a go-slow policy on the sale and settlement of public lands. In 1840, the Whigs elected William Henry Harrison but Harrison he died soon after election and his vice president John Tyler would follow the Whig platform. he party. In 1844, the Democrats' candidate Polk recaptured the White House.

406. Taylor, had been the Commander of the United States forces in Mexico and DeMorse had roundly criticized him for being too lenient with the Mexicans whom he and other Texans, with memories of Goliad and the Alamo scarcely 10 years old, continued to hate. Moreover, Taylor was a newcomer to politics, having never been associated with any of the political parties. Indeed, he had never even voted before he was put up as a candidate for President. DeMorse considered the attention being given Taylor as a form of "man worship" as he called it. He thought it dangerous that the electorate could put its trust and the Nation's health in an unknown, untested commodity at the expense of a party which had a clearly annunciated platform. But, most of all, DeMorse's involvement was motivated by a sincere belief that the Whig party was the representative of the rich and powerful and the Democratic Party acted for the best interests of America and her people.

407. January 8, 1848

408. August 5, 1848

409. July 1, 1848

410. Former President Martin Van Buren and his third party Free Soilers appear to have gotten none of the popular vote in Red River, but they fared a little bit better nationally, gaining 10% of the popular vote and some seats in Congress. They were comprised of the anti slavery elements of both the Whig and Democratic parties, abolitionists, as they were termed. Unlike most third parties in American history, this one would not

disappear, but, in time, would have an affect on elections to come follow.

411. December 2, 1848

412. Perhaps, President Taylor's sudden death in July, 1850, the victim of a violent stomach disorder following an attack of heat prostration, deprived DeMorse of someone to criticize. *The Standard* reader would have been hard pressed to learn much about the President's death, if he relied solely upon *The Standard*. The epitath for Taylor there was neither laudatory or sympathetic:

> *Some of the Taylor papers are awfully shocked at some of their brethren who failed in putting on a show of sorrow on the death of the President. We did not put our paper in mourning for the simple fact that we, and the community in which we live, felt no sorrow and did not regard his death as a national calamity, but, if anything, quite the reverse of that. Texas papers had better be clothed in mourning for the blood of her citizens, which is daily being shed on our western frontier by the hands of ruthless savages and whose appeals to the late President for protection were unheeded and unanswered. In the language of the citizens of Bexar county "Texas lost no friend when General Taylor died."* September 7, 1850

413. His father had been a veteran of the American Revolution and had introduced his son to the ranks of the Jacksonian Democratic party. Soon the younger Pierce emerged as a state leader in New Hampshire, then served two terms in the U.S. House of Representatives and, in 1837, took his seat in the U.S. Senate as the youngest member of that body. When the Mexican War broke out, Pierce volunteered and was commissioned, first a colonel, and then a brigadier general. Ironically, in 1847, Pierce, with a brigade of 2,500 men, joined Gen. Winfield Scott in his campaign against Mexico City. After his return to civilian life, Pierce's endorsement of the Compromise of 1850 and the

Fugitive Slave act made him "a Northern man with Southern principles."

414. October 23, 1852

415. October 30, 1852

416. Little doubt why. In 1849, for example, the immigrants landing in New York numbered 115,991 Irish, 55,705 Germans, and 52, 393 from all the other countries of Europe. DeMorse printed a letter he had received from Bridgeport Connecticut (the movement had begun in New England). that explained the movement's name and its strategy at the polls: "Up here in Yankeedom, American nativism has revived under a new form, known by the name and title of Known Nothings. They are strong enough in numbers to carry all the local elections and so very secretly so that their candidate are not known until after the elections and the members of the party are not even known. Hence, they are called Know Nothings, for ask them what you will they "will know nothing about it." May 6, 1854. *The Standard* reported that the Know Nothings had elected the mayor of Louisville with a 950 majority. According to their fashion, he was not known to be a candidate until the morning of the election.

417. Two million Irish peasants fled famines in Protestant controlled Ireland from 1845 to 1860, a big bite for a host nation to digest. What made in even more upsetting was that these were Catholics, those people associated with the Spanish Inquisition, the tyranny in Italy and repressed Liberty in France. They were not welcome in America, at least in the views of some. In Minnesota reportedly, free blacks were to be vote, while all foreigners and Catholics (even those native born) were to be denied it.

418. November 17, 1855. Clarksville had some support for Know Nothingism and even a newspaper, the *Weekly Messenger*, to spread its word.

419. The Compromise of 1850 had kept peace for a few years between the North and the South as to what to do with slavery. The coalitions in Congress necessary to pass this Kansas-Nebraska Act, had divided the territory in two, with the inhabitants of each having the right to choose to be slave or free states, scrambled the existing party lines. The Whig party ceased being of any force. Its southern members became Democrats. Its northern members either joined the Known Nothing Movement, called the American Party, or joined a new party of self proclaimed "Anti-Nebraska Democrats and Anti-Nebraska Whigs", who began to call themselves "Republicans". Many northern Democrats joined this party too. For newcomers to the scene, the Republicans had been immediately successful. For example, in the elections of 1854, often cooperating with the Know-Nothings, they had elected a majority to the U.S. House of Representatives and won control of a number of Northern state governments.

420. October 25, 1856

421. November 22, 1851

422. November 22, 1851

423. One side could argue its value. It could be profitable. Slaves were the ultimate in cheap labor - chiefly food and maintenance after the initial purchase. And they reproduced, dividends of sorts for the slave owner. A lad or maid of 15 could be purchased in African interior for four yards of Manchester cotton, valued six pence. *The New Orleans Crescent* reported "that Messrs J.A. Beard & May auctioneers of his city, sold on Tuesday last, 32 Negro men for the sum of $47,450, or an average of $1,482, and 15 of all descriptions for $15,630, making an average of $1,042 each." March 22, 1856

424. Slavery was perceived to be essential to the economic production of cotton in the United States. Free people, with a wealth of land available at little or no cost for them to farm as their own, were not about to crouch all day in the sun, harvesting

the bolls from the plants to make another man rich. Without cotton, the spinning mills of New England Old England alike would close, throwing hundreds of thousands of mill workers out of work and far from their family farms or foreign lands they had abandoned to go to the cities. Especially in England, which had been spared the Revolutions that crossed Europe in 1848, having an unemployed, hungry urban population would be ill advised. In 1852, three and a half million people, one-eighth of her population, depended on the production of cotton. March 15, 1851

425. There were two and a half million slaves, overwhelmingly American born. In fact, only 20,000 of them had been born in Africa. Out of every 100 of those who were involved in agriculture, 2 worked with hemp, 5 with rice, 6 sugar, 14 tobacco and 73 with cotton and other products. Who owned the slaves in America in the 1850s? Three hundred and forty seven thousand families, consisting of some two million people, owned slaves. One fifth of the families owned but a single slave and nearly one half of the families had fewer than five.

426. The Pro-Slavery Argument, was a collection of intellectual justifications for the institution of slavery, which, boiled down, maintained the Slavery was a positive good, not an evil for which the South must apologize or the North should criticize. The slave, being inferior, was treated better than he could be on his own. He was fed, clothed and housed, as one would a piece of property that had cost nearly a thousand dollars. Certainly, he was better treated than factory workers in Massachusetts, or the imprisoned debtors of that same state. America profited as well from the institution of slavery. Southern cotton was the fuel the fired the prosperous Northern mills. Nor was the practice immoral. Did not the ancient Hebrews have slaves, and in the New Testament, did not Paul tell advise, "Servants, obey your masters"?

427. Despite a ban some slaves were still being smuggled in from Africa, at least according to this hearsay by the Caddo

Gazette, which had it second hand from another journal: " We have been credibly informed by *the V.B. Intelligencer* that there is a constant trade in kidnaping Negroes, going on between Africa and Texas. Year before last, there were several vessels, well loaded with Negroes brought from Africa and landed near the Mouth of the San Bernard and the Negroes there sold. This black scheme should be looked into by the government and those engaged in it punished according to law. June 23, 1849

428. June 15, 1850

429. The South is dependent upon the North. The fault lies with itself. It has the remedy in its own hands. Heretofore it has only grown the raw materials. The north hands manufactured them and reaped all the profit. It has grown rich and prosperous beyond measure, the South has grown poor. There should be a change. Necessity and duty alike demand it. Self respect and self preservation require it. The South should manufacture first all of its necessaries, its heavy articles. It has the raw material, the water power and all proper facilities in abundance. When it will have done this, the North will have learned a lesson and we shall be independent and prosperous. July 21, 1849

430. November 2, 1850

431. June 29, 1850

432. June 23, 1860

433. December 22, 1860

INDICES

People

BLACKWELL, Joseph - 137
BOYCE, Mr. - 20, 207

A
ADAMS, John - 165, 166
AKE, John - 273
ALLEN, David - 207
ALLEN, Hugh - 272
ALLEN, Joseph - 273
ANDERSON, Rev. John - 99, 154, 170, 171
ANDERSON, Dr. W. N. - 146, 149
ANDERSON, Mr. - 96
ANDERSON, Mrs. - 100, 155, 168
ATKINSON, Jas. - 176
AUSTIN, Stephen F. - 103

B
BAGBY, John A. - 167
BANGS, Mr. - 289
BARRUS, Rev. H. C. - 24
BARRY, Jasper A. - 167, 171, 178
BARRY, Dr. - 170
BATTON brothers 273
BEDFORD, John R. - 175.
BELL, John - 253, 254
BELL, Gov. Peter H. - 133
BELL, W. H. - 231
BERRY, Bill - 273
BERRY, Nat - 273
BINE, Lieut. - 215
BIVINS, Sheriff - 133

BRADLEY, Rev. Mr. - 111
BRECKINRIDGE, John - 253, 254
BREM, G. B. - 259
BROWN, Maj. - 229
BUCHANAN James - 246, 247
BURKS, J. H. - 168, 170
BURNETT, Austin - 208
BUSH, Miss Mary - 157
BUTLER, Charles - 208
BUTLER, William O. - 240

C
CALDWELL, James C. - 46
CANDLE, Green - 136
CARL, Prince of Sohm-Braunfels - 213, 214, 287
CARNCROSS, Miss - 157
CARNCROSS Family - 157
CASS, Lewis - 239, 240, 241
CASTRO, Henri - 220
CATON, Cynthia - 13, 20
CHAMBERLAIN, Mr. Rev. - 291
CLARK, Benjamin - 103, 250
CLARK, Frank H. - 167, 171
CLARK, Gilbert - 32, 103
CLARK, Isabella Hanks - 7, 11
CLARK, James - 7, 11, 13, 17, 59, 103, 125, 250

CLARK, James Rogers - 103
CLARK, Pat B. - 58, 131
CLARK, Col. - 87, 173
CLAY, HENRY - 294
COE, MR. - 157
COX, Jim - 273
COLUMBUS, Christopher - 51
COOKE, Miss Francis - 172
COOKE, Louis P. - 232
COOPER, Peter - 264
CORLEY, Rev. Mr. - 142, 170, 171
CRAWFORD, Sheriff - 138
CRITTENDON, William - 20, 72
CROCKETT, Davy - 217, 258
CROOKS, A.M. - 140
CROWNOVER, Benj. - 44
CRUMP, Capt W. G. - 219

D

DALE, C. C. - 14
DALE, J.P. - 14
DARNALL, J. .H. - 23
DEAN, Reuben - 273
DECORDOVA, Jacob - 211
DELAHUNTY, James - 143
DeMorse, Charles - 1, 2, 6, 8, 16, 17, 19, 21, 23, 28, 29, 31, 34, 38, 39, 41, 42, 43, 44, 47, 48, 49, 50, 51, 54, 61, 62, 64, 65, 66, 67, 68, 69, 50, 51, 54, 61, 62, 64, 65, 66, 67, 68, 69, 71, 72, 73, 74, 76, 77, 78, 79, 82, 85, 87, 88, 89, 90, 91, 92, 95, 96, 97, 101, 106, 109, 115, 118, 120, 121, 123, 125, 126, 127, 129, 132, 133, 135, 138, 145, 146, 150, 152, 153, 155, 156, 158, 161, 162, 166, 173, 174, 176, 177, 184, 185, 190, 191, 193, 194, 196, 198, 200, 203, 204, 205, 206, 210, 211, 212, 213, 218, 227, 234, 235, 238, 239, 241, 242, 243, 244, 245, 246, 249, 250, 251, 252, 253, 260, 261, 264, 268, 269, 271, 272, 274, 279, 282, 285, 292, 294, 295, 296, 297

DESPAIN, Dr. - 105
DICKSON, Joseph J. - 172, 180
DICKSON, Wm. P. - 14, 20
DILLAHUNTY, Charles - 167
DILLAHUNTY, Hervey - 152
DILLAHUNTY, Judge - 42
DIXSON, Susanna Louisa - 149
DONNE, John - 203
DONOHO, William - 270
DONOHO, Mrs. - 12, 15, 21, 180, 183
DOUGLAS, Stephen - 253, 254
DUKE, William G. - 104
DUKE, Mr. - 101
DUNCAN, Thomas H. - 50
DURST, Maj. - 290
DYSART, Rev. Mr. - 110

E

ELLETT, A. K. MD. - 113, 168
ELLIOT, Dr. - 179
ENGLISH, Col. - 38
ENMONSON, William - 43
EPPERSON, B. H. - 173
ESTILL, REV. MILTON - 103

F

FARRET, John - 15
FERGUSON, MR. - 215
FILLMORE, MILLARD - 242, 246, 247
FITZPATRICK, Col. Rene - 49
FLEMING, MR. - 121
FLEMMING, PERRY H. - 104
FORAT, MR. - 221
FORBES, Thom. C. - 38
FOWLER, Brad - 54
FREDERICK, Prince of Prussia - 215
FREDSON, George - 20
FREMONT, John C. - 246, 247
FREYER, Mr. - 157
FULLER, B. F. - 170
FULLER, Mr. - 138

G

GAFFENEY, William - 140, 141
GAINES, Jno. P. - 168
GAINES, Wm. C. - 21
GATTIS, Mrs. - 98
GIBSON, Mrs. - 182
GILL, Mr. - 260
GORDON, Dr. George - 11, 20, 59, 72, 131
GORDON, Isabella - 104
GORDON, James - 14
GORDON, John - 16
GRAFT, Mr. - 101
GRAHAM, S. - 114
GRAHAM, Mrs. - 99

GREGG, Mr. - 32
GRIFFIN, Capt. - 294
GRIFFITHS, Mr. - 273

H

HALL, Dr. J. F. - 105
HAMLIN, Hannibal - 254
HAMPTON, a Negro man - 136
HANSBROUGH, W. S. - 208
HARNEY, Gen. - 286
HARRIS, J. F. - 133
HARRIS, Rev. Mr. - 110
HARRISON, M. - 98
HARRISON, William H. - 39
HARRISON, William Henry - 295
HARRISON, Wm. M. - 16
HART, J. C. - 20, 189, 190, 240, 269
HART, Joseph C. - 23, 36
HART, W. F. T. - 136
HART, Mr. - 222
HAYS, Jack - 220, 226, 227
HEATER, Mr. - 215
HENRY, Mr. - 157
HERNANDO, Gov. - 214
HEWLETT, Mr. - 108
HIGHSMITH, Capt. - 116
HODGE, Col. - 281
HOOVER, Mr. - 115
HOPKINS Capt. J. E. - 46
HOPKINS, R. M. - 38
HUMPHREYS, Wm. - 136
HUNTER, Capt. Edward - 294
HUSBAND, Miles - 143, 144, 275
HUTTON, William - 273

HYDE, John K. - 208

J

JACKSON, Andrew - 394, 296
JEFF, a Negro man - 136
JEFFERSON, Thomas - 260, 294
JOHN, a Negro man - 140, 141, 142
JOHNSON, Benj. - 190
JOHNSON, Isaac W. - 221
JOHNSON, Jean - 162
JOHNSON, Ned - 138
JOHNSTON, Wm. S. - 45, 49

JONES, Henry - 48, 258
JONES, Wm. - 207
JONES, Capt. - 196, 197
JONES, Parson - 145
JOSEPHINE, Mademoiselle - 285

K

KING, Martin Luther - 165
KING, William R. - 243
KING, Lieut. - 222
KING, Mr. - 159
KINNEY, Henry L. - 224, 225
KIRBY, Colonel's - 273

L

LANE, Maj. - 231
LATIMER, Gunboat - 125
LATIMER, Henry R. - 167
LATIMER, James W. - 278
LAWTON, Geo. F. - 13

LEIGH, Charlie - 200
LINCOLN, Abraham - 253, 254, 294
LITTLE, Mrs. - 273
LOK, Mr. - 285
LOMBARDO, Mr.- 289
LOOK, Dr.- 133, 144, 185
LOOK, Mr. - 32
LOTT, Col. - 223
LOVEJOY, Rev. John Lemeul - 104
LOVEMORE, Col.- 224
LYNCH, MR. - 134
LYNCH, Judge - 233

M

MABBIT, William - 7
MAREVAULT, Father - 108
MARTIN, H. B.- 209
MARTIN, Rev. Father - 142
MAXEY, Sam Bell - 154
MCANIER, Samuel - 169
MCCORMICK, Cyrus - 40, 237
MCCULLOCH, Capt. H.E. - 222
MCGOWAN, Edward - 173
MCKENZIE, John Witherspoon Pettigrew - 36, 101, 102, 104
MCLARAN, J. H.- 152
MCNURTY, Mr. - 231
MENFREE, Mr.- 209
MERCER, Mr. - 209
MEUSEBAUCH, John O. - 214
MEUSEBACH, Baron -214, 215, 217
MIDDLETON, Tom - 272, 273
MILLS, John T. - 20, 129, 145,

152, 178
MINTURE, Dr. J.P. - 115
MONTGOMERY, J. J. - 13
MONTGOMERY, John - 169
MOORE, Dr. - 15
MOORE, Justice - 144
MORRIL, A. - 20
MOSES, a Negro man - 140, 141, 142
MURCHINSON, Capt. - 215, 216
MUSGROVE, Mr. - 13

N
NALL, Miss - 135

P
PADON, Dr. - 105
PARTAIN, M. H. - 153
PATTERSON, Mr. - 34
PEABODY, Charles H. - 142, 143, 145, 167, 170, 186, 275
PEASE, Gov. - 183
PIERCE, Franklin - 242, 243, 244, 296
PITTS, John D. - 50
POLK, James - 239, 295
PORTER, Maj. - 281, 282
PORTER, Rev. Mr. - 180
PUTNAM, Hillard - 273
PUTNAM, Vandy - 273

R
RAGIN, G. [see also Regin] - 152
RAGIN, Reason - 136

RAGSDALE, Smith - 185
RALSTON, Wm. - 38
REDDING, Dr. A. J. - 46
REGIN, Gilbert [see also Ragin] - 15
REYNOLDS, Mr. - 163, 285
RHINE, Howard - 14, 24, 25, 54, 62, 187
RICE, A. J. - 45
ROBBINS, John - 45
ROSS, Capt. - 211
RUNNELS, Henry G. - 208
RUSSELL, A. J. - 173
RUSSELL, J. W. - 167, 171
RUSSELL, Mr. - 99, 135

S
SALTER, Mr. - 157
SAMPSON, Rev. James - 48, 96
SAMUELS brothers - 273
SAUTUSKA, Capt. - 196, 197
SCOTT, Gen. Winfield - 242, 244, 296
SCURRY, Thomas - 175
SHANAHAN, J. B. - 21
SIMS, F.M. - 16
SIMS, James W. - 104
SIMS, Wm. - 45
SLAUGHTER, Howard - 291
SLEDGE, Col. Wm. - 273
SMATHERS, Isaac - 7
SMATHERS, John Wesley - 133
SMITH, B.B. - 176
SMITH, George - 15
SMITH, S. - 232
SMITH, Samson - 45
SMITH, Dr. - 262

SMITH, Judge - 262
SNEED, B.J. - 15
SNIDER, J. J. - 34
SPENCER, Walter S. - 58
STEVENSON, Rev. William - 103
STEWART, Mr. - 294
STOUT, Henry - 7
SWEENEY, Mr. - 209
SWINDELLS., John W. - 203, 278

T
TAYLOR, Joseph - 46
TAYLOR, Thomas - 273
TAYLOR, Zachary - 239, 241, 242, 295, 296
THOMAS, Jas. W. - 170
THOMPSON, Richard - 167
THOMSON, C.P. - 181
TITUS, A. J. - 39
TITUS, Jack - 154
TODD, Mrs. Eliza A. - 98
TODD, Col. William - 98
TODD, Judge - 29, 141
TOMKINS, Mr. - 156
TYLER, John - 295

V
VAN BUREN, Martin - 239, 241, 295
VESTELL, Mr. - 290
VICTORIA, Queen - 287
VINING, Mary Jane - 129
VIOLETTE, P. - 232
VON MEUSEBACH, Ottofried Hans - 214, 215, 217

W
WALKER, Dr. - 172
WALKER, Mr. - 290
WALLACE, Ernest - 269
WALLACE, William - 278
WALLACE, Mr. - 219
WALLIS, E. P. - 45
WARD, Dr. - 13
WARRENER, Rev. Mr. - 105
WEATHERRED Martha W. (Maum) - 98
WEATHERRED Robert - 98
WEBSTER, Daniel - 294
WENTWORTH, Mr. - 54
WESTERN, Albert - 143, 144, 274, 275
WETMORE, Alex - 7
WETMORE, George - 7
WHARTON, Dr. - 172
WHITE, Mr. - 273
WILCKE, Lieut.- 216
WILLIAMS, Wm. - 48
WILLSEY, Capt. Benjamin - 289
WILLSEY, Mrs. - 289
WILSON, Thos. R. - 20
WINLOCK, Wm. H. - 294
WOMBLE, Mr. - 289
WOODSWORTH, H.D. - 33
WOOLRIDGE, Lodiska C. - 97
WOOTTEN, G. H. - 167
WOOTTEN, Judge - 38
WRIGHT, Claiborne - 6, 103
WRIGHT, Hardy - 6

WRIGHT, Jin - 6
WRIGHT, Capt. T.G. - 175
WRIGHT, Travis - 64, 125
WRIGHT, Mr. - 135

YOUNG Rev. Mr. - 107

Z

ZAMORA, Doreteo - 289

Y

YOUNG, Rev. J. - 151

PLACES WITHIN TEXAS: TOWNS, COUNTIES, REGIONS AND WATER COURSES

Alamo - 217, 295
Albion - 32
Austin - 1, 12, 35, 76, 116, 117, 131, 210, 211, 212, 213, 264, 272, 282, 285
Barton Springs - 213
Bastrop - 109, 272
Bexar county - 296
Bezzata - 282
Blossom Prairie - 44
Bonham - 66, 79, 204, 265, 294
Bosque river - 210
Boston - 76, 98, 108, 199
Bowie county - 23, 37, 40, 48, 104, 127, 172, 185, 205, 262
Brazoria county - 25, 52, 208
Brazos River - 41, 61, 206, 209, 211, 229
Brownsville - 117, 228, 229, 230, 232, 289
Brushy Creek - 284
Buck Horn - 272
Buffalo - 210, 280
Burham's Settlement - 6

Burleson county, - 272, 273
Caney Creek - 48

Carlshafen - 287
Cass county - 36, 40, 127, 205
Castroville - 220, 221
Cedar Hills - 94
Chappell Hill - 273
Cherokee county - 40
Cincinnati - 32, 119, 206
City of the Three Forks of the Trinity - 6
Clarksville - 1, 2, 5,6,7,8, 10, 11, 12, 14,16, 17,19, 22, 23, 24, 25,27, 28, 29, 30, 30, 31, 32,33, 36, 43, 44, 54, 57, 61, 62, 63, 64, 66, 69, 70, 71, 72, 73, 74, 75, 76, 78, 79, 80, 81, 82, 83, 84 87, 91, 95, 96, 97, 98, 101, 103, 104, 105, 106, 109, 110,113, 114, 115, 118, 119, 120, 121, 122, 123, 124, 125, 126, 127, 128, 129, 131, 133, 136, 138, 145, 149, 150, 152, 153, 154, 155, 156, 157,

158, 159, 161, 162, 165, 166, 167, 172, 173, 178, 184, 186, 189, 190, 191, 193, 195, 198, 200, 203, 205, 206, 234, 235, 238, 241, 247, 255, 257, 258, 259, 268, 269, 284, 292, 297

Clarksville
- Broadway - 11
- Church Street - 16, 104
- cemetery - 131, 259
- Locust Street - 11
- Main Street - 11
- Mulberry Street - 16
- Methodist Cemetery - 17
- North Locust street - 104
- Pecan street - 11
- public square - 11, 10,29, 35, 73, 103, 104
- Washington Street - 17
- West Washington Street - 259

Collin county - 127, 128, 130, 205
Cooke county - 93, 127, 128, 205
Colorado River - 1, 161, 206, 209, 225, 273, 285
Comal River - 214, 215
Corpus Christi - 209, 224, 225, 226, 290
Corsicana - 211
Cow House bayou - 221
Cross Timbers - 294
CutHand Bottom - 57
Daingerfield - 74
Dalby Springs - 198, 199, 200
Dallas county - 6, 127, 128, 131, 198, 199, 200, 205
Dallas, town of - 2,7,61,94, 209, 210, 211, 278
DeKalb - 104

Delaware Creek - 11, 24, 71, 87, 92, 120, 121, 191, 192, 193, 194
Denton county - 125, 128, 130, 135, 205
Doaksville - 185, 235, 292
Eagle Pass - 228
Ellis county - 130, 205
El Paso county - 227, 228, 244
El Paso, town of - 50, 84, 227, 228, 237
Fannin county - 79, 87, 127, 128, 175, 204, 208
Fort Ringold - 232
Fort Ewell - 232
Fort Worth - 2, 226
Fort Towson - 104, 108, 185
Fort Inge - 232
Fort Brown - 228
Fort Washita - 41
Fredericksburgh - 215, 216
Fulton - 64
Gainesville - 93
Galveston - 51, 52, 117, 120, 121, 205, 206, 208, 209, 224, 232, 265, 286
Galveston Bay - 52, 81
Georgetown - 102, 211, 212, 284
Goliad county - 221, 222
Goliad, town of - 221, 222
Grayson county - 28, 128, 130, 205, 245, 294
Grimes county - 50
Jasper county - 262
Gonzalez - 285
Guadalupe River - 50, 61, 214, 218
Gulf of Mexico - 1, 61, 221, 224, 226, 228

Halesboro - 32

Hamilton's Valley - 285

Harrison county - 40, 49, 208, 270

Henderson county - 280

Hopkins county - 49, 127, 128, 205

Houston - 7, 120, 121, 205, 206, 207, 208, 232, 264, 280

Hunt county - 127, 128, 205

Huntsville - 135

Indianola - 119, 120, 209, 214, 287

Jefferson - 74, 75

Johnson county - 130, 205

Jonesboro,[Jonesborough] 6, 12, 49, 82, 104, 125, 137, 257, 258, 260

Kaufman county - 127, 131, 134, 205

Kaufman, town of - 281

La Bahia - 221

La Grange, 125, 273

La Salle county - 232

Lake Shannahan - 191, 192

Lamar county - 33, 79, 87, 92, 98, 125, 128, 129, 145, 175, 205, 233, 254, 294

Lamartine - 211

Laredo - 228, 289, 290

LaVaca - 119

Lavaca Bay - 287

Leona River - 232

Limestone county - 221

Lost Creek - 273

Madras - 32, 125, 258

Maple Springs - 32

Marshall - 71

Matagorda county - 25, 48

Matagorda, town of - 1, 119

Medina River - 219, 220

Millville - 32, 175

Montague county - 128, 205

Mount Pleasant - 71, 133

Navarro county - 146, 149

New Braunfels - 214, 215, 216

Nueces county - 225

Nueces River - 61, 226, 232

Palo Alto - 289

Paris - 33, 54, 69, 111, 154, 162, 265, 294

Parker county - 128, 130, 205

Pecan Point - 7, 36, 38, 64

Pecos River - 226

Pickney - 125

Pine Bluffs - 282

Pine Creek - 43, 121, 172

Plano - 94

Port LaVaca - 208

Port Isabel - 289

Porter's Bluff - 210, 211, 281

Praesidio - 228

Preston - 77, 294

Puerco stream - 233

Rancho delos Indois - 289

Rancho Capitaneo - 290

Rancho de Dolores - 290

Red River county - 1, 6, 10, 23, 27, 28, 29, 30, 32, 35, 36, 38, 42,43, 44, 47,48, 49,51, 54. 57, 58, 68, 70, 81, 93, 95, 103, 113, 121, 130, 131, 133, 136, 137, 149, 151, 165, 166, 167, 170, 174, 175, 189, 196, 203, 205, 235, 237, 241, 247

Red River - 12, 16, 57, 58, 61, 62, 63, 64, 65, 66, 77, 78, 79, 82, 83, 88, 89, 101, 103, 104,

120, 120, 137, 138, 195, 210, 226, 292

Red River District - 12, 127

Red River Valley - 2, 6, 7, 10, 35, 39, 59, 66, 78, 89, 93, 109, 116, 123, 127, 154, 161

Refugio county - 222, 223

Rhine River - 220

Richland - 149

Rio Bravo del Norte - 229

Rio Grande - 61, 117, 225, 226, 227, 228, 229, 230, 231, 232, 239, 289

Rio Grande City - 232

Robbinsville - 32

Roma - 229

Rowland - 32, 59, 68, 77, 87, 196

Rusk county - 40

Sabine River - 61, 271

San Antonio - 9, 51, 54, 61, 116, 117, 118, 120, 212, 214, 217, 218, 219, 221, 226, 227, 232, 237, 273, 285, 289, 290

San Antonio street (New Braunfeld) - 214

San Bernard river - 300

San Gabriel river - 233, 284

San Patricio county - 224

San Patricio Hibernia - 223

Santa Olaya ranch - 289

Savannah - 32, 38, 175

Seguin - 50, 285

Sel Colorado - 225

Sequin Street, New Braunfels - 214

Shelby county - 40

Sherman - 65, 125, 268

St. Patrick of Ireland - 223

Sulphur Creek - 47, 50, 61, 71, 198, 270

Taos, Tex, - 210 , 281

Tarrant county - 6, 128

Tehuacana Springs - 211

Texas Hill Country - 213

Titus county - 48, 75, 118, 127, 128, 205

Trinity - 61, 79, 97, 119, 206, 209, 210, 211, 280

Tyler - 119, 130

Upper Brazaos - 200

Upper Colorado - 285

Upper Cross Timbers - 2

Upper Trinity River - 79, 206

Upshur county - 40, 125, 205

Uvalde county - 232

Victoria - 119, 208, 209, 271

Waco - 12, 135, 211

Walker county - 119

Washington county - 25, 273

Waller Creek - 286

Washita River - 41

White River - 74

Williamson county - 211, 212

Wharton county - 25

Wise county - 205

PLACES OUTSIDE TEXAS, TOWNS, STATES, NATIONS, REGIONS AND WATER COURSES

Africa - 51, 184, 251, 257, 298, 299, 300
Alexandria, Louisiana - 68
Arkansas - 6, 12, 16, 37, 61, 74, 95, 97, 103, 105, 191, 192, 193, 270, 294
Arkansas river - 74
Astor Hotel (New York City) - 203
Atlantic Ocean -154, 236, 292
Bath, Maine - 245
Benton county, Alabama. - 283
Boston, Mass. - 245
Braunfelds, Province of Germany - 214
Bridgeport Connecticut - 297
California - 54, 80, 115, 227, 233, 237, 238, 239, 284
Chihuahua - 206, 229, 288
Choctaw Nation - 34, 40, 59, 79, 101, 108, 138, 235
Clinton, Mississippi - 97
Comargo - 290
Connecticut - 1, 250, 257
Cuba - 48, 262
Delaware - 250
Denmark - 271
Durango - 229
Ellsworth, Maine - 245
England - 35, 178, 234, 238, 251, 277, 278, 287, 292, 299
Europe - 10, 50, 51, 117, 149, 209, 212, 221, 228, 234, 235, 236, 239, 251, 297, 299

France - 10, 185, 234, 235, 251, 291, 297
Georgia - 101, 241
Germany - 10, 214, 220, 287, 291
Guanajuato - 229
Havana - 15, 209
Hempstead county, Arkansas - 294
Illinois - 250
Independence, Missouri - 226
India - 117, 234, 268
Indian Territory - 6, 101, 104, 235, 251, 292
Indiana - 250, 271
Iran - 6, 234
Ireland - 97, 223, 235, 251, 292, 297
Italy - 100, 160, 291, 297
Kansas - 298
Kentucky - 51, 105, 262
Little Rock - 12, 74
London - 63
Louisville, Ky. -57
Low Land countries - 287
Lynchburg, Va. - 52
Maryland - 247
Massachusetts - 1, 148, 237, 245, 264, 294, 299
Matamoros - 228, 229, 230
Mexico - 7, 9, 76, 103, 134, 166, 168, 169, 218, 221, 222, 223, 234, 228, 229, 230, 232, 239, 243, 257, 265, 271, 272, 295

Mexico City - 296
Michigan - 247
Miller county, Arkansas - 104
Minnesota - 297
Mississippi River - 53, 61, 62, 73, 74, 99, 117, 120, 195
Missouri - 53, 288
Monterey - 229
Natchez - 121
Newark - 245
New England - 1, 35, 63, 91, 230, 237, 247, 293, 297, 299
New Hampshire - 242, 296
New Haven, Connecticut - 17
New Mexico - 61
New Orleans - 6, 12, 15, 27, 40, 51, 62, 65, 66, 74, 89, 117, 119, 120, 121, 122, 229, 271, 282
New York - 1, 109, 117, 156, 157, 229, 234, 242, 247, 250, 251, 257, 278, 292, 293, 297
North Carolina - 135, 191
Ohio - 103, 247, 278
Oklahoma - 101, 235, 259, 292
Pacific railroad - 79, 80
Pacific Ocean - 80, 227
Palestine - 234
Parras - 231
Patterson, New Jersey - 254, 293
Pennsylvania - 246, 250

Persia - 234
Philadelphia - 113, 191, 245
Plymouth Mass. - 237
Poland - 291
Prussia - 215, 234, 286
Richmond, Va. - 113
Rome - 125
Russia - 82, 234, 291
Saltillo - 229, 231
San Luis Potosi - 229
Santa Fe - 226, 227, 229
Santa Fe county - 282
Shreveport - 1, 56, 62, 66, 67, 71, 74, 78, 79, 119, 121, 280
South Carolina - 129
Spain - 9, 51, 218
Spring Hill, Arkansas - 97
St. Louis, Missouri - 245
Switzerland - 291
Taos, N. M. - 280 -81
Tennessee - 6, 53
Turkey - 234
Vermont - 107
Vicksburg, Miss. - 264
Wall Street - 1
Washington D.C. - 76, 241, 242
Wisconsin - 107, 247, 250
Zacatecas - 229

SCHOOLS, CHURCHES, FRATERNAL INSTITUTIONS, NEWSPAPERS, VESSELS, AND BUSINESSES

Alexander's Ladies Dress Shop - 14

Alma House and Penitentiary -113
Alma House and Hospital - 113

American Bible Society - 105
Anderson School - 168
Austin State Gazette, The - 119, 212
Barry & Moore, Drs. -15
Battle of Goliad - 221, 272, 295
Belfast University - 97
Brim's Cabinet Shop - 16
Bryarly and Co. - 88
Buffalo, the - 63
Caddo Gazette - 299-300
Choctaw, The - 68
Christian Church - 105
Clarksville Academy - 96, 100
Clarksville Band - 168, 172
Clarksville Classical Mathematical and Mercantile Academy - 96
Clarksville Female Academy - 97, 155, 172
Clarksville Female Institute - 98, 100, 155
Clarksville Hotel - 96, 99, 143, 160, 172, 174, 178
Clarksville Male Academy - 96, 99
Clarksville Male and Female Academy - 99
Clarksville Music Society, The -155
Cumberland Presbyterian Church - 103, 110, 142
Daily Bulletin, The - 1
Dallas Herald. The - 204, 278
Dickson, W.P. & Co. - 14
Donoho House - 21, 121, 122, 180, 183
Dublin Nation, The - 29

Eagle Hotel - 100, 160, 161, 172
Emery's Wheat Thresher - 40
Fanny Fern, the - 62
Father Matthews Branch Temperance Society - 108
Female College at Clinton, Mississippi - 97
Ferguson and Heater, Messrs variety store - 215
First Presbyterian Church of Clarksville - 103, 104
Freemasons - 151
Fulton, the - 63
Galveston Civilian, The - 51
Georgia University - 101
Hanger's Mail Stages - 74
Harrison's Blacksmith shop - 16
Hopkins and Hamilton - 38
Houston Telegraph - 205, 206
Houston and Texas Central Railroad - 211
Huntsville Banner - 54
Independent Order of Odd Fellows - 110, 152, 153, 171, 177, 179, 180, 181, 182
Institution of the Blind in New York City - 157
J. A. Beard & May Messrs auctioneers - 298
Jim Turner, the - 68, 77
Johnson & Aik - 190
Johnson's Southern Minstrels - 162
Johnson's store - 137
Jonadab Temple of Honor of the Knights of Templar - 152
Knights Templars, The - 151
Lee's confectionary - 15

Look & Gregg - 32
Masonic Hall United - 104
Masons - 154, 184
McCormick Reaper - 237
McDonna, Rhine & Bros. - 14
McKenzie College - 12, 101, 104
Memorial, The (Plymouth Mass) - 237
Mercer and Menfree, Messrs plantation - 209
Methodist Episcopal Church, South - 104
Mills & Murray - 20
Montgomery Barnett & Co - 33
New York Herald, the -278
New York Sun, the - 278
New York Tribune, the - 249, 257
New Orleans Crescent - 298
Oliver & Chatfield - 14
Paris Times, the - 278
Peabody Silver works - 15
Peabody's Jewelry store - 186
Picayune, The - 8
Pine Creek Academy - 98
Pioneer, the - 6
Preston, the - 77
Raines Blacksmith shop - 16
Reynolds & Company - 163
Reynolds and Lok, circus - 285
Rhine & Co. - 14
Rhine & Brothers, - 14, 24, 25, 54, 62, 187
Richard Watson, the - 292
Ringwood Female Seminary - 98

Rogers & Co. of Patterson NJ - 254, 293
San Antonio Texian - 221
San Antonio Western Texian, The - 257
Shanahan's blacksmith shop - 16
Shiloh Cumberland Presbyterian Church - 103
Shiloh Community - 103
Sims Hotel - 162, 178
Sisters of Eliza Walker Social Temple - 153
Sligo Champion, the - 292
Society of Odd Fellows - 104
Sons of Temperance - 107, 108, 150, 172, 174, 178, 182, 185, 250
Southwestern University - 108
Star Hotel - 13, 19, 20, 172, 173, 185
State Times, the - 286
State Gazette, the - 225
Steamer Globe - 213
Templars - 107, 151, 153,170
Texas, the - 68
Thompson livery stable - 16
Thompson's Hotel - 12, 15, 144
Tom Thumb - 264
Trimble & Hudkins, law office - 19
Victoria Advocate, The - 219
Washburn's Circus - 162
Weekly Messenger, the - 297
Wells & Fuller - 138
West's black smith's shop - 16
Western Star, The - 238
Western Texian, The - 257

GENERAL

Adelsverein - 237, 238
Alamo, the - 217, 295
American Party, the - 298
Anti-Nebraska Whigs - 298
Anti-Nebraska Democrats - 298
Apaches - 9, 54, 225, 227
Armenians - 234
Association of Noblemen - 238
Battle of Palo Alto - 28
Battle of Refugio, - 222
Battle of Palmito - 228
Battle Resaca de la Palma - 228
Battle of San Jacinto - 134
Bowie knife - 143, 146, 286
Bradshaw's Telegraphic Sewing Machine - 237
buffalo - 7, 57, 92, 222
bull fights - 218
Caddos - 6, 9
Catholic - 245, 291, 297
Cherokees - 138
Choctaw Indian Ball Play - 195, 196
Choctaws - 9, 104, 137, 195, 235, 251
cholera - 31, 32, 115, 116, 117, 118, 119, 122, 208, 218, 219, 232, 268
Church of Holy Sepulcre - 234
Civil War - 51, 54, 95, 98, 102, 123, 210, 236, 246, 253
Comanches - 9, 216, 221, 223, 230, 231, 233, 290
Compromise of 1850 - 242, 296, 298
Confederacy - 177, 255
Constitutional Union party - 253
Delaware Indians - 6, 7, 9
Democratic Republican party - 238
Democratic party - 294, 295, 296
dysentery - 114, 122, 213
El Dorado - 285
El Nino - 81, 84, 88, 93
Electoral College - 241
Episcopal Union - 251
Episcopal Church - 104, 105, 250
famine in Ireland - 117, 235, 292
Father of Texas Journalism - 1

Father of the Democratic Press in Texas - 294

fauna - 213

Five Civilized Tribes - 195, 259

flora - 213

fossils - 211, 213

free blacks - 7, 8, 294, 297

Free Soil Party - 239, 241, 242, 243

Fugitive Slave Law - 255, 297

German Emigration and Railroad Company - 214

gold - 53, 133, 200, 213, 227, 233, 237, 270, 285

Greeks - 234, 277

Hail Columbia - 170

History of Clarksville and Old Red River County, Texas, the - 131

Houston and Texas Central Railroad - 211

Indian Relocation Act - 235

Industrial Revolution - 236, 249

influenza - 116, 213

Irish - 62, 128, 222, 235, 245, 272, 292, 297

Jennnings repeating rifle - 237

Kansas-Nebraska Act - 298

Kickapoo - 6

Know Nothingism - 245, 246, 297

Louisiana Purchase of 1803 - 6

lynch law - 131, 147, 272

Manchester cotton - 298

May Day - 101, 178, 179, 182, 183

McCormick wheat reaper - 237

Missouri Conference of Methodist Church - 103

Nall vs Russell - 135

National Democrats - 253

Nativism - 245, 297

New York National Democrat - 293

Non Intercourse Act of 1789 - 287

Northern Whigs - 242

Northern Democrats - 298

Nullifiers - 252, 253

Osages - 6

Popery - 245

Princeton University - 195

Pro-Slavery Argument - 299

Protestants - 106

Quart law - 108

Red River Volunteers - 101

Republican Party - 238, 239, 244, 246, 247, 253, 294, 298

Revolutions of 1848 - 234

Rutgers University - 195

Santa Fe Expedition of 1841 - 288

Sharp patent rifle - 237

Shikhs - 234

small pox - 121, 122

Southern Democrats - 253, 254

Spanish Inquisition - 297

Star Spangled Banner, the - 152, 170, 253

Tawakoni Indians - 211

Texas Revolution - 1, 166, 168, 169, 223, 228

Tornado Alley - 93

Uncle Tom's Cabin - 249, 251

Union - 10, 34, 69, 75, 78, 85, 166, 218, 229, 243, 244, 246, 247, 250, 252, 253, 255, 257

Waco Indians - 211

War with Mexico - 168, 169, 223, 226, 228, 232, 239, 265

Whig party - 238, 242, 294, 295, 298

White House - 294, 295

yellow fever - 31, 119, 120, 122, 208

AGRICULTURE

acorns - 47

apples - 15, 43, 44, 227, 261

beets - 45, 46

cattle - 9, 18, 51, 52, 53, 54, 77, 94, 117, 135, 208, 212, 221, 223, 225, 238

corn - 8, 9, 10, 15, 27, 34, 35, 36, 38, 41, 42, 45, 46, 55, 56, 69, 77, 86, 131, 204, 224, 285, 293

cotton - 9, 10, 12, 14, 23, 27, 32, 34, 36, 37, 38, 39, 40, 41,

42, 45, 46, 47, 48, 49, 50, 51, 53, 54, 55, 56, 59, 62, 63, 64, 65, 66, 68, 70, 72, 83, 87, 89, 206, 207, 210, 251, 280, 293, 298, 299

eggplant - 46

figs - 227

fruit - 9, 15, 42, 43, 46, 47, 92, 227, 243, 261

grain - 9, 10, 27, 32, 38, 41, 42, 45, 48, 209

grasshoppers - 54, 55, 213

hogs - 49, 59

lemons - 209

live stock - 49, 83

Longhorns - 51

muskmelon - 45

oats - 9, 41

oranges - 207

peaches - 43, 44, 46, 92, 227

pears - 92, 227

pecan mast - 47

plum - 44, 62, 89, 92, 261

quinces - 227

radishes - 44, 56

sheep - 9, 50, 197, 282

sugar cane - 48, 49

sugar - 9, 48, 49, 53, 67, 209

sweet potatoes - 45

tobacco - 15, 47, 102, 107, 262, 299

vegetables - 9, 42, 44, 46, 86

vineyards - 209

wheat - 9, 10, 34, 39, 40, 41, 42, 44, 46, 48, 55, 56, 77, 87, 90, 204, 237